U0136620

心南向
一家人

Bonds of Friendship,
Bonds of Love
—Taiwan and Southeast Asia

光華畫報雜誌社 編著

目次
CONTENTS

推薦序 一步一腳印，落實新南向──鄧振中 　　006
One Step at a Time: The New Southbound Policy in Action

推薦序 台灣最美的風景，應該要是人──林麗蟬 　　008
Taiwan's Greatest Beauty Should Be in Its People

編者序 為新南向注入「心」意──陳亮君 　　010
Adding "Heart" to the New Southbound Policy

Part 1

新住民 · 台灣新職人
VOCATIONS

泰國移工的心靈導師：台泰溝通橋梁──陶雲升　　014
Asoke Srichantr: Spiritual Mentor to Thai Migrant Workers

戲舞掌中乾坤：葉蘇珊操偶圓夢　　022
A World in Her Hands—Yek Sansan

泰拳教育在台灣：台灣泰拳教父──李智仁　　030
Ran Lee, Taiwan's Father of Muay Thai

台越一家，共創新味：客家媳婦阮氏秋的美味人生　　038
A Taiwanese–Vietnamese Fusion:
Hakka Daughter-in-Law Nguyen Thi Thu's Delicious Life

特別篇 爪哇特色捏麵人：移工捏出創業夢　　046
Dough Sculpting the Java Way
—A Migrant Worker Kneads Her Dreams

Part 2

新采風 · 文學交流
LITERATURE

說不準的台北人：陳又津的漫遊書寫　　056
Taipei People to Be—Writer Chen Yuchin

來自彩虹大地的筆：印尼筆會台灣分會　　062
Rainbow Land Writers:
Indonesia's Forum Lingkar Pena Shines in Taiwan

移民工文學在台灣　　070
Immigrant Literature in Taiwan

特別篇 東南亞文學圓桌會：生命的關懷，書寫的原點　　080
Southeast Asia Literature Roundtable:
Writers Inspired by Concern for Humanity

Part 3

新藝向 · 藝術交織
ARTS

「菲尼」不可：鄒隆娜的電影世界　　092
Rina Tsou's World of Film

影藝 · 趙德胤：影像敘寫故鄉 成就電影夢想　　098
Midi Z: Taiwan, Cradle of My Cinema

雨過天晴：阮金紅用影像記錄人生　　108
Basking in Sunshine After Rain
—Videographer Nguyen Kim Hong

越南安妮：新移民的歌仔戲人生　　116
A New Immigrant Performs on a New Stage

看見天堂鳥的姿態：生命的舞者李庭莉　　124
Passing Down the Legacy of Balinese Dance in Taiwan

Part 4

新商機 · 產業開創
ENTREPRENEURSHIP

「印」是要去：台商探見印度內需　　134
Taiwanese Businesses Eye India's Domestic Market

布局東協新商機：台商搶搭泰國 4.0 列車　　146
Next Stop, ASEAN Opportunities!
Taiwanese Companies Board the Thailand 4.0 Train

新創產業走出台灣：搶攻印尼內需市場　　154
Beyond Taiwan: Realizing Entrepreneurial Dreams in Indonesia

農業領軍：綠金生技創新局　　162
Green Gold: Farming Enterprises Take Root

特別篇 93 師咖啡：延續泰北孤軍的故事　　172
93Army Coffee: Granddaughter of a Forgotten Army

Part 5

心守護・為新住民發聲
POLITICS

制度化建置的推手：司法通譯硬漢──陳允萍　　184
Making the Case for Judicial Interpretation—Peter Chen

為新住民姊妹發聲：首位新住民國策顧問──胡清嫻　　192
National Policy Advisor Ho Thanh Nhan
—Speaking Up for New Immigrants

倡議姊妹權益的守護者：邱雅青　　200
Her Sisters' Guardian—Yadrung Chiou

台灣第一位新住民立委：　　208
柬埔寨「灰姑娘」林麗蟬勇闖國會
Taiwan's First New Immigrant Legislator: Lin Li-chan

特別篇　台灣 NGO 扎根越南：教育改變孩子未來　　216
Taiwanese NGOs in Vietnam:
Changing Children's Futures Through Education

一步一腳印，落實新南向

承蒙受邀為《台灣光華雜誌》出版之《心南向‧一家人》撰序，備感榮幸。誠如書名所言，已一語道出「新南向政策」之核心理念。猶記兩年半前蔡總統上任後推動「新南向政策」初始，自社會各界湧進各種不同之建言與異議，這兩年多來，我們始終秉持謙卑之心並以一步一腳印之精神，竭力落實新南向政策，以不負台灣人民對政府之期許。

台灣之外交處境艱難，面對國際情勢瞬息變化，倘不善用台灣軟實力之優勢，積極參與區域事務，亟可能被國際社會邊緣化。中國大陸之「銳」實力並以「錢」為本所推動之「一帶一路」，正對當前國際秩序帶來衝擊與挑戰；美國總統川普爰於2017年提出「印太戰略」（Indo-Pacific Strategy），延續歐巴馬「重返亞洲」對東協、印度之重視，以及韓國總統文在寅於2017年11月喊出「新南方政策」（New Southern Policy）。從美、韓咸將東南亞與印度作為重要國家戰略目標之面向觀之，我國「新南向政策」之前瞻性與正確性已十分明確。

兩年多來，我接待了許多來自美國、日本、韓國與東協等國之產官學界，以及媒體朋友們，他們除了對政府推動新南向政策給予肯定與鼓勵之外，亦盼瞭解我推動新南向政策之具體作法。目前，政府除了在雙邊關係上積極推動與我理念相近（like-minded）之國家，於新南向夥伴國進行合作，亦利用 APEC 場域，推展新南向議題之國際合作。

為推動新南向政策，我造訪了許多地方與人士，在西門町街頭、台北捷運、大學校園看到了更多的穆斯林朋友，醫院、學校、交通樞紐等亦新設了祈禱室；以及欣見台商與青年學子勇闖向南等，我與新南向夥伴國在區域農業、醫衛合作、產業創新、產業人才培育，以及文化觀光等合作成效已逐漸浮現。除了在國人眼前呈現這些亮麗的經貿與交流統計，我們更需要的是，將這些背後的感人故事與國人分享。

感謝《台灣光華雜誌》出版之《心南向‧一家人》，我們也深信以「人」為本之新南向政策，將會讓台灣與新南向夥伴國的心相串連，成為一家人，雙贏共榮。

行政院政務委員暨
兼任行政院經貿談判辦公室
總談判代表

鄧振中

2018 年 11 月 12 日

One Step at a Time:
The New Southbound Policy in Action

I am honored to have been asked to write a preface for *Bonds of Friendship, Bonds of Love—Taiwan and Southeast Asia*. The book's focus reflects the core ideals of the New Southbound Policy. When President Tsai Ing-wen first launched this initiative, a variety of suggestions and objections flooded in from throughout society. For the past two-plus years we have remained humble and devoted to putting the policy into practice, to honor our citizens' expectations of their government.

Taiwan faces a difficult diplomatic situation. In a rapidly changing world, if we do not make good use of our soft power and take an active part in regional affairs, we may well become marginalized. Mainland China's "sharp power" and its One Belt One Road program are a challenge to the current world order. This is why in 2017 U.S. President Donald Trump proposed his Indo-Pacific Strategy, and South Korean President Moon Jae-in declared his New Southern Policy. With these two countries now treating Southeast-Asian nations and India as important strategic partners, it is clear that the launch of Taiwan's New Southbound Policy was both prescient and correct.

Over the last two years I have hosted many people in industry, government, academia and the media from countries such as the U.S., Japan, South Korea, and the ASEAN nations. Besides affirming our promotion of the New Southbound Policy, they have also sought to understand the concrete methods we use to promote it. Today, Taiwan is actively pursuing bilateral cooperation with like-minded partner countries, while also promoting international cooperation on issues related to the policy through APEC.

While promoting the policy I have visited many places and people, and have seen increasing numbers of Muslim friends on the streets of Ximending, on the Taipei MRT, and on university campuses, as well as the setting up of prayer rooms in hospitals, schools, and transportation hubs. I have also been happy to see more Taiwanese businesses and students heading southward. The fruits of our cooperation with our partner countries in agriculture, healthcare, business innovation, skills training, culture and tourism are becoming ever more visible. But beyond citing brilliant statistics about trade and other interactions, it is even more important that we share with our people the moving stories happening behind the scenes.

I wish to thank *Taiwan Panorama* for publishing this book. We firmly believe that a people-centered New Southbound Policy can connect the people of Taiwan with those of our partner countries, and that we can bond together into a prosperous family of nations, to the benefit of all.

John Chen-Chung Deng
Minister without Portfolio and concurrently
Chief Trade Representative
November 12, 2018

台灣最美的風景，應該要是人
——新移民與移工的理想憧憬

中華民國是亞洲第一個民主共和國，成熟之民主發展及曾為亞洲四小龍之首的經濟實力，讓前總統李登輝在 1990 年代主導之南向政策，吸引大批跨國婚姻與移工，創下台灣移民史上的第一個高峰。首波黃金移民潮迄今，已過廿餘年，婚姻移民之總數已達五十四餘萬，藍、白領移工數量的總和也超過七十萬，致使廣義的新住民人口，躋身台灣五大族群之一，也成為多元文化在我國蓬勃發展的重要力量。

筆者本為柬埔寨人，正是在南向政策的風潮下，於 1997 年嫁來台灣成為新住民，且有幸於 2016 年獲國民黨提名為不分區立法委員，並以為所有移民與移工，建構一個友善和諧的生活環境為己任，讓每一位新住民朋友，都能享有一個得以安居樂業的家。

筆者十分瞭解，作為一名外籍工作者或婚姻移民，要迅速融入異地環境絕非容易，期間與當地文化之互動、社會刻板印象之破除，以及在新環境中獲得群體之認同與歸屬感，皆需若干時間加以適應；像是部分僑居海外的華人，在外地被歸類為華僑，但在定居台灣後，卻仍被視為外來者，這對到哪都被當成華僑的他們而言，家究竟在哪？

筆者認為，台灣具有大量的多元移民人口，因此我們具備成為一個族群友善社會的條件與必要性，而這樣的社會，則需以縮短新住民適應當地環境的時間、充分給予權益保障與歸屬感，以及杜絕一切形式之歧視為三大基礎；這不但是筆者投身公共事務的最大使命，亦為所有新住民朋友的理想憧憬，更會是台灣最美的景色——一個不視口音、不論籍別、不分種族的友善寶島。

本刊之內容，即綜整近年東南亞國家之相關報導，包含移民與移工的人物專題，以特寫的方式，描述我們來台奮鬥打拚的過程，藉以記錄台灣的新住民故事，同時也勉勵未來的移入者；更重要的是，讓社會多多瞭解我們，以消弭所有誤解與刻板印象，共創和諧台灣。

立法委員 林麗蟬

2018 年 11 月於台北

Taiwan's Greatest Beauty Should Be in Its People

The Republic of China is Asia's first democratic republic. Its mature democracy and its economic power as the leader of Asia's "four tigers" laid the foundations for President Lee Teng-hui to launch the "Go South Policy" in the 1990s, attracting large numbers of foreign spouses and migrant workers to Taiwan in the first peak in immigration since the National Government relocated here in 1949. Today, there are over 540,000 immigrant spouses and more than 700,000 migrant workers in Taiwan. These numbers make "new immigrants," broadly defined, one of the island's five major ethnic groups, as well as a major force for the flourishing development of multiculturalism

I myself am originally from Cambodia. In 1997, at the peak of the Go South Policy, I married into a Taiwanese family and became a "new immigrant." In 2016 I was nominated by the Kuomintang to stand for election as an at-large legislator. I take it as my personal duty to construct a friendly and harmonious environment for all immigrants and migrant workers, so that each new resident can enjoy a tranquil, happy life.

I understand how difficult it is for immigrants to rapidly blend into an alien environment. It takes time to adapt to local culture, break down stereotypes, and gain a sense of acceptance and belonging. This is similar to the experience of some ethnic Chinese living overseas: they are regarded as Chinese migrants in their countries of residence, but after coming to live in Taiwan they are still seen as outsiders. If these people are seen as "overseas Chinese" wherever they go, then where can they call home?

I believe that Taiwan, with its large and diverse immigrant population, has both the potential and the need to become a welcoming multiethnic society. Such a society must meet three basic conditions: it must reduce the time it takes for new immigrants to adapt to the local environment; guarantee the rights and interests of newcomers while also providing a sense of belonging; and put an end to discrimination in all its forms. This is not only the goal that has drawn me into public affairs, it is also the ideal that all immigrants long for. This would be the most beautiful feature of Taiwan—being a friendly island that ignores accents, makes no issue of nationality, and does not discriminate based on ethnicity.

This book brings together articles related to Southeast Asia that have appeared in *Taiwan Panorama* magazine in recent years. It includes reports on individual immigrants that take a close-up look at our struggles and hard work after coming to Taiwan, telling the stories of Taiwan's new immigrants and also serving to give encouragement to future migrants. The most important thing is to allow society to better understand us, and eliminate misunderstandings and stereotypes, so that together we can build a harmonious Taiwan.

Lin Li-chan

Legislator

Taipei, November 2018

為新南向注入「心」意
——《光華》東南亞報導30年

繼《光華》第一本叢書《面對當代人物》於1984年推出後,市場反應熱烈,開啟國內雜誌將系列報導集結成書之先河,至今「台灣光華叢書」已輯印三十餘種,包括:《國際漢學與漢學家》、《台灣原住民文化》、《台灣好滋味》等,可謂每本《光華》叢書皆為台灣不同面向之縮影。

而《光華》中英文版月刊早在1990年3月號就已刊出〈大馬的過埠新娘〉,關注台灣跟東南亞國家於文化上的交流議題,同年4月號〈目標鎖定「東協龍頭」:印尼投資篇〉、1991年12月號〈新加坡華語運動再進階〉及1998年3月號〈東南亞的台商心聲〉,報導面向已逐漸擴及至東南亞的教育、經貿層面。

一直到2014年12月,為符應我國新南向趨勢與需求,創刊《光華》東南亞三語文版(越南文、泰文、印尼文)雙月刊,除報導東南亞台商的成功故事,也關注在台東南亞移工、新住民之生活,如〈來自彩虹大地的筆〉、〈阮金紅用影像記錄人生〉、〈泰拳教育在台灣〉……等,讓議題更趨在地化,報導的角度也從台灣看東南亞,逐漸轉變為台灣多元族群中的一份子。

此外,為了讓議題更加全面與深入,《光華》編輯團隊親赴印尼、馬來西亞、越南、泰國、印度等新南向國家,分別就台商、產業、華教、國際援助、文學、藝術等面向進行探訪,讓心與心的連結,跨越距離,展現雙邊交流之豐富層次與深度。

如此精采多元的報導內容,將以「新住民」、「新采風」、「新藝向」、「新商機」、「心守護」為經緯,透過各篇深入淺出之人生故事,交織出台灣與新南向國家人民交流之具體成果。從政府到民間,在這一波波新南向的浪潮中不斷地前行,開闢出不同以往的嶄新境界。

《光華》副總編輯　

2018年11月於台北

Adding "Heart" to the New Southbound Policy
—Thirty Years of Reporting on Southeast Asia

When *Portraits of Now*, a collection of articles from the bilingual monthly magazine *Sinorama* (now *Taiwan Panorama*), was published in 1984, the market response was very enthusiastic, and it launched a trend for magazines in Taiwan to collect reports together in book form. Since then more than 30 titles have been published in the Taiwan Panorama Collection. Each presents a microcosm of a particular aspect of Taiwan.

As long ago as March of 1990, the Chinese–English edition of *Sinorama* published the article "Malaysian Husbands, Taiwan Wives," highlighting issues of cultural interactions between Taiwan and Southeast-Asian countries. With the publication of "Investing in Indonesia" in April of the same year, "Singapore's Promoting Chinese Campaign Shifts into High Gear" in December 1991, and "Taiwan's Business People in Southeast Asia Talk About the Crisis" in March 1998, the subjects covered by the magazine's reports on Southeast Asia were expanded to include education, economics, and trade.

In December of 2014, in response to Taiwan's increasing engagement with Southeast Asia—now reflected in the "New Southbound Policy"—*Taiwan Panorama* began publishing bimonthly editions in Vietnamese, Thai, and Indonesian. Besides reporting on the success stories of Taiwanese businesses in the region, we also have focused on Southeast-Asian migrant workers in Taiwan and the lives of "new immigrants," in articles such as "Rainbow Land Writers," "Basking in Sunshine After Rain—Videographer Nguyen Kim Hong," and "Ran Lee: Taiwan's Father of Muay Thai." The subject-matter of our reports has become more localized, while their perspective has shifted from how Taiwan sees Southeast Asia to the experience of Southeast Asians as members of Taiwan's multicultural society.

In addition, to provide more comprehensive, in-depth coverage, *Taiwan Panorama* journalists have traveled to New Southbound Policy partner countries including Indonesia, Malaysia, Vietnam, Thailand, and India to report on many topics, including Taiwanese businesses, industry, Chinese-language education, international aid, literature, and the arts, showing how people-to-people connections transcend distance and demonstrating the richness and depth of bilateral interactions.

Grouped into five themes—"Vocations," "Literature," "Arts," Entrepreneurship," and "Politics"—the diverse articles in this collection use approachable human interest stories to weave a tapestry of the interactions between the peoples of Taiwan and of our New Southbound Policy partner countries. As government and people continue to deepen these ties in different ways, our relations will surely take on fascinating new dimensions.

Ivan Chen
Deputy Editor-in-Chief, *Taiwan Panorama* magazine
Taipei, November 2018

Part *1*

//////////////////

新住民·台灣新職人
VOCATIONS

泰國移工的心靈導師：台泰溝通橋梁──陶雲升
Asoke Srichantr: Spiritual Mentor to Thai Migrant Workers

戲舞掌中乾坤：葉蘇珊操偶圓夢
A World in Her Hands—Yek Sansan

泰拳教育在台灣：台灣泰拳教父──李智仁
Ran Lee, Taiwan's Father of Muay Thai

台越一家，共創新味：客家媳婦阮氏秋的美味人生
A Taiwanese–Vietnamese Fusion: Hakka Daughter-in-Law Nguyen Thi Thu's Delicious Life

特別篇 爪哇特色捏麵人：移工捏出創業夢
Dough Sculpting the Java Way—A Migrant Worker Kneads Her Dreams

Asoke Srichantr:
Spiritual Mentor to Thai Migrant Workers

泰國移工的心靈導師

台泰溝通橋梁——陶雲升

文·郭玉平　圖·林旻萱

Camille Kuo / photos by Lin Min-hsuan / tr. by Bruce Humes

「我本身是泰國人，又有中華民國國籍，盡自己的力量做有助於兩邊社會的事，我想這是義不容辭的。」在泰語廣播及政府活動舞台上熱情主持的陶雲升，私底下卻寡言少語，時常沉思；而當電話響起，又肩負起為泰國貿易經濟辦事處（簡稱「泰辦處」）服務的雙重身分，多方聯繫，處處機鋒，作為政府與移工的溝通橋梁。

//////////////////////////

"As a Thai who is also a citizen of the Republic of China, I spare no effort to do things that benefit both societies. I believe this is my duty," says Asoke Srichantr, who enthusiastically hosts Thai-language broadcasts and takes the stage at government events. In private, he is reticent and often contemplative; but when the phone rings, he shoulders the additional role of working for the Thailand Trade and Economic Office in Taipei, liaising widely and speaking articulately as a bridge facilitating communications between Thai migrant workers and the Thai and Taiwan governments.

泰國公共電視台來台採訪，
由陶雲升翻譯解説。
（中央廣播電台提供）

Srichantr interpreting for an interview
conducted in Taiwan by the Thai Public
Broadcasting Service. (courtesy of RTI)

隨著政府對東南亞移工及新住民愈發重視，每年開齋節和潑水節等東南亞重要節慶，國內各縣市紛紛舉辦大型活動吸引萬人齊聚，經常參加泰語活動的人，一定會認得陶雲升高亢的聲音。

陶雲升來台近 40 年，「聲」跡縱橫泰語主持界，長期為泰籍移工解決問題，是移工公認的心靈導師。他默默付出，不居功名，如2018 年 4 月震驚社會的桃園敬鵬工廠大火事件，有 2 名泰籍移工及 6 名消防員罹難，沒人曉得為桃園市政府與罹難移工家屬奔波聯繫的人，就是他。

佛家慈悲思想與捨我其誰的承擔，如何深植陶雲升心底，這得從他的童年說起。

與收音機的不解之緣

低調的陶雲升鮮少說起自己的過去，身為泰國華人，他從小生活在泰國清邁，對電子產品很感興趣，尤其是收音機。陶雲升每次看父親開啟家裡那台老式飛利浦收音機，「我就覺得裡面是不是有人啊？可是爸爸把他拆開來曬太陽，我看又沒人啊！」也在父親的教育下，養成每天收聽美國 VOA、英國BBC、澳洲 ABC 等國際廣播的習慣。

Asoke Srichantr came to Taiwan nearly 40 years ago, and today the sound of his voice is omnipresent at events presided over by Thai-language presenters. He has long solved problems for Thai migrant workers, among whom he is recognized as a spiritual mentor. He makes his contribution quietly, oblivious to recognition. For example, in the Chin Poon factory fire in Taoyuan that shocked society this April, two Thai workers and six firefighters tragically died. Few people know, however, that it was Srichantr who undertook the busy task of liaising between local officials and the families of the Thai victims.

To understand how Buddhist compassion and a willingness to selflessly throw himself into such challenges took root in Srichantr's heart, we must look to his childhood.

Unbreakable bond with radio

Low-key Srichantr rarely speaks of his past, but he reveals that as an overseas Chinese growing up in Chiang Mai, Thailand, from his earliest years he was particularly fascinated by the radio. Guided by his father, he developed the habit of listening to international broadcasters such as the Voice of America, the British Broadcasting Corporation, and the Australian Broadcasting Corporation.

The unbreakable bond between Srichantr and radio didn't end there. At 11 years of age, he was ordained as a novice monk. Whenever he had free time, he took radios apart to observe their structure, and learned on his own how to assemble a battery-free unit containing a crystal radio receiver. After graduation and once again a layman, he went on to major in electrical engineering at a technical college. It was the 1980s, when Taiwan's electronics industry was just taking off, so Srichantr came to the island to put his studies to good use.

Six years after his arrival in Taiwan, the radio once again played a pivotal role in his life. Srichantr applied for the position of Thai announcer at the Voice of Asia, then managed by Taiwan's Broadcasting Corporation of China. Thanks to his many years listening to overseas news broadcasts and his familiarity with international political and economic terminology, he stood out among the 70 applicants.

With this appointment, Srichantr's remarkable career in broadcasting took off. He established excellent relations with many listeners, and attained the pinnacle of success in 2013 when the program he was hosting won a Golden Bell Award.

Monkhood: A Thai custom

Srichantr's childhood experience of spending a short period as a monk, followed by reversion to lay life, is not typical in Taiwan, where Mahayana Buddhism is widespread, but it is commonplace in Thailand.

陶雲升和收音機的不解之緣不僅於此，11歲出家當沙彌，每天研讀佛法和小學課程，一有閒暇就拆解收音機研究構造，無師自通，學會組裝免用電池的礦石收音機。畢業還俗後，繼續到技術學院主修電子工程學，1980年代正逢台灣電子業起飛，陶雲升順勢來台發揮所學。

來台6年後，收音機再度成為他的人生轉捩點，陶雲升勇於嘗試，報考亞洲之聲廣播電台的泰語主持人。

亞洲之聲是當時行政院新聞局委託中國廣播電台管理的海外電台，報考泰語主持的競爭對手多達70人，很多是在台留學畢業的泰籍華人，人才濟濟。由於陶雲升長年收聽國際廣播，熟悉國際政經專業用語，以及在台工作經歷豐富，脫穎而出，成為亞洲之聲泰語主持人。

或許陶雲升從沒想過，童年好奇開啟收音機，也開啟了他精彩的廣播人生。從電子業到廣播圈，讓他與聽友締結善緣，也攀上高峰，2013年獲得廣播金鐘獎的肯定。

泰國出家風俗

陶雲升童年曾短期出家、還俗的經歷，在普傳大乘佛教的台灣並不常見，但在泰國是相當稀鬆平常的事。

小乘佛教是泰國最主要的宗教信仰，「男子一生中要當一次和尚」是不成文的「義務」。出家3天、3個月或3年都隨個人志願，隨時可以還俗，前泰國國王拉瑪九世蒲美蓬亦曾按習俗短期出家15天。

泰國人認為，當和尚能夠學習作人的道理，尤其在年輕時研修佛學，可養成良好的道德觀念。所以很多女孩子認為男朋友要先去當和尚，才能結婚。此外，也有人希望藉由出家修行，以報答父母的養育之恩。

至於家境貧困促成出家機緣，是泰國民間的另一面向。許多經濟狀況不佳的家庭，為了讓孩子接受更好的教育，會把孩子送到寺廟當沙彌。

陶雲升靦腆地說自己出家是「因為家裡不富有啦！吃飯沒問題，但是要供你去上學是不太可能，所以我從小跟著師父到廟裡去出家兼念書。」

陶雲升藉著出家才能讀書，貧困並未打倒他的心志，反將逆境轉變為積極求學的墊腳石。他在短時間內研習完國中及高中課程，畢業後就在廟裡教其他小沙彌英文、科學和電子學。

廣播人不再隱身台後，因應媒體新潮流，轉型推出網路影音直播節目。（中央廣播電台提供）

No longer invisible: Joining the trend toward new media, Srichantr appears before viewers as he launches live video programming. (courtesy of RTI)

The Theravada school of Buddhism is Thailand's principal religious faith. "A man must serve as a monk once in his life" is an unwritten duty. Be it for three days, months or years, it is an individual choice, and one can return to lay life at any time. Even the late King Bhumibol Adulyadej, who passed away in 2016, did a 15-day stint as a novice monk.

Thais believe that serving as a monk can nurture a healthy set of values. Many parents hope that via monkhood, their sons can learn how to lead a proper life; the boys, for their part, hope to show their gratitude to their parents for raising them. Poverty can also be a motivating factor. "My family wasn't well off! They couldn't pay for my education," says Srichantr bashfully, "so when I was young I left home to become a monk and study with a master at the temple."

Recalling his six years as a monk, spent reciting the Buddhist classics alongside his high-school studies, Srichantr comments that "those years were very useful in shaping my outlook on life and my behavior" now that he is an adult.

Spiritual mentor to the Thai migrant community

Buddhism has planted a sense of compassion

儘管寫信人口銳減，泰語聽友每月仍有三、四百封來信。
Despite a sharp decline in letter writing, Thai-language listeners still send in three or four hundred each month.

in Srichantr's heart. Recognizing the needs of his migrant worker audience, he devoted a segment during his show to imparting basic legal knowledge and invited listeners to call in and seek advice. He even invited the director of the Thailand Trade and Economic Office in Taipei (TTEO) to explain legal regulations. Beginning with Voice of Asia right down to today's show on Radio Taiwan International (RTI)—covering three decades—he has been demystifying the law for his listeners.

Before the current 24-hour "1955 Hotline" was put in place for migrant workers to seek advice or lodge complaints, Thai workers would call Srichantr's show to clarify information and resolve misunderstandings between workers and their employers. Previously, the percentage of Thai workers who abandoned their jobs was the highest among those coming from Thailand, Indonesia, Vietnam and the Philippines; but after the show began broadcasting, the rate fell sharply to become the lowest among the four nationalities that year.

Regarding his role in facilitating intercultural communication, Srichantr recounts an incident that left a strong impression. In 1999, a serious conflict involving Thai and Filipino workers broke out at Formosa Plastics' Naphtha Cracking Plant #6 in Yunlin County. Srichantr and senior TTEO officials rushed to the scene that night. Seeing that the rioters had clubs in their hands and showed no sign of retreating, Srichantr borrowed a megaphone from the police, and explained to the Thai participants that the Thai and Taiwan governments would intervene in order to resolve the issue of the employer's high-pressure management practices. "I hope that everyone can respect our traditional Thai virtue of moderation. When I count to three, place the things in your hands on the ground and return to your dormitories. Could I have your cooperation, please?" His voice seemed to possess a magical calming quality, and at the count of three, the migrant

陶雲升說，出家那 6 年自己年紀太小不懂大道理，只會背誦，長大之後才發現當年背讀的佛學經典，「對人生哲學和作人處事方面，還滿有幫助的。」

泰籍移工的心靈導師

佛學在陶雲升心底埋下一份慈憫的情懷，他體察到移工聽友的需求，在廣播節目中開設法律常識單元，開放聽友 call in 諮詢，甚至邀請泰辦處處長來解說法規。節目從亞洲之聲，一直延續到後來的中央廣播電台（簡稱「央廣」），30 年來為眾多聽友解惑。

不像現在可撥打「1955 勞工專線」諮詢申訴，早期泰籍移工都是透過這個節目來釐清資訊，並化解許多勞資誤會。陶雲升說，有些誤會是由於台泰習俗差異造成的，例如泰國人認為頭部是很神聖的，不能亂摸，而台灣人多以拍肩摸頭表示親切，就有移工因為雇主輕輕摸頭的動作而生氣逃跑或離職返鄉。

「我有廣播的資源，又有泰辦處的正確資訊來源，我想結合這兩方面去幫助他們。」陶雲升說，原本泰籍移工的逃跑率在印泰越菲 4 國裡是最高的，節目播出後即大幅下降，成為四國最低。

關於協助溝通，陶雲升談到另一件印象深刻的事，1999 年雲林台塑六輕廠爆發嚴重的移工衝突事件，來自泰國和菲律賓的工人互丟石塊、汽油彈，大批警力無法遏止，泰辦處長官和陶雲升趕到現場與泰籍移工溝通。陶雲升看暴動人群手持棍棒沒有退散的態勢，跟鎮暴警察借用擴音器，用泰語和移工說明政府單位會介入，以解決廠商高壓管理的問題，「希望大家能夠遵循泰國人的溫良美德，我數到三，你們就把東西全部放下回去宿舍，能不能配合？」陶雲升的聲音彷彿有鎮定的魔力，他一數到三，移工們陸續放下棍棒回宿舍，解除危機。

其實陶雲升當下也很擔心逾千名的移工不願意配合，不過因為「我們在節目中說明法律常識、跟聽友聊天、幫他們解決問題，所以他們比較信任吧！」

他鄉遇故知的喜悅有如久旱逢甘霖，移工遠從泰國飛到台灣，在陌生的環境聽著不熟悉的語言，儘管遭遇糾紛也有苦難言，藉由陶雲升的泰語廣播節目，能暢所欲言、受益解惑，實是旱地甘霖之喜。林口發電廠工作十多年的泰籍移工梅山說：「我們都叫他『陶老師』，聽陶老師說話，就像爸爸媽媽在旁邊教你一樣，大家都會聽。」陶雲升如移工在台的第二父母，溫柔的叮嚀都銘記在移工們的心裡。

率先轉型經營新媒體

隨著時代轉變，使用收音機收聽廣播的人口減少，泰語聽友來信也從一個月兩、三千封減少到三、四百封，而網路收聽廣播的人數增加，網路的留言訊息也倍增。

陶雲升在外語廣播圈首開先例，他召集央廣泰語主持人一起經營 Facebook 粉絲專頁，從後台的「洞悉報告」可以看出粉絲互動十分熱絡，光是一則颱風資訊的貼文就有超過一千五百多個讚。

但陶雲升不是刻意「率先」，傑出的點閱率其實是無心插柳。起初是體恤泰籍朋友看不懂中文，希望藉由網路分享台泰的氣象、匯率及國家大事，善盡第二父母的職責，叮嚀「颱風要來了，要小心！」、「新台幣升值了，現在匯錢回泰會多更多」……等，實用的生活資訊吸引來三萬多人追蹤，甚至泰國媒體會直接引用他們粉絲專頁上的新聞，於泰國推播泰人在台灣的狀況。

轉型經營新媒體如 Facebook、YouTube，是廣播和電視媒體的趨勢，因應觀眾收聽收看型態，推出更貼近民眾需求的影音節目。雖然跨領域經營對陶雲升又是新的嘗試，但「得到的反應都是正面的，我們覺得很值得！」陶雲升仍抱著熱情，在媒體新潮流中揚帆前行。

2018 年 8 月刊出

由泰辦處與央廣合辦的「泰想見到您」活動，已提供五十多名泰籍優良勞工的子女來台省親。（中央廣播電台提供）

Thanks to the "Thai Workers Family Reunion" activity cosponsored by the TTEO and RTI, more than 50 Thai children have come to Taiwan to visit a parent who is working here. (courtesy of RTI)

workers gradually did as requested and returned to their housing, thereby ending the crisis.

In fact, at that instant Srichantr himself was worried that the workers—numbering over 1000—might not cooperate. But "since we popularize the basics of the law via our show, and chat with the audience and help them resolve problems, they're fairly trusting of us!"

Srichantr goes the extra mile, serving as a Taiwan-based surrogate "parent" for migrant workers on the island, so his gentle admonitions are imprinted in their hearts.

Pioneering switch to new media

Srichantr set a precedent among foreign-language broadcasters in Taiwan by mobilizing Thai presenters at RTI to jointly host a Facebook fan page. Based on the page's analytics, it is evident that it is highly interactive. One post alone—providing information on a typhoon—has notched up more than 1000 "likes."

Srichantr's initial motivation was that he sympathized with Thai listeners who couldn't read Chinese, and he simply hoped he could help share information via the web about local or Thai weather reports, currency exchange rates and major political events. But unexpectedly, these practical tips attracted more than 30,000 followers, and even Thai media began citing the news on this fan page, updating Thais back in their home country about the status of their fellow citizens in Taiwan.

Transitioning to operating new media like Facebook and YouTube is the trend in radio and television. This calls for launching audio and video programs that more closely match the needs of people, and the way listening and viewing audiences consume them. Cross-media management is a fresh experience for Srichantr, but he is enthusiastic about it as he surfs the waves of this new media tide.

Published in August 2018

A World in Her Hands—Yek Sansan

戲舞掌中乾坤

葉蘇珊操偶圓夢

文・鄧慧純　圖・莊坤儒

Cathy Teng / photos by Chuang Kung-ju / tr. by Geof Aberhart

上午，她穿上雨鞋，進果園裡摘番茄、到田裡照顧秧苗；下午，驅車到鄰村的包公廟前，搭好舞台，在舞台後搬演布袋戲。她是來自印尼的葉蘇珊，19歲時嫁來台灣雲林，一轉眼已經 15 個年頭了，最讓人嘖嘖稱奇的是，她練就了一手操演布袋戲的工夫，是一位專業的布袋戲操偶師。

In the morning, she pulls on her gumboots and heads out to the orchard to pick tomatoes, and then to the paddies to tend to her rice seedlings.
In the afternoon, she and her husband drive to a temple in a neighboring village, set up their stage, and put on a *po-te-hi* Taiwanese glove puppet show. Her name is Yek Sansan, and she moved to Taiwan from Indonesia at the age of 19 after marrying a Taiwanese man. Fast forward 15 years and, to the amazement of many, she has become a trained professional *po-te-hi* puppeteer.

夫唱婦隨，葉蘇珊與先生陳志能一起經營布袋戲團。

Yek Sansan and Chen Chih-neng are an inseparable couple, even running their own *po-te-hi* troupe together.

　　布袋戲是台灣重要的傳統表演藝術之一，它不僅是庶民大眾重要的娛樂，也與民間宗教信仰有緊密的關係。葉蘇珊的先生陳志能經營一個布袋戲班，每逢酬神廟會時節都要出場表演。葉蘇珊是先生的賢內助，除了操持家務外，還跟先生一起演布袋戲。

來自印尼的布袋戲操偶師

　　採訪當天，陳志能受邀到雲林縣斗南鎮的玄興宮（包公廟）幫江姓家族酬神還願，感謝神明過去一年對家族老小的保佑。夫妻倆開著載有全部生財家當的小貨車出發，到了會場，10 分鐘內，一台貨車像變形金剛變身一樣，夫妻倆一個升起車頂，一個攤開木支架，貨車順勢化身為金光閃閃的舞台。

　　開演前，需先焚香祭拜，而後燃燒金紙，此稱之為「淨台」。陳志能當天身體不適，高燒到 39 度，他撐著病體寫完千秋牌（上頭明述演出日期、列位神明與出資者）、向神明秉告此次酬神的緣由、說些吉祥話後，後續的酬神戲就委由葉蘇珊上場。

　　她依著程序，首先開演「扮仙戲」，利用木偶扮演神仙，向天上神明傳達人民的訴求。葉蘇珊一一將福仙、祿仙、壽仙三仙請上台就定位。因為是神明的角色，戲偶移動要威嚴且徐步，她一邊示範一邊解釋。接著她將一尊尊要出場的戲偶，在後台準備好，攤開滿是印尼文註記的腳本，確認每尊戲偶出場的順序。每尊戲偶有專屬的音樂，葉蘇珊聽著音樂就知道誰該出場，她還示範男女戲偶的走路方式，女偶要有妖嬌的姿態，男偶走路則豪邁大器且快步。

Po-te-hi—or *budaixi* in Mandarin—is one of Taiwan's most important traditional performing arts. Not only has it served as a big source of entertainment for the ordinary people, it also has close ties with folk religion. Yek's husband Chen Chih-neng runs a *po-te-hi* troupe, traveling to temples to perform during various festivals. Yek has become an invaluable partner to Chen, not only taking care of the household but also performing alongside him.

The puppet master from Indonesia

On the day *Taiwan Panorama* visited the couple, Chen had been invited to perform at the Bao Gong Temple in Dounan Township, Yunlin. The performance was to be part of a ceremony held by a local family to thank the gods for their protection over the past year. With everything in their truck, the couple drive to the venue, and within ten minutes of arriving, everything is ready to go. Like a Transformer, the truck changes as the couple lift up the roof and set out a wooden frame, and just like that the little truck has become a glittering stage.

Before the show starts, they light some incense and joss paper, praying for the stage to be "cleansed." Feeling ill and running a fever of 39°C, Chen steels himself and finishes writing the playbill that lists the date, the gods being honored, and the donors. Then he says a few auspicious words and turns the performance over to Yek.

The show begins with the customary "*pan-sian*" (*banxian*) curtain-raiser, using wooden puppets to portray gods relaying the wishes of the people to the heavens.

One by one, Yek introduces immortals representing wealth, fortune, and longevity, making sure they move with a majesty that befits their status as deities. All of the puppets she will be using are set up behind the stage, alongside script sheets with notes in Bahasa Indonesia to make sure she gets them out in the right order. Each puppet has its own distinctive music and rhythm, and so Yek can tell just from the music who should be coming out next. Explaining her process later, she demonstrates the different gaits of male and female puppets, with the females walking more sensually and the males more quickly and heroically.

在廟前的廣場搭好舞台，布袋戲主要是替請主酬謝神明，是演給神明看的。

Performed in booths set up in front of temples, *po-te-hi* shows are usually intended to thank the gods for their protection and good grace.

每一場布袋戲，
葉蘇珊都全神貫注而認真，
一如她生活、學習的態度。

Yek gives her all to each
and every performance,
just as she does
with everything else in life.

葉蘇珊說，到台灣後，才知道先生是布袋戲班的班主，印尼沒有布袋戲，她看著一尊尊的木偶十分有趣，就跟著先生與二伯學戲，先生把她當弟子教，嚴厲且不留情面。學偶戲要記得偶的臉部特徵與角色、出場的時機及如何動作。「初學戲時，每個戲偶的臉都搞不清楚，再加上語言不通，不時戲偶會上錯場，要靠先生在一旁緊急救援。」葉蘇珊不好意思地說。

她還記得初登場的戲是演濟公的故事，當時既緊張又害怕，怕出醜砸了場子。練習時被木偶砸到頭是家常便飯，手指要撐著木偶的頭，弄得指間紅腫也都是常有的事。問她練布袋戲最困難的地方時，葉蘇珊卻說：「只要有心要學，沒有學不會的事。」布袋戲口白多是台語，來台之初，聽不懂台語，就是一句一句問。現在跟著先生四處去酬神表演，

葉蘇珊還是會用眼睛偷學，她說這種實戰的經驗最記憶深刻。

葉蘇珊的個性認真且認分，經過多年的練習，現在的她可以兩手操三個木偶，獨挑大梁沒問題。

19歲的飄洋渡海

葉蘇珊來自印尼西加里曼丹省山口洋市，是客家華僑。多年前，印尼發生排華暴動，媽媽擔心女兒的未來，透過媒人引介，讓葉蘇珊飄洋過海嫁到台灣來。

葉蘇珊回想剛到台灣時，中文、台語都聽不懂，加上當時先生貪杯，無心於事業，布袋戲客源不穩定，讓她曾想當個落跑新娘。但女兒出生了，家庭經濟多靠葉蘇珊四處打工撐起，後來先生戒了酒，願意全心投入事業，夫妻倆胼手胝足地把三人小家庭再次撐起。

Yek says she only found out that her new husband was the head of a puppet theater troupe after she arrived in Taiwan. *Po-te-hi* doesn't really exist in Indonesia, so she found the puppets intriguing. She started learning the art from her husband and his uncle, with Chen taking her on as an apprentice and not letting their relationship soften his strict teaching style. Learning puppetry involves learning the special facial features and characters of each of the puppets, as well as when they take the stage and how they move. "At first I couldn't keep the puppets' faces straight in my head, and the language barrier made it even harder," says Yek, embarrassed. "I would send them out at the wrong times, and had to rely on my husband to rescue the show."

Her first performance was the story of the mad monk Ji Gong, and she still remembers how nervous and scared she was, afraid she'd screw up and ruin everything.

When asked what the hardest part of learning *po-te-hi* was, though, Yek responds that "as long as you really, really want to learn, there's nothing too hard to figure out." Getting hit in the head by puppets during practice is common, and as their heads are propped up by the fingers, swollen fingers are far from unusual. On top of that, when she first arrived Yek spoke no Taiwanese, and had to ask what every sentence meant. A believer in the idea of "no pain, no gain," she stuck to it, and now she travels all over the island with her husband to perform, but even still she is always watching and learning—real-world experience is the easiest to remember, she says.

A hard worker by nature, Yek has invested years into her practice, and now can control three puppets with just two hands, enough to put on a full show solo.

葉蘇珊用戲偶逗弄著孩子，稚嫩的孩子好奇又畏懼她手中的戲偶。

Yek Sansan entertaining a small child with one of her puppets, the child at once curious about and wary of the puppet in her hands.

開心農場當副業

布袋戲的邀演不是每個月都有，只逢2、3、8、9這幾個重要月分才有較多的酬神活動，所以葉蘇珊跟先生商量，跟村裡的老人家租了幾塊地，自己耕作增加收入。

一分二的地（近1,200平方公尺）開墾種植小番茄，另外一塊地種花椰菜，開始了自己的開心農場。只見葉蘇珊巡著田園，把差不多可收成的白花椰菜用旁邊的葉子摺起來蓋住，防止鳥來啄食，壞了賣相。還有一塊地正在打田放水，等整完地之後，就可以插秧了。

一路上，葉蘇珊解說著，哪一種番茄的種苗較好，這方田地種完番茄之後要改種其他的作物，以養地力。問她怎麼懂這麼多？之前在印尼下過田嗎？她說沒有，以前在印尼每天都是穿著亮麗在店裡當銷售員，在台灣雖然辛苦，但學習更多、收穫更多。

認真且認分的天才

路上不時遇到村裡的長者，他們總是停下腳步跟葉蘇珊話家常，分享著田裡的花椰菜何時收成才能賣得好價錢、纍纍的番茄已經在藤上可以採收了、那方水田已經準備好，可以翻土插秧了，葉蘇珊也以熟練的台語應對著。

村裡耆老對於陳志能娶到這個厲害又勤奮的妻子都多所稱讚，「葉蘇珊肯做事，又會演布袋戲，真的是天才。」鄰居對記者這麼說。但這一切的稱讚都是葉蘇珊認真生活、努力勤奮換來的。

來到台灣15年了，她全心融入台灣的生活。家裡的神桌上供奉著西秦王爺，祂是戲曲界的保護神，葉蘇珊每日早晚虔誠上香，祈求庇佑全家平安、事業興隆。

種番茄和演布袋戲哪個比較賺錢呢？「馬馬虎虎啦！」葉蘇珊說，只是不管布袋戲或農作，都是看天吃飯。酬神是跟神明的約定，所以只要訂好日子，除非真是狂風暴雨，都要依約演出。儘管現在看布袋戲的人少了許多，葉蘇珊覺得這是跟神明與請主的約定，每場戲都是賣力搬演著戲偶。

戲台後，狹長的空間，看著夫妻倆伴著音樂，交錯穿梭操弄戲偶的身影。這是在台灣的一方角落中，幸福的背影。

2016年8月刊出

夫妻倆承租了幾塊地，種點番茄、蔬菜，貼補家用。

Yek and her husband rent a few plots of land where they grow tomatoes and cauliflower to supplement their income.

Leaving home at 19

Yek is originally from the city of Singkawang in Indonesia's West Kalimantan Province, and is of Hakka descent. After the 1998 anti-Chinese riots in Indonesia, Yek's mother began worrying about her daughter's future and contacted a matchmaker to marry her off to a Taiwanese man.

When she arrived in Taiwan, Yek recalls, she spoke neither Mandarin nor Taiwanese, and her husband's puppet theater business was on rocky terrain as he was a bit of a drinker and not committing himself to his work. For a while, she even considered running away. After their daughter was born, for a while the family finances rested predominantly on Yek's shoulders. Then her husband quit drinking and invested himself back into his puppetry, and the three of them began rebuilding their new family.

There isn't call for *po-te-hi* shows all the time, though. February, March, August, and September are peak time for thanksgiving events, so Yek and her husband negotiated a few blocks of land from a local family to start a small-scale farm and complement their income.

Their little "Farmville" is half used for growing tomatoes, while the other half is dedicated to cauliflower. Yek inspects their plot carefully, looking for cauliflowers that are almost ready to harvest and folding their leaves over them to protect them from birds, keeping their salability up. Previously they had another plot dedicated to Chinese flowering cabbage, but right now that part is unused, with irrigation being set up to make it ready for planting later.

As we check out their plants, Yek explains which types of tomato grow better here and how they fertilize the soil in preparation for the next crop to go in their place. When asked how she knows so much about farming and whether she had worked on a farm back in Indonesia, Yek replies that she hadn't,

and that in fact she had worked as a nicely dressed sales assistant. Life in Taiwan has been hard work, she says, but has also taught her a lot.

Genius is 99% perspiration

From time to time, elderly folk from the village will stop by and have a chat with Yek, talking about when the cauliflower will be ready, how the tomatoes are about ripe enough to harvest, about turning the soil once the other plot is properly irrigated.... Throughout all of this, Yek chats along in smooth Taiwanese. These old villagers have nothing but praise for the hardworking, impressive woman that local boy Chen has married, with neighbors telling us: "Yek Sansan is a hard worker and a *po-te-hi* performer, she's a real genius." Such praise is hardly unfounded, given the diligence and hard work Yek has shown in her time here.

In the 15 years she has been in Taiwan, Yek has fully thrown herself into local life. In their home, the couple have a shrine to Lord Xiqin, who could be considered the "patron saint" of *po-te-hi*, and every morning and evening they light incense and pray to him to support their family and their business.

So which is the better money earner, tomatoes or *po-te-hi*? "They're both alright," Yek responds. "Either way we rely on the heavens to make enough to put food on the table." A thanksgiving ceremony is essentially an appointment with the gods, so once the day is set, barring violent storms the show must go on. While few people watch *po-te-hi* shows today, Yek still takes every show seriously, considering them deals with both their clients and the gods, and as such she gives each performance her all.

Watching from backstage as this husband-and-wife team cram themselves into a tiny space and maneuver their puppets around, we get a glimpse of real happiness in this small corner of Taiwan.

Published in August 2016

Ran Lee, Taiwan's Father of Muay Thai

泰拳教育在台灣

台灣泰拳教父——李智仁

文・郭玉平　圖・林旻萱

Camille Kuo / photos by Lin Min-hsuan / tr. by Geof Aberhart

你印象裡的泰拳是什麼樣的運動呢？一向以凶悍著稱的泰拳，在高雄仁李泰拳館裡，並沒有電影中的殘暴對打景象，反而是連高血壓患者都能天天操練的武術。

館長李智仁是緬甸華僑，年輕時於緬甸及泰國習得正統泰拳功夫，在國際泰拳風氣興起之際將泰拳帶進台灣，因此獲「台灣泰拳教父」的尊稱。他教拳超過 17 年，桃李滿門，包含總統貼身隨扈在內，學員們積極參與國內外泰拳和散打賽事，打出泰拳一片天。

What comes to mind when you hear the name "muay Thai"? Despite its reputation for ferocity, the muay Thai practiced at Ran Lee Muaythai Gym in Kaohsiung is nowhere near as brutal as what you've seen in the movies. In fact, even people with high blood pressure can take part!

Gym leader Ran Lee studied orthodox muay Thai in Myanmar and Thailand. As the art began to grow in popularity internationally, Lee brought it to Taiwan, earning him the title of "father of muay Thai in Taiwan." He has taught muay Thai for over 17 years now, and among his many students in that time he can count even a bodyguard of an ROC president. Lee's students have also put in excellent showings at both muay Thai and sanda (Chinese kickboxing) events at home and abroad, building quite a reputation for their art.

走進台灣仁李泰拳館，空氣中瀰漫著痠痛藥膏的氣味，館長李智仁席地為學員敲打釘補護具，午後日光灑落，這和平的場景和多數人對泰拳的印象大相逕庭。泰國的傳統搏擊技術相對於拳擊、散打等技擊術，比賽規則少，可在極短距離使用拳、腳、膝、肘進行攻擊，保有戰鬥民族徒手搏擊的殺傷力，因此受傷流血的機率高，所以，泰拳常被評為「狠辣兇殘」。

現今流行的「擂台泰拳」，又稱「商業泰拳」，規定選手必須配戴拳套，安全性提高，並在 60 年代風靡全球。雖然如此，台灣接觸泰拳的人卻不多，於是有東南亞血統的李智仁首開先河，將泰式拳法運用在拳擊比賽中，被公認是台灣泰拳史最悠久的開山祖師。

向泰國拳王亞批勒拜師學拳

李智仁是緬甸華僑，受到李小龍電影的啟迪，10 歲開始在緬甸學習中國功夫和緬甸拳。

轉型練泰拳則是在移民台灣後。李智仁看到《國家地理雜誌》頻道介紹泰國國寶級拳王亞批勒‧寶希蘭（Apidej Sit-Hirun），亞批勒一生累積 340 場勝績，蟬聯全泰拳擊、西洋拳 7 項冠軍，更進軍國際拳壇，迄今拳壇仍無人能出其右。李智仁深受其吸引，立即飛往泰國拜亞批勒為師。

在泰國培訓，每天早上 5 點起床跑步、練拳，一天下來將近 10 小時的激烈特訓，身體疲憊到快無法負擔。李智仁談到學拳：「最苦的是克服受傷的後遺症，像是脛骨會受傷，就是脛骨練得不夠硬，要再加強。」療傷後還要克服心理陰影加強訓練，這種苦只有自己能體會。

所幸有緬甸拳的基礎，李智仁得以縮短學程，很快就學成歸台，李智仁說：「我非常喜歡泰國，泰國風情又接近緬甸，所以我將泰國當作第三個故鄉，台灣是第二個。」

親身經驗台、泰學拳的差異

在泰國，泰拳十分普及大眾，甚至一個泰國家庭 6 個小孩，就會有 2 個自小生活在道館，以終身志業的方式培養，成人後再將比賽所得平分回饋給道場。

反觀台灣，因為泰拳未商業化，泰拳選手無法將其作為職業維持生計。所以，大部分的台灣人是抱著健康練習或體型雕塑的心態學習泰拳，練習模式跟泰國當然不同。

但是在台灣學泰拳有一大優勢，環境相對富裕，加上政府推行的全民健康保險，所有人民都享有平價醫療的權利，對於時常受傷的泰拳選手，有很大的醫療保障。學員黃于修在泰國拳賽曾看到選手受傷，當地醫生

泰拳界傳奇人物亞批勒（右），晚年投身泰拳教育，教導過多位世界級拳手及影視明星。（李智仁提供）
Muay Thai legend Apidej Sit-Hirun (right) dedicated his later years to teaching the art, with his students including a number of world-class fighters and movie stars.
(courtesy of Ran Lee)

李智仁首開先例，
將泰拳運用在台灣拳擊比賽中，
被尊稱為「台灣泰拳教父」。

Ran Lee was a pioneer of muay Thai in Taiwan, putting his skills to use in boxing matches around the country and earning himself a reputation as the father of Taiwanese muay Thai.

Stepping into Ran Lee Muaythai Gym, I am immediately struck by the smell of liniment that fills the air. Gym leader Ran Lee sits on the floor repairing protective gear for his students as the afternoon sun pours in. It is a peaceful scene quite at odds with most people's impressions of muay Thai. In comparison with other combat sports like boxing or sanda, there are fewer rules in competitive muay Thai. Punches, kicks, knees, and elbows can all be used at extremely close range, which means the fighters' blows remain incredibly powerful and the chance of drawing blood is high, contributing to the general perception of muay Thai as a brutal art.

The modern, ring-based form began to gain popularity worldwide in the 1960s. However, relatively few people in Taiwan engaged with the sport,

so Ran Lee began by putting muay Thai techniques to use in boxing matches. It was this that earned him recognition as the founding father of Taiwanese muay Thai.

Learning from a master

At age ten, the Myanmar-born Lee began studying Chinese kung fu and lethwei (Burmese kickboxing), only switching to muay Thai after he moved to Taiwan, where he saw a piece on the National Geographic Channel about muay Thai legend Apidej Sit-Hirun of Thailand. Sit-Hirun racked up an impressive 340 career wins and at one point held a total of seven muay Thai and boxing titles at the same time. To this day, no one in the muay Thai world has been able to match Sit-Hirun's achievements. Lee

只給了一包便宜的綠色藥水，選手喝完馬上腹瀉排出體內瘀積的熱氣，雖然有效但成分不明，令人擔憂；相形之下，在台灣學泰拳「你沒有後顧之憂，只要有心練，還是可以變拳王。」李智仁說。

習武先習德——李教練的教學現場

台灣各拳館教授泰拳的風格和技術都各有千秋，有些會側重摔技，有些側重肘或膝，而仁李泰拳館則是著重於加強拳腳，李智仁說：「摔是泰拳的精髓，拳腳是泰拳的基本功。」因為腳步打穩，出拳才會紮實。且根據醫學理論，全身70％的肌肉在下半身，訓練泰拳步伐能加強大腿肌力，不僅有助於血液循環，也能培養泰拳需要的大量體力。

基礎工夫奠定後，李智仁會親自拿靶一對一教學。護身靶具的重量再加乘拳踢的力量，戴靶者需承受的攻擊力道相當大，一堂課二十多位學生練下來，受傷是常有的事；但李智仁知道，沒有一個學生的弱點是一樣的，親自戴靶才能因材施教。所以在李教練的教學現場，沒有固定教法，只有專屬每一位學員的叮嚀。

仁李泰拳館的宗旨：「學藝先學禮，習武先習德」。不尊師重道或心存邪念的人，都曾被李智仁逐出師門。

好勇的人學習泰拳，反而會在基礎訓練的過程學到「降伏其心」。教練黃于修國中時期學過太極拳，自認為程度不差，一進泰拳館就好大喜戰，挑戰其他學員，結果卻一敗塗地，之前所習的技藝全部洗牌重練。黃于修學拳7年的體悟是「泰拳帶給我的是生活上的態度，我更懂得沉澱、思考，避戰但不懼戰。」

「教練教導我們要守倫理、孝順，學拳不可爭強鬥狠。」學員們都稱呼「邱哥」的邱訂助

仁李泰拳館學員
一進拳館，
即自動自發暖身練拳。

//////////////////////////

When students enter
Ran Lee Muaythai Gym,
they immediately get started
on their warm-ups.

Experiencing the differences

To the Thai people, muay Thai can be a profession, while most Taiwanese study it as a form of exercise or to get in shape, and so their approach to it is vastly different from the Thai approach.

That said, there is one big advantage to learning muay Thai in Taiwan—with Taiwan being comparatively more affluent and having a national health insurance system, there are better healthcare options open to oft-injured fighters. "You don't have to worry about the medical side; you can just focus on training and becoming a champion," says Lee.

Respect above all

Ran Lee Muaythai Gym focuses on fist- and footwork. "Clinches are the essence of muay Thai," says Lee, "and fistwork and footwork are the fundamental techniques." If your footwork is solid, then your punches will be too. Some 70% of our muscles are in the lower body, and by strengthening the thighs through legwork, you can not only improve circulation but also develop the physical strength muay Thai demands. Once the foundations are laid, Lee then works with students one on one, because only by wielding the pads himself can he really tailor the training to the student.

Ran Lee Muaythai Gym's guiding principle is, "When learning an art, first learn the rules; when learning to fight, first learn to be moral." Those eager to learn muay Thai will learn through basic training to "subdue their minds," as Buddhist scripture puts it. Trainer Aldo Huang began his martial arts studies learning tai chi in junior high. By his own estimations, he got pretty good at it. Then he joined Ran Lee's gym and challenged the students there, but they mopped the floor with him. He felt he had to go back to basics and reevaluate everything he'd learned. In his seven years studying muay Thai, Huang says his biggest takeaway has been that "muay Thai has given me a new attitude toward life.

侯怡君（上圖）歷經數場賽事，與克服病痛的莊福仁（下圖），都在在體現堅持到底的運動家精神。

Ann Hou (top) has competed in several tournaments, while Chuang Fu-jen (above) has overcome poor health to learn muay Thai. Both exemplify the athletic spirit of perseverance.

was immediately drawn to Sit-Hirun and jumped on a flight to Thailand to ask the champion to take him on as a student.

His training in Thailand saw him spend ten hours in intense muay Thai training each day. It was almost too much to physically bear. "The hardest part was getting over injuries. If I injured my shin, for example, then I had to take it as a sign I hadn't toughened that area up enough, so I had to train harder," says Lee about that time.

Fortunately, with his background in lethwei, Lee was able to learn at a more rapid pace, and soon he was back in Taiwan. "I love Thailand. I consider Thailand my third home; Taiwan's my second."

說。他笑稱自己是仁李最老的學生，跟隨李智仁學拳多年，他形容李教練不管是武術或待人處事各方面，都值得大家學習，因此桃李滿天下，職業含括法官、陸海空軍人、維安特勤和警察等。

學生積極參加國際泰拳賽事

「泰拳講求實用性，一定要實戰對打。」李智仁說，他從自身經驗深深理解到：閉門修煉無法提升拳技與心智，唯有參加正式比賽才能跳躍性的成長。李智仁常鼓勵學生參加國內外賽事，經歷過多次比賽的學生分享：「會更認識自己，愈打愈謙虛，因為知道自己懂很少。」侯怡君說。

侯怡君年僅 28 歲，看到她靈活的身手，很難想像剛進拳館的她體重高達 85 公斤，教練一句：「要不要去比賽？」讓她卯足全力一年多內瘦身至可參賽的 57 公斤，「我覺得比賽最苦的是減重，看別人狂吃，自己只能喝水。」侯怡君說。然而辛勞在上場後就被拋到腦後，尤其是在獲勝時，什麼都不苦了。

另一位仁李泰拳館的榮耀拳手羅啟榮，在 2012 年香港皇者拳霸賽打進決賽，與香港拳王陳啟迪爭奪亞洲拳王金腰帶。陳啟迪是世界業餘泰拳冠軍，技術和氣勢都勝過羅啟榮，「但是阿榮從頭打到尾，而且勢均力敵。」李智仁讚譽羅啟榮能在國際賽事奪下亞軍，實屬難得。

生活實踐泰拳精神：堅持

和泰拳相提並論的散打，其比賽規則採用三戰兩勝制，只要前兩回得勝，就不用進入第三回合；但泰拳不同，泰拳五回合以最後一局定勝負，儘管前四回合連敗，只要在第五回合奪勝就是贏家。賽制所呈現的正是泰拳精神──堅持，如李智仁常說的：「前後未分，終點為定。」

練習泰拳其實是在練習一個人的意志力，新進學員莊福仁表白：「訓練真的很痛苦，我光是拉筋就常常痛到哭。」莊福仁患有高

現代泰拳比賽規定選手須配戴拳套，提高安全性。
Modern competitive muay Thai rules require fighters to wear gloves, improving safety.

血壓，為了健康而來學習泰拳，短短 4 個月內，病情得到控制，也經醫生許可調降高血壓藥量。痛苦的訓練都能堅持下來了，生活及工作上還有什麼過不去呢？

在台灣推廣泰拳至全球

隨著時代推移，推廣泰拳的方式也逐漸轉變，李智仁常受邀至健身房示範，或是到孤兒院跳泰拳戰舞、在大專院校擔任泰拳社團顧問等，讓更多人瞭解泰拳。

仁李泰拳館就像是個小熔爐，有日、法、西……等二十多國的拳手慕名來台拜師，甚至有沙烏地阿拉伯、北京等地方贊助商邀請李智仁去指導，但他都一一拒絕，「畢竟這邊屬於我們，我的家在台灣。」李智仁說。

李智仁認定台灣為最終的家鄉，泰拳教育是他生活的全部，每晚課程開始，學員汗水氣息漸漸覆蓋拳館空氣中的藥膏味，儘管昨日練習的傷痛依舊，李智仁仍用行動貫徹泰拳的精神──努力、堅持到底！

2018 年 7 月刊出

It's taught me to be more settled and more thoughtful, and to try to avoid fighting, but not fear it."

"Coach teaches us to be ethical and filial." Another of Lee's students, Chiu Ting-chu, has been studying with Lee for many years and describes him as someone worthy of learning from in terms of how he interacts with people and deals with situations as well as in muay Thai. Lee works with a wide variety of people, with students from over 20 countries whose professions include judges, professional military personnel, and police officers.

International tournaments

"Muay Thai emphasizes practicality and must be tested in combat," says Lee. Studying in isolation can never create true improvement of skills or mentality—only by challenging yourself in actual competition can you really grow. Lee frequently encourages his students to compete. "The more you fight, the better you know yourself and the more humble you get, because you realize you don't actually know all that much," says student Ann Hou.

Seeing how nimble the 28-year-old Hou is, it's hard to imagine that when she first joined the gym she weighed 85 kilos, yet the coach asked straight out if she wanted to compete. Over the next year and change, she spared no effort to get to her fighting weight, 57 kg. "The hardest part of competing, I would say, is cutting weight. I see everyone pigging out and I'm stuck just drinking water," says Hou. However, once she stepped into the ring, all those worries were behind her, and the hard work proved to be all worth it when she stepped out a winner.

Another of Lee's students, Luo Qirong, made it to the final match of the 2012 Hong Kong Supreme Fight Championship, ultimately being defeated by HK fighter Chan Kai Tik for the Asian Gold Belt. Chan was a world amateur muay Thai champion, and was technically superior to Luo, "But Luo kept at it the whole way through and was an even match for him," says Lee in praise of Luo's impressive achievement.

Living the muay Thai spirit

Competitive muay Thai fights go five rounds, with the last one deciding the winner. Even if you lose all four of the previous ones, if you can take that fifth round, you win. This setup is a display of the spirit of muay Thai: perseverance. As Lee says, you don't know the final score until the end.

New student Chuang Fu-jen admits that "the training is really grueling; even just doing the stretches makes me want to cry." Chuang suffers from high blood pressure and took up muay Thai for his health. In just four months he has been able to get his condition under control, and his doctor even gave permission for him to cut down on his medication. Studying muay Thai is about training your willpower, and that is then reflected in both life and work. If you can make it through the pain of training, what can't you make it through?

Promoting Taiwanese muay Thai

How muay Thai is promoted is something that has been changing with the times. Lee is now often invited to gyms to give demonstrations; to orphanages to show his *ram muay*, the traditional "dance" performed before fights in honor of the fighter's teacher; and to college muay Thai clubs as a consultant, helping more and more people get familiar with the sport.

Even now that he has settled in Kaohsiung and is raising a family, Ran Lee's life is still focused on muay Thai education. Every night as class gets under way, the scent of the students' sweat replaces the smell of liniment that otherwise pervades the gym. Even when the pain of yesterday's practice is still fresh, Lee pushes on, realizing the spirit of muay Thai: perseverance, to the very end!

Published in July 2018

A Taiwanese–Vietnamese Fusion:
Hakka Daughter-in-Law Nguyen Thi Thu's Delicious Life

台越一家，共創新味
客家媳婦阮氏秋的美味人生

文 · 張瓊方　圖 · 林格立
Chang Chiung-fang / photos by Jimmy Lin / tr. by Scott Williams

阮氏秋，一位越南永隆鄉下出生長大的姑娘，15 年前隻身越洋遠嫁來台，雙十年華、秀氣的小姑娘，憑著聰慧伶俐與刻苦耐勞的本性，勇闖台中東勢料理世家，在夫家開設的「淺嚐時尚料理廚房」裡，開始了她在台灣的美味人生。

////////////////////////

Nguyen Thi Thu came to Taiwan 15 years ago after wedding a Taiwanese man. A delicate Vietnamese woman from rural Vinh Long Province, she was then just 20 years old, but quick-witted and hardworking. She put those traits to good use at Light Taste, her husband's family's Taichung restaurant, where she began what has become her delicious life in Taiwan.

2009 年，阮氏秋與高齡 88 歲的婆婆廖劉桃巒攜手參加客家美食創意大賽，婆媳聯手烹調客家名菜「客家小炒」，拿下國際組冠軍，傳為佳話。

戀戀木瓜香

2011 年公共電視以阮氏秋與先生廖慶星的故事為藍本，拍製公視人生劇展《戀戀木瓜香》單元劇，請來重量級資深演員梅芳飾演客家婆婆，夏靖庭飾演先生，越南知名演員海倫清桃飾演越南媳婦。劇組商借台中東勢廖家及位於潭子的餐廳「淺嚐時尚料理廚房」實地拍攝。

當年 4 月中旬，《戀戀木瓜香》上檔播出，阮氏秋一時間成了家喻戶曉的「名人」，故事發生地「淺嚐時尚料理廚房」的生意也因此提高了兩成。

阮氏秋爆紅，她受邀上遍各大美食節目，示範如何烹調冠軍菜「客家小炒」。但婆婆廖劉桃巒卻受了點委屈，《戀戀木瓜香》為求戲劇效果，劇情高潮起伏，刻意誇大了婆媳間的衝突，劇中梅芳飾演的廖奶奶宛如一位蓄意刁難媳婦的「惡婆婆」。

拍攝期間，在一旁觀戲的阮氏秋幾度心驚直言：「我婆婆沒有這麼壞啦！」劇組向廖家及廖老太太解釋劇情鋪陳和衝突跌宕的需要，不過看戲的人們不明箇中蹊蹺，以為阮氏秋真的被婆婆欺負了。「我到市場買菜都有人過來問我：『妳是怎麼熬過來的啊？』」阮氏秋無奈地笑說。

情定胡志明市

受欺負不至於，但隻身來到人生地不熟、語言又不通的異地他鄉，難免要經過一段辛苦的適應融入期。

話說這一段台越情緣，起源於 15 年前。

現任弘光科技大學餐旅管理系教授的廖慶星，當年是圓山飯店主廚、離婚多年的他，隻身與朋友到越南旅遊，經介紹在胡志明市認識了阮氏秋，50 歲的廖慶星動了再婚的念頭，娶回當年才 21 歲的阮氏秋。

「十幾年前永隆好多人嫁來台灣，」阮氏秋說，現在台中就有十幾位來自越南的姊妹，大家會定期聚會話家常。阮氏秋在家中 4 個孩子裡排行第二，大哥業已成家，「當時心想嫁到台灣來也不錯，不過這幾年這種現象已經漸漸少了。」

阮氏秋初到台灣，廖慶星還任職台北圓山飯店，將她單獨留在台中潭子才開張二、三個月的「淺嚐時尚料理廚房」幫忙。「多多跟人接觸，中文才能學得比較快。」廖慶星說，當年阿秋（阮氏秋）是廚房裡的開心果，經常說錯話逗得大家哈哈大笑。

阮氏秋白天在餐廳幫忙，晚上到學校念「新住民中文班」，就這樣一路念到國中畢業，中文能力進步不少，不但聽、說沒問題，還能寫，已非當年吳下阿蒙。

阮氏秋的學習能力很強，很快就能進入狀況，廖慶星後來乾脆將餐廳採買的重責大任交給她，市場攤商都認識她，見到她來採買，總會親切地招呼：「阿秋來了！」、「阿

這道阮氏秋的創意開胃菜，取名「戀戀木瓜香」。

Nguyen Thi Thu created this appetizer, which she calls "Papaya Love."

公視劇組在台中「淺嚐時尚料理廚房」實地拍攝，婆媳二人與劇組合影。右二為海倫清桃，右三為梅芳，左一為夏靖庭。（淺嚐時尚料理廚房提供）

Nguyen and her mother-in-law worked with a Public Television Service production team while it filmed on location at the family's Light Taste restaurant in Taichung. The photo captures the actors playing the family: Helen Thanh Dao (second from right), Mei Fang (third from right), and Hsia Ching-ting (far left). (courtesy of Light Taste)

阮氏秋與婆婆廖劉桃鑾聯手拿下 2009 年客家美食創意大賽冠軍。（淺嚐時尚料理廚房提供）

Nguyen and her mother-in-law Liao-Liu Taoluan won top honors at the 2009 Creative Hakka Gourmet Food Competition. (courtesy of Light Taste)

阮氏秋的個性執著，從備料開始就要求盡善盡美。

Nguyen demands perfection at every stage of preparation.

In 2009, Nguyen Thi Thu and her then 88-year-old mother-in-law, Liao-Liu Taoluan, took first prize in the Creative Hakka Gourmet Food Competition's international category with their Hakka Stir Fry, a signature Hakka dish.

Papaya Love

In 2011, Taiwan's Public Television Service based an episode of its *Life Story* program on the lives of Nguyen and her husband, Liao Ching-hsin. The producers called the episode "Papaya Love" and cast several well-known actors in the leading roles: the Vietnamese actress Helen Thanh Dao as Nguyen, Mei Fang as her Hakka mother-in-law, and Hsia Ching-ting as her husband. The team even shot portions of the program in the Liaos' home in Taichung and at the family's Light Taste restaurant in the city's Tanzi District.

The episode turned Nguyen into a household name, and led to appearances on many of Taiwan's biggest cooking shows to demonstrate how she makes Hakka Stir Fry. But her mother-in-law suffered a bit from the attention. The producers deliberately overplayed conflicts between Nguyen and her mother-in-law to create dramatic tension, and portrayed the latter as being very hard on Nguyen.

Watching the cast shoot the episode, Nguyen

秋的個性比較執著，食材都要精挑細選漂亮的，『仁仁仁』（台語，意即完美無瑕）的才要。」廖慶星笑說。

越南媳婦的拿手菜

南下台中潭子拜訪廖慶星與阮氏秋夫妻前，電話中請求她現場為我們示範幾道拿手菜，她二話不說，選擇示範店裡的兩道招牌菜：「客家小炒」與「戀戀木瓜香」。

客家小炒幾乎是所有客家餐廳必備的名菜，但真正做得道地的卻少之又少。

魷魚、三層肉、豆干、蔥、蒜、芹菜、紅蔥酥、蝦米、辣椒……阮氏秋備好料，切菜下刀俐落不含糊。這道 7 年前她與婆婆一起奪冠的客家菜，阮氏秋可是下足功夫苦練過，「我炒了三十幾隻魷魚才去參加比賽。」阮氏秋笑談當年。

起鍋、下料、翻炒，阮氏秋架勢十足，身為五星級飯店主廚、大學餐旅管理系教授的先生廖慶星只在一旁微笑觀看、拍照，英雄無用武之地。「三層肉要煸出油，讓香氣出來，接著炒豆干、芹菜等配料才會香，」阮氏秋透露，客家小炒成功的祕訣在於：「小小火、慢慢炒，將食材煸出香氣來。」

「戀戀木瓜香」指的就是越式涼拌青木瓜，這道菜是阮氏秋開發的創意開胃菜，公視人生劇場走紅後，店裡乾脆將菜名改成與劇名「戀戀木瓜香」一樣。

材料以青木瓜和紅蘿蔔為主角，刨絲之後加上糖、酸辣醬、檸檬、花生、香菜等配料，就大功告成。阮氏秋在酸辣醬裡加入了家鄉味：魚露，讓這道涼拌菜有了越式風味，她還不忘提醒：「青木瓜和紅蘿蔔絲必須冰鎮 15 分鐘才會爽脆可口。」

歲數相差一甲子的婆媳，
聯手烹調，其樂融融。
（淺嚐時尚料理廚房提供）

Nguyen and her mother-in-law take great pleasure in cooking together in spite of their 60-year age difference. (courtesy of Light Taste)

客家小炒是客家名菜，但要懂得
「眉角」才能做得道地。

An authentic Hakka Stir Fry, a
signature Hakka dish, takes a
good deal of skill to make.

often thought: "My mother-in-law was never that bad!" But viewers came away with the impression that Nguyen had been bullied. "People I ran into while out grocery shopping would always ask: 'How did you bear it?'" she recalls with a frustrated laugh.

Love in Ho Chi Minh City

Nguyen was a stranger in a strange land when she first came to Taiwan. Adapting was difficult because she didn't speak the language.

She met her husband some 15 years ago.

Now a professor with the Department of Hospitality Management at Hungkuang University, Liao was then head chef at Taipei's Grand Hotel, and was divorced. He got to know Nguyen in Ho Chi Minh City while on a trip to Vietnam with friends. The two fell in love, and 50-year-old Liao asked the 21-year-old Nguyen to marry him.

"A lot of women from Vinh Long married Taiwanese in those days," says Nguyen, noting that she has a dozen or so Vietnamese "sisters" in the Taichung area who often gather for chats.

When Nguyen arrived in Taiwan, Liao was still working at the Grand Hotel in Taipei. Nguyen went down to Taichung without him, helping out at the family's recently opened Light Taste restaurant in Tanzi. "She was interacting with people a lot, which helped her pick up Mandarin quickly," recalls Liao. He says that Nguyen injected humor into the restaurant's kitchen, where her malapropisms made everyone chuckle.

Nguyen worked in the restaurant during the day, and took Mandarin classes for immigrants in the evening. She eventually completed a middle-school equivalency certificate, becoming fluent in spoken Mandarin and learning to read and write the language along the way. Liao later turned the restaurant's food-buying duties over to her. Nowadays, all the vendors in the market know her and greet her warmly when she comes in to make purchases.

Her best dish

Nearly every Hakka restaurant serves Hakka Stir Fry, but very few serve a really authentic version of the dish.

Squid, pork, dried tofu, scallions, garlic, celery, crispy shallots, dried shrimp, chili peppers... Nguyen wields her cleaver with skill while preparing the ingredients. She worked hard to learn to make the dish with which she and her mother-in-law won a competition seven years ago. "I cooked more than 30 squid before entering the competition," she recalls with a laugh.

"You fry the pork belly to render the fat and bring out the aroma, then fry the dried tofu, celery and other ingredients to give it flavor." Nguyen reveals that the trick to Hakka Stir Fry is cooking it "low and slow" to bring out the flavors of the ingredients.

「淺嚐」位於台中潭子加工區對面，走的是多元路線，每到假日座無虛席。

Located opposite Taichung's Tanzi Export Processing Zone, Light Taste offers a wide-ranging menu and is always packed on the weekends.

共炒美味人生

台越聯姻在台灣不是新聞，婚姻生活的箇中滋味也不盡相同。若以「淺嚐」的兩道招牌料理來形容阮氏秋在台灣的生活況味，那麼「客家小炒」便如同她們婆媳之間的相處，愈煸愈香，回味無窮；「戀戀木瓜香」則像他們夫妻之間的情感，酸中帶甜，微辣帶香，這是一種台、越調和後，雙方都喜歡的融合滋味。

現在高齡 94 歲的婆婆廖劉桃鸞多居住在東勢老家，偶而還會自己坐公車來店裡看看。或許是料理人的靈魂不老，廖慶星雖然替媽媽請了印傭，但老人家嫌她不會煮菜，堅持自己煮飯跟印傭一起吃。

媳婦阮氏秋也從第一線退下來，一方面為了讓自己的中文更精進，另一方面為了多點時間照顧現念國二的女兒，阮氏秋平日到人力仲介公司擔任翻譯，假日才到餐廳幫忙。

今（2016）年 65 歲的廖慶星則計劃明年退休，退休之後呢？會不會回到阿秋的娘家越南開餐廳？或者乾脆去越南養老？「我真的想過，這也是一種可能！」廖慶星說。

將來無論在台灣或越南，相信廖慶星與阮氏秋夫妻依然會繼續分享他們的美味人生。

2016 年 11 月刊出

The title "Papaya Love" was a reference to a Vietnamese-style chilled appetizer that Nguyen created with green papayas. When the Public Television Service program became popular, the restaurant renamed the dish to match the title.

Papaya Love's main ingredients are green papayas and carrots, which are julienned, then mixed with sugar, hot sauce, lemon, peanuts, and cilantro. Nguyen adds a little fish sauce to her hot sauce to make it a little "homier" and more Vietnamese. She also reminds us that the julienned papaya and carrots need to be iced for 15 minutes to ensure that they are crunchy.

A delicious life

If you were to describe Nguyen's life in Taiwan in terms of Light Taste's specialties, you might say her relationship with her mother-in-law is a bit like Hakka Stir Fry: it has a flavor that stays with you, and the longer it "cooks" the more character and nuance it develops. Her relationship with her husband is reminiscent of Papaya Love: it is a Taiwanese–Vietnamese fusion with sweetness in the sour and flavor in the heat.

These days, Nguyen has pulled back from the restaurant's front lines, in part to improve her Mandarin still further and in part to spend more time with her eighth-grade daughter. Nowadays, she spends her weekdays working as an interpreter for a labor broker, and only helps out at the restaurant on the weekends.

The 65-year-old Liao plans to retire next year. Will he open a restaurant in Nguyen's homeland after he retires? Or perhaps just move there and take life easy? "I've thought about it," says Liao. "It's a possibility."

Whether in Taiwan or Vietnam, Nguyen and Liao will no doubt continue to enjoy their delicious life together for years to come.

Published in November 2016

客家小炒 vs. 戀戀木瓜香，
廖慶星與阮氏秋夫婦共創台越美味人生。

//////////////////////

As with their Hakka Stir Fry and Papaya Love,
Liao Ching-hsin and Nguyen Thi Thu have fused
the flavors of Taiwan and Vietnam together
in their personal lives.

Dough Sculpting the Java Way
—A Migrant Worker Kneads Her Dreams

爪哇特色捏麵人

移工捏出創業夢

文‧陳群芳　圖‧林格立
Chen Chun-fang / photos by Jimmy Lin / tr. by Scott Faul

源自祭祀文化裡的捏麵人，原是不忍殺生而改以麵粉和水捏製成豬、魚等祭祀牲禮，在近代演變成可以賞玩的小物，如動物、人偶、卡通人物等，是許多人的兒時記憶。現在，有位來自印尼的移工 Pindy，不僅學習中華文化的傳統技藝，還將自己的文化融入。在她的巧手下，爪哇婚禮、甘美朗樂器等全成了精巧的捏麵人，這些色彩繽紛的人偶，正是文化碰撞的精采火花。

Traditional dough sculpture from China has its origins in the culture of sacrificial rites. The first forms were shaped from rice flour dough to take the place of animals, like pigs and fish, that people were no longer willing to kill as offerings. Today these figurines have evolved into collectible miniatures of all kinds, including animal motifs and cartoon characters. And now a migrant worker from Indonesia has not only learned this traditional folk art, but even infused it with themes from her own culture such as Javanese wedding attire or Gamelan musical instruments. Her exquisite and colorful dough sculptures are like glorious sparks released by the convergence of cultures.

在楊清仁（左）的鼓勵下，Pindy（右）漸漸培養出對捏麵人的興趣與成就感。

With encouragement from Young Chingjen (left), Pindy (right) became increasingly interested in dough sculptures and built up a repertoire of her own.

　　假日的台北車站大廳、台中大小文創市集裡，常常能見到一位頭戴穆斯林包巾，有著開朗笑容的女孩，她身穿印尼服飾、講著印尼語，手上卻做著台灣本土的技藝──捏麵人。她是來自印尼的移工 Pindy，「這是中爪哇婚禮服飾，那是小時候騎著牛穿過農田去上課的場景。」Pindy 親切地向民眾介紹她的捏麵人作品，許多人因而對印尼有多一點的認識。

開朗少女離家記

　　來自印尼中爪哇省的 Pindy 是家中長女，高中畢業便主動向父親提起出國工作的規畫，希望能為家中減輕負擔。她知道留在印尼的薪資不高，必須走出去才能為自己創造比較好的待遇。於是沒有工作經驗的 Pindy，第一站就近前往新加坡磨練英文，累積工作經驗，一年多後返家，回到印尼的人力仲介

公司學中文、學習照顧病人及小孩的相關技能。這次，她出發來到台灣。

　　Pindy 回憶自己來台的第一份工作，「我在宜蘭照顧阿嬤，6 個月都沒辦法講話。」中文不好的她因為怕講錯話，剛來的前半年都不敢開口。在雇主的支持下，建議她看電視，鼓勵她開口溝通練習，一方面 Pindy 也積極看書學習中文，現在中文難不倒她，連台語也聽得懂。

　　問起適應的問題，Pindy 笑笑地說：「台灣的米飯比較好吃。」而常讓移工困擾的宗教問題，Pindy 會選擇不影響雇主的場合來膜拜阿拉，以樂觀的態度克服異鄉的種種不同。

　　之後 Pindy 陸續到工廠或其他家庭工作，當時移工政策規定的三年時限一到，Pindy 就帶著努力工作存下來的報酬回到印尼。

　　這一待就是 5 年，期間她結婚並生下兩個孩子，應該要幸福快樂的回鄉生活，最後卻

During weekends and holidays in the main concourse of the Taipei Railway Station or at craft markets large and small around Taichung you are likely to come across this radiant young woman wearing a traditional *kerudung*. Clothed in Indonesian dress and speaking Bahasa Indonesia, her hands are occupied with a traditional folk craft popular in Taiwan, sculpting dough figures. Her name is Pindy Windy, a migrant worker from Indonesia. "This is a bride and groom in central Javanese wedding dress, and that is a scene from my childhood, riding to school on the back of a water buffalo across the rice paddies." A good many people have been introduced to Indonesian culture through Pindy's enthusiastic descriptions of her dough works.

Leaving home

Pindy is the eldest daughter of a Central Javanese family. After graduating from high school she told her father that she wanted to help the family by working abroad. Her first stop was nearby Singapore, to practice English and gain some work experience. After a year she returned to Indonesia to study Chinese and to learn the proper skills for taking care of invalid patients and small children. Her next assignment was in Taiwan.

Pindy recounts her first work experience in Taiwan, "I took care of an elderly woman in Yilan without talking for six months." Not having a very good command of Chinese, she feared saying the wrong thing and rarely opened her mouth to speak throughout her first half year in Taiwan. With the support of her employer, who suggested she watch Chinese-language television and encouraged her to speak out and learn by practice, along with her own active learning through reading and study, she eventually mastered Chinese and even understands Taiwanese.

She returned to Indonesia with her hard-earned savings after reaching the three-year limit under the regulations for migrant workers at that time. She stayed there for five years, during which time she got married and gave birth to two children. But what should have been a happy life back home ended in divorce.

Losing all before finding dough

Pindy's husband spent all her savings, making her a penniless single mom struggling to bring up two small children. She wanted a better life for her two-year-old toddler and less-than-a-year-old infant, and so she made the difficult choice to place them in the care of her own mother while she went to Taiwan for work. Pindy's eyes well up with tears as she tells the story of parting from her children.

Pindy 將印尼文化融入創作，捏出獨一無二的美麗作品。

Pindy incorporates images from Indonesian culture into her works, sculpting exquisite one-of-a-kind creations.

是以離婚收場。問起這段破碎的婚姻，Pindy 輕描淡寫地表示，因為先生太懶散，都不工作，她出錢讓他做生意也花光光，給過他好幾次機會，試圖挽救彼此的關係，但最終還是以分開收場。

歸零重來，開啟捏麵人生

先生花光了 Pindy 的積蓄，獨自扶養兩個小孩的她，為讓孩子過好一點的生活，忍痛將兩歲及還沒一歲的孩子，託給自己的媽媽照顧，隻身來台工作。談起當時與孩子分開的心情，Pindy 想起來還是紅了眼眶。

再次來台，Pindy 一樣擔任看護工作，但沒想到一次醫院的看護工作，竟意外開啟她不一樣的人生。

鄰床的家屬，是在醫院照顧母親的捏麵人師傅楊清仁。照顧病人的工作疲憊又漫長，原本就關心移民工議題的楊清仁，主動邀請 Pindy 學習捏麵人，讓她能打發時間。

一開始，Pindy 只是好玩，她覺得自己做的玩偶並不漂亮，一度感到挫折，是楊清仁不斷地鼓勵，直到她嘗試製作印尼文化的人偶，Pindy 才真正找到興趣。

捏麵人原有的素材裡只有紅白藍黃黑五原色，為了詮釋故鄉婚禮的傳統服飾，Pindy 跟著楊清仁學習更進階的調色技巧。白色加紅色揉成粉紅色，需要咖啡色的話就將黃、紅、黑三種顏色的黏土團相加……隨著各種原色比例的不同，就能調出各種深淺的五彩黏土。

Pindy 結合家鄉的記憶以及四處蒐集的印尼圖片，在她的巧手下，化身成充滿異國風情的捏麵人。印尼島嶼眾多，深厚的文化底蘊，讓 Pindy 的創作靈感源源不絕。

除了印尼相關的創作，Pindy 也將她在台灣的生活與觀察放進作品，如由她貼身照顧的阿嬤與阿公、雇主的家庭成員，巧妙地捕捉每個人的神韻與特色，逗得大家直說好像。Pindy 說她最喜歡人物創作，每張臉孔都有不同表情，讓她覺得有趣且充滿挑戰。

印尼服飾的時裝秀，在 Pindy（後排中）主辦的東協市集「印尼站」，熱鬧登場。

Pindy (back row, center) takes the stage for a group photo after the fashion show at the Indonesian Pageant she organized for the Bazaar Asia Tenggara in Taichung.

人偶表情、服裝飾品、印尼風情的背景，每個作品都能見到 Pindy 的用心與巧思。

Pindy's dedication and skill are on display in the lively expressions of her figures, the vivid motifs of their costumes and the Indonesian essence of her backgrounds.

This time in Taiwan, Pindy was once again assigned work as a caregiver, but what she didn't anticipate was how a spell nursing her patient in a hospital would open the door on a whole new life.

In the neighboring bed an elderly woman was being attended to by her son, Young Chingjen, a master in the art of dough sculpture. Young, who understood the endless hours of hard work that go into invalid care and had long been deeply committed to the issues of migrant workers, invited Pindy to take on dough sculpting as a leisure activity to help her unwind.

At first Pindy just thought it was fun and didn't consider her toy figures all that attractive. Through Young's constant encouragement and her first attempts at crafting subjects from Indonesian culture, though, Pindy soon discovered a passion for the art form.

There are essentially five pigments used in dough sculpture: red, white, blue, yellow and black. In order to bring out the vivid colors of the traditional wedding attire worn in her native land, Pindy studied advanced color mixing techniques with Young. For example, if she had a need for the color brown, she could make it by mixing yellow, red and black into the sculpting media. Colorful hues in a variety of shades and tones can all be achieved by adjusting the ratio of the basic colors used.

Pindy's skillful hands have transformed subjects that combine memories of her local region with photos of Indonesia from all over, into dough sculptures. Her creations capture the distinctive essence of her native culture. The subject-matter for Pindy's creations is replenished from the deep wells of diverse cultural content that originates in the myriad islands of the Indonesian archipelago.

Kneading hope to share joy

Pindy doesn't only make dough figures on request for friends, but has also gotten many of her migrant-work sisters involved in the craft. She relates how Indonesia also has a similar craft but the quality

Pindy 期望能用捏麵人，
捏出自己與同胞的未來。

Pindy hopes to use her
dough-art creations to sculpt out
a future for herself and
for her compatriots.

樂於分享，捏出希望

對捏麵人愈做愈有興趣的 Pindy，不只接受朋友的委託製作，也拉著移工姊妹們一起學。Pindy 表示，印尼雖有類似捏麵人的商品，但品質沒有台灣好，小巧、變化性高的捏麵人，易於保存與收藏，若能結合印尼的風土民情，應能在印尼的觀光地區受到遊客青睞。如此能為印尼當地創造工作機會，也許能改變同胞們出國工作謀生的命運。

於是，駐台北印尼經濟貿易代表處、台中東協廣場、文創市集等地，都有 Pindy 捏麵人教學的身影。甚至放假回印尼時，也到幼稚園教小朋友捏麵人，竭力推廣捏麵人技藝。

週日與朋友相聚在台北車站大廳時，Pindy 也會帶著捏麵人的材料，大方地向有興趣的朋友免費教學；有時國內外旅客路過，也會被眼前充滿南洋風情的捏麵人吸引而駐足，小小的捏麵人牽起不同文化與國籍間的友誼。

2017 年 4 月 Pindy 在台灣朋友的協助下，在台中舉辦了捏麵人偶的個展「指創精彩」，色彩豐富的印尼婚禮服飾、印尼傳統音樂甘美朗的樂器等，令人眼睛為之一亮。除了展覽，8 月時 Pindy 更在台中市政府邀請下，主辦東協市集「印尼站」活動，她規劃了印尼服裝時尚秀、印尼舞蹈表演、印尼樂團演出、小吃攤等，濃濃的家鄉味讓現場氣氛更顯熱鬧歡騰，希望為同胞提供表演的舞台，也藉此讓台灣民眾能更了解印尼文化。

Pindy 對同胞的熱心付出，讓她成為許多在台印尼移工口中的老師。在楊清仁的眼中，Pindy 的認真與努力，讓她的捏麵人充滿特色而閃耀。未來，Pindy 也將繼續舉辦移工的歌唱比賽等活動，並持續在台灣及印尼推廣捏麵人，期望自己能在印尼做點捏麵人的小生意。望著 Pindy 在創作時專注而自信的神情，我們在她身上看到了無限的希望。

2017 年 11 月刊出

is not as good as Taiwan's. If these minutely detailed and highly malleable dough miniatures were to incorporate Indonesian themes they would surely add to the appeal of Indonesia's tourist destinations. Their contribution to employment opportunities within the country might also have a transformative effect upon the fate of her fellow Indonesians, currently forced to seek work overseas. With this in mind venues such as the Indonesian Economic and Trade Office in Taipei and Taichung's ASEAN Square have welcomed educational visits by Pindy the dough sculptor. Even during holiday visits back to Indonesia she takes time out to promote her craft by teaching small children dough sculpting at kindergartens.

In April of this year, through the support of Taiwanese friends, Pindy organized a dough figurine exhibition, "Fingers Creating Brilliance," in Taichung. At the invitation of the Taichung City Government she also organized an Indonesian Pageant at the city's Bazaar Asia Tenggara (ASEAN Market) in August. The event showcased Indonesian fashion, music, dance and ethnic cuisine, successfully realizing Pindy's hope of giving her Taiwan-based compatriots a stage to promote greater understanding of Indonesian culture amongst the people of Taiwan.

Pindy's passion for helping her fellow Indonesians has earned her the sobriquet of "teacher" amongst many of her country's migrant workers in Taiwan. In the view of Young Chingjen, Pindy's determination and focused effort have resulted in unique works that stand out from the crowd. For the future, Pindy will continue to promote dough sculpture in both countries, with plans in the future to open a small shop in Indonesia. When viewing Pindy's extreme focus and confidence in sculpting dough we can see in her an example of unfettered hope.

Published in November 2017

Part 2

新采風・文學交流
LITERATURE

說不準的台北人：陳又津的漫遊書寫
Taipei People to Be—Writer Chen Yuchin

來自彩虹大地的筆：印尼筆會台灣分會
Rainbow Land Writers: Indonesia's Forum Lingkar Pena Shines in Taiwan

移民工文學在台灣
Immigrant Literature in Taiwan

特別篇 東南亞文學圓桌會：生命的關懷，書寫的原點
Southeast Asia Literature Roundtable: Writers Inspired by Concern for Humanity

Taipei People to Be—Writer Chen Yuchin

說不準的台北人

陳又津的漫遊書寫

文・林念慈　圖・林旻萱
Lin Nianci / photos by Lin Min-hsuan / tr. by Geoff Hegarty and Sophia Chen

初見陳又津，於是知道「少女」是一種結合調皮與慧黠的特質，
比起「文學女人」這類太過綿密的辭彙，她爽朗俏皮的語言，以
及嘩啦啦傾瀉的笑聲，更近似於少年的質地。

With a refreshing irreverence, bright and witty chatter and almost
nonstop laughter, writer Chen Yuchin comes across more as a
perky "young thing" rather than what most would imagine as a
serious and somber literary artiste.

陳又津開朗的性格與笑聲，
更趨近於少年的爽朗明亮，
同時也反映在作品中。

（陳又津提供）

Always bright and smiling, Chen's sparkling personality is
also reflected in her writing. (courtesy of Chen Yuchin)

　　母親是印尼華僑，小時候陳又津就要面對別人的提問：「媽媽是哪裡人？」然後她就要想出一個答案，回答變成一種習慣；後來，她可以編寫出無數的答案，母親忽然有三億化身，映照萬千，這或許是她開始寫小說的契機。

質疑歸類　只願如實呈現

　　「後來我就奪回話語權了，所以回答變成一種樂趣。」陳又津促狹一笑，關於身為新二代這件事，她更是輕鬆以待：「關於這個標籤，大家都說這群人好特別，但我真看不出哪裡特別，每個人本來就都不一樣，不管是我的身世也好，我喜歡的文類也好，有什麼好歸類的？應該說，歸類到底有什麼正向作用？」

　　有人問，《準台北人》到底是散文還是小說？她的答案亦復如是：「你怎麼看就怎麼是，作家頂多是作品的第一個經紀人，我沒有更高的位置，只能如實呈現我所看見的。」至於分類，她無奈地攤攤手，說：「那是研究生的工作，不是寫作者的工作啊！」

沉默父親、勇敢媽咪、樂觀女兒

　　《準台北人》深刻書寫「新移民二代」身分以外的故事，榮民爸爸跟身為印尼華僑的媽媽在三重落腳，陳又津就是在測量這些步伐有多深，走得多遠。

　　父親太沉默了，或許就因為如此，才有了〈跨界通訊〉作品，文章中擬喻一個死去的父親忽然傳來消息，如數家常地說起「那個世界」，正如那個年代裡的男人，只能隔著遙遠的歲月傳話，也不知道別人聽清楚了沒有，只顧著自語。

　　相較於無言以對的父親，陳又津的母親有著強悍的生命力。她把自己的未來，都賭在一張機票上，在觀光簽證過期以前，想盡辦

With a Chinese-Indonesian background inherited from her mother, as a child she became accustomed to being asked where her mother was from. Answering questions like this became a normal part of her life, so to deal with it she began making up fanciful replies. Eventually her mother's image became a realm of unlimited possibilities, and perhaps it was this experience that inspired her to begin writing.

No categorization necessary

Chen is quite relaxed about her ethnic background. "Lots of people think that being a second-generation migrant is somehow special, but I can't imagine what could be special about something so remote from my life today. Everyone is different, and I'm myself regardless of my background or what type of literature I like. Why should we try to put people and things into categories? Does it bring any greater understanding?" asks Chen.

Some people question whether her book *Taipei People to Be* is an essay or a novel. The writer's answer is always the same: "It's up to the reader to categorize the book however they want to. As a writer, I reflect on what I see and feel about the world in my writing, and I have no greater qualification than a reader to make such judgments."

Quiet father, bold mother, optimistic daughter

Taipei People to Be tells the plain and simple story of the writer's parents. Her father was a military veteran from mainland China and her mother a Chinese-Indonesian, who together settled in New Taipei City's Sanchong District. The book departs from previous works which tended to focus on second-generation migrants and their lives.

Chen's father was a very quiet man, and perhaps this served as an inspiration for one of her other books, *Communication Without Borders*, which portrays a deceased father who sends constant and detailed mystical messages from the next world. It seemed that men of her father's generation would often communicate through shared memories remote from the young.

In contrast to her father, Chen's mother had a strong and resilient personality. Having gambled her future on a one-way flight to Taiwan, she arrived in the country on a tourist visa knowing that she needed to find a husband before her visa expired. Eventually, she settled down in Sanchong. Regardless of whether she actually won a better life with her husband, at least she had the courage to make her own way.

Chen is similar in many ways to her mother. She

身為印尼華僑的媽媽（右），總能四兩撥千斤地化解種族間的尷尬，也是陳又津創作的契機之一。

Chen's Chinese-Indonesian mother (right) has always had the sharp wit to deal with sensitive racial issues, often providing inspiration for Chen's writing.

沉默爸爸、勇敢媽咪、樂觀女兒，陳又津幼時與家人合影。（陳又津提供）

This family snap, taken when Chen was a child, shows a quiet father, a bold mother and an optimistic daughter. (courtesy of Chen Yuchin)

法把自己嫁了,好在台灣落地生根,輸贏不論,那勇氣就足以頂天立地的活著;每次遇到多事的鄰居補上一句:「她是印尼來的。」那語氣裡或多或少夾帶輕蔑,母親總是能妙語化解,讓對方當下一愣,甚至無話可說,再也不敢招惹「印尼來的」。

陳又津也有這樣舉重若輕的本領,她把悲哀、痛苦的議題,比如最邊緣的小人物、最巨大的死亡,都以幽默的筆法迴旋帶過,流暢輕巧卻步步到位。「生活絕不是整天愁眉苦臉的,人生苦短啊!你寫得那麼沉重悲哀,誰看?」她哈哈一笑,盡顯樂觀陽光的個性。

保留選擇的權利

她不諱言,這些年有幾次機會回印尼,其實更像回一個度假村:殷勤的母系親人、鄉下老宅與郊區購物中心,還有熟悉的客家聲腔,問她「看見了什麼?」她笑了笑:「還真沒看見什麼!」就跟你我記憶中的返鄉一樣,幾分新鮮、幾分尷尬,叫不完的叔伯阿姨與鄉村風光,就是沒那些大家以為的「二代血淚尋根記」。

當然,身為新二代,陳又津的書寫免不了會面對母國或家鄉,好在對她而言,這不過是轉身之間的事情,而非失根、迷途;她甚至拋出一個問題:什麼是新二代?「說不定根本沒有新二代啊!」她說。每個人都如此獨一無二,誰不是新的一代?那就邊走邊找

吧,一邊漫遊,一邊尋找自己的座標。

陳又津在自己的文字裡悠然自得,更像散步、玩耍,所以顯得更有餘裕。她承認自己是幸運的,那些標籤不曾傷害她,但也許傷害過其他孩子,她也希望政府打造一個友善的環境,而非是血緣上的友善。

血緣上的強制友善,是因為你的身分,給予特別的優惠,反而令人沉重;而環境的友善,就像是菜單上並列四種語言,台灣人、印尼人、菲律賓人、柬埔寨人同時都看懂了,這過程不需要一點聲音,每個人自然能溫柔會心。

陳又津表示,新二代不是非要政府做些什麼,而是希望能保留選擇的權利,生命是溫熱的,不是一份專案,需要更多自由,去找尋自己的出口。

如果新二代的旅程還在繼續,那麼,「準」台北人會有「跨過去」的那一天嗎?「這可能是一場積分賽吧,永遠都在準備跨越,但愈是意識到自己在準備區,就會一直停留在那一區。」陳又津如是說。

少女繼續在城市漫遊,看似漫不經心,其實步步縝密。正如細川匯聚成河,每一個細碎的字句都指向情感記憶;亦如大橋連結台北與三重兩端,只要連上了,就能溝通。準確或者不準確無從定義,但至少願意傾聽,已經足夠。

2017 年 2 月刊出

陳又津在自己的文字裡悠然自得,更像散步、玩耍,所以顯得更有餘裕。

Chen is happily immersed in her writing, which for her is more recreation than work.

has an assertive streak that allows her to deal with the serious issues of life with a humor and lightness of being that is reflected in her writing.

Freedom of choice

Chen has visited Indonesia several times in recent years and says her mother's hometown is more like a holiday resort for her. There she can enjoy the hospitality of her mother's family in their old house, and relaxed shopping in a nearby shopping mall, all in a familiar Hakka-speaking environment. It's just like most people's experience of returning to their ancestral home, with mixed feelings of curiosity and awkwardness and so many people who are addressed as uncles and aunts. There are none of the sad stories about second-generation expats searching for their roots that many people might imagine.

However, as a second-generation immigrant, Chen's writing inevitably touches on issues surrounding her origins. But it's not a big issue for her as her roots are strong and sure. Everyone is unique. Everyone has roots somewhere. So, Chen says, just take it easy. As you travel the road of life, each person needs to find their own coordinates by which to navigate.

Chen admits that she is quite fortunate. She has never been hurt by labels of any sort, but she is well aware that others may have been. While she welcomes current government efforts towards building and maintaining an openhearted and friendly environment, she would prefer less emphasis on ethnicity and more on inclusion.

Second-generation immigrants want nothing from the government except to allow them full rights to choose their own way. Life is full of warmth, but people need the freedom to find their own direction.

As second-generation migrants continue to seek a sense of identity in their new home, when will come the day for these "Taipei people to be" to narrow this rift? "It's like a race for life. People are always trying to eradicate divisions, but the more you become aware that you are still stuck at the starting line, the more likely you are to remain there," says Chen.

A young woman roams the city, following a seemingly random path. But in fact her every step is meticulously planned. As a river is fed by small streams, every word and line in Chen's writing is an expression of her emotional remembrances. Like the bridges connecting Taipei City with Sanchong, as long as two sides are connected, they can communicate. Regardless of whether Chen's stories accurately reflect the real lives of Taipei people, as long as readers are willing to read, that's enough for the writer.

Published in February 2017

Rainbow Land Writers:
Indonesia's Forum Lingkar Pena Shines in Taiwan

來自彩虹大地的筆
印尼筆會台灣分會

文・黃淑姿　圖・林格立
Sanya Huang / photos by Jimmy Lin / tr. by Bruce Humes

隨著大量的外籍移工與逐年增加的留學生，來自異國的寫作組織默默地在台灣開花、結果，最初從 1999 年菲律賓移工詩社至今，這群堅持以母語寫作的異鄉遊子累積出許多精彩作品與創作能量，印尼筆會台灣分會（Forum Lingkar Pena Taiwan, FLP Taiwan）更是其中的佼佼者。

///////////////////////////

In the wake of the arrival of increasing numbers of migrant workers and overseas students, writing organizations have unobtrusively blossomed and borne fruit on Taiwanese soil. Beginning in 1999 with the Taiwan chapter of the Philippine poetry club Samahang Makata International, these groups of wanderers from foreign lands who have a passion for writing in their mother tongues have amassed much positive energy and created many wonderful works. Among these bodies, the Taiwan chapter of Indonesia's Forum Lingkar Pena ranks as one of the most outstanding.

印尼筆會（Forum Lingkar Pena）是由印尼作家 Helvy Tiana Rosa 於 1997 年在雅加達創辦，分會遍布印尼 32 省與海外五大洲 12 國，全球共約一萬三千名會員。筆會常保開放性，活躍於文化出版領域，除了與出版商、代理商交流，公開舉辦文學研討會、寫作工作坊等，為社會帶來各種時代性的議題。對筆會成員而言，寫作不只是抒發個人情感，更是禮敬神祇的神聖展現。

台灣分會的成立，則與印尼的經濟發展緊密相關。1980 年代起，印尼每年有大量勞動人口輸出至馬來西亞、台灣等地從事勞力密集與居家照顧產業。印尼筆會海外分會的成員，自然多數也是由勞動者所組成。

台灣分會的成立

FLP Taiwan 前身「寫作空間」（"Bilik Sastra"）由 YuheRina Gusman 所創辦，當時她留學台灣，研究印尼移工的精神生活，發現印尼移工所學多為英語或中文及電腦技術等實用課程，精神上卻很匱乏。2010 年，YuheRina 向印尼國家電臺（Radio Republik Indonesia，RRI）提出「寫作空間」計畫，申請了一批印尼語文學書籍提供在台移工閱讀，吸引了許多創作與閱讀愛好者聚集。爾後，「寫作空間」集結了許多成員共同於 2012 年加入印尼筆會，成為海外分會一員，活動內容也自閱讀交流擴大為寫作課程與作品分享與評論。

FLP Taiwan 沒有明顯階級或固定聚會場所，之所以能發揮效能，除了創辦人 YuheRina 與先生都是在台灣求學的留學生，相對於來台工作的勞動者而言，夫妻倆生活穩定，而有餘力可以貢獻時間、精力給 FLP Taiwan，參與者的積極、主動投入，也佔有重要因素。

此外，團結力量大，透過在台灣的印尼同胞之間的人脈網路，獲得各種非正式的場地、人力、物資等資助。比如，2017 年 11 月第一場聚會，因為原本常使用的台北車站場地同時舉辦印尼英雄日的慶祝活動，而將聚會場地改到印尼同胞推薦的 BNI（Bank Nasional Indonesia）位在台北市忠孝西路的辦公室中，就是一例。

高度自我要求

移工們平常工作就很忙，可能連休息時間都不夠了，為何還願意抽時間出來閱讀、寫作，更何況是花很多時間與別人討論作品？YuheRina 說，筆會成員的人格特質與一般人不同，最大的差別就在高度自我要求：「他們的學習動機很強烈，希望能更進步，有一天可以帶著在台灣、在國外所學習到的一切知識與技能，回到家鄉做出更好的貢獻。」

移工們珍惜台灣的學習環境，有些知識在印尼是學不到的，或沒有途徑可學。她指了指 BNI 的場地說，這裡有兩間教室，免費提供印尼移工在此學英文、學電腦；印尼文雜誌 "Indosura" 雜誌編輯 Mira Luxita 因辦公室場地同樣位在 BNI 的地利之便與同鄉情誼，更主動為筆會找來寫作教學書籍，無償提供給需要的人借閱。如何在繁忙工作中爭取創作

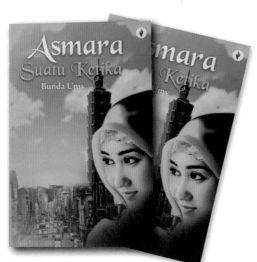

"Asmara Suata Ketika" 是 Bunda Umy 以台灣移工經驗寫成的印尼文小說，文字淺白易懂，故事頗富趣味。

Bunda Umy's novel *Asmara Suata Ketika* is an easy-to-read but compelling tale of romance that draws on her experience as a migrant worker.

筆會聚會當天，眾人翻閱 Mira Luxita 帶來的寫作教學書籍。

Aspiring authors examine the writing textbooks that Mira Luxita has brought to an FLP Taiwan gathering.

Founded by Indonesian writer Helvy Tiana Rosa in 1997, Jakarta-based Forum Lingkar Pena (FLP) has established chapters in all but two of Indonesia's 34 provinces, and in 12 countries on five continents. Members number about 13,000 globally. Though founded in religious belief, FLP is open to the world. It is active in the field of cultural publishing and in addition to interacting with publishers and agents, it hosts literary seminars and writing workshops to introduce to the community at large a host of topics relevant to our times.

Establishment of Taiwan chapter

The forerunner to FLP Taiwan, Bilik Sastra ("Literary Salon"), was founded and managed by YuheRina Gusman. At the time, she was studying in Taiwan and researching the lives of Indonesian migrant workers here. She found that many were taking practical courses such as English, Chinese and computer technology, yet a spiritual dimension was missing. In 2010, YuheRina submitted a proposal to Radio Republik Indonesia to initiate a "Writing Space" program, and requested Indonesian literary texts for the country's migrant community in Taiwan. The program attracted many fans of reading and writing in their mother tongue, and these meetings led many participants to join FLP as overseas members. Activities grew from reading and socializing to encompass courses where they could share and discuss their own writing.

FLP Taiwan possesses no clearly defined hierarchy or fixed meeting place. Its successful role and continued existence are rooted not only in the positive, proactive engagement of its participants, but also in the fact that both in the past

空間？YuheRina 提及 Bunda Umy 的國語流利且擅長語言溝通，是她能夠有彈性時間發揮創作的重要因素。Bunda Umy 自己則說，「如何與雇主溝通」是一門重要的藝術。

多才多藝的 Bunda Umy 能寫還能唱，2016 年擔任《聲線計畫：史貝克斯的歌──「唱」》（Sound Route: Songs of SPECX—The Singing）主唱，與三位台灣藝術家合作，用歌聲演出跨國混血孤女史貝克斯的故事。當她用印尼語腔調唱出台灣人耳熟能詳的台語老歌〈安平追想曲〉，既陌生又熟悉的語言表達，意外成為表演中的高潮；聽的人、唱的人，一起在共同的歌聲裡託付各自的歷史記憶與身世情感。演出需要很多排練，Umy 一週只有一天的休假遠遠不夠用。因此，她與雇主討論，在不影響工作的空檔中邀請藝術家到雇主家中進行排練。

Bunda Umy 預計在台灣工作契約到期後，返回印尼中爪哇 Solo 附近的家鄉開一間書店，與熱愛搖滾樂的兒子一起創作歌曲。類似的正向循環，在筆會成員們身上特別明顯。這些人結束海外工作返回印尼家鄉，帶著在異地生活的堅強與知識回到母國，創造良好的正面影響。YuheRina 告訴我們，許多筆會成員回到印尼，因為具備多種技能以及語言專長，加上在筆會中學到的書寫、表達以及溝通技巧，都能幫助他們找到比當初出國前更好的工作。

高水準創作與交流

實體聚會之外，FLP Taiwan 成員在臉書私密社團中亦積極互動。筆會安排寫作課程，現任社長 Justto Lasoo，以及 YuheRina、Bunda Umy 等資深成員也會出功課給其他成員練習，並點評作品、分享創作技巧。僅有高中畢業的 Bunda Umy，卻能教授印尼古典文學中每首 4 句的詩歌「板頓」（pantun）技巧；除了她本身熱愛寫詩，與東南亞國家的學生普遍從小就開始學寫詩有關。首創在台開辦移工詩文比賽的前任台北市勞工局局長鄭村棋在深入了解後發現，「在泰、菲、印尼，寫詩就像台灣學生寫週記般尋常。」

來自印尼爪哇中部的筆會成員 Nna Achlam，正專心閱讀寫作教學書籍。

Nna Achlam, a native of Central Java, diligently consulting a how-to text for writers.

逐年成熟的 FLP Taiwan，也開始延續總會的對外互動傳統，邀請以母語徵件的移民工文學獎（Taiwan Literature Award for Migrants）策展團隊，從台灣攜帶 2014 至 2016 的移民工文學獎印尼得獎作品、紀錄影片、作品集等成果，前往雅加達舉辦兩場成果發表會，並參與「台印移民工文學論壇」。2016 年則與四方文創合作，邀請「移工文學之母」Pipiet Senja 來台舉辦寫作工作坊。

異中求同的文學語言

印尼國徽中，神鷹腳下牢牢抓住的古爪哇語「Bhinneka Tuggal Ika」，意指「異中求同」，這句話出自古老的印尼神話：據說，很久很久以前有位國王，他每天都要吃掉一個人，使人民經常活在死亡恐懼中，不知道哪一天自己將要受死。

as overseas students in Taiwan, and now in their settled life together, YuheRina and her husband have more time and energy to devote to its operations than do most migrant workers.

Aspiring writers: Distinguished by self-discipline

Typically quite busy, migrant workers often haven't enough time to rest, so why are they willing to devote their free time to reading, writing and discussing written works with others? YuheRina explains that FLP members' personalities are not those of a typical person. The greatest difference lies in the high demands they place on themselves. "Their motivation to learn is very intense. They hope to make greater progress, so that one day they can take all the knowledge and skills they've learned in Taiwan and elsewhere, and return to their hometowns to make a meaningful contribution."

Versatile Bunda Umy can write and sing too. In 2016, she collaborated with three Taiwanese artists on *Sound Route: Songs of SPECX—"The Singing,"* as the lead vocalist in the role of Saartje Specx, a daughter born in 17th-century Nagasaki to a regional governor in the Dutch East India Company and his Japanese concubine. Raised largely in what was then the Dutch East Indies (modern-day Indonesia), she later lived in Taiwan before her death at just 19. When Umy used Indonesian-accented Taiwanese to sing the old Taiwan favorite, "Romance of Anping Port," her alien yet oddly familiar rendition of the unrequited love of a half-Dutch, half-Asian girl for a fickle Dutchman unexpectedly became the high point of the show. Her representation of the legend resonated with both performer and spectators in terms of collective and individual memory and identity—for Tainan's Anping was briefly occupied by the Dutch, while Indonesia was for centuries. The show required a lot of practice, and Umy's standard weekly day off was far from enough time. With her employer's permission—on condition that it did not interfere with her work—she invited the artists to her workplace for rehearsals.

When her Taiwan contract ends, Bunda Umy plans to return to her hometown near Solo in Central Java, where she will open a bookstore and co-author songs with her son, a big fan of rock 'n' roll music. A similar positive cycle is evident among other FLP members. When these individuals return to their hometowns, they take back to their motherland the perseverance and know-how they have acquired in a foreign land, with the intent to make a positive impact.

創辦人 YuheRina Gusman 從草創至今不間斷地參與筆會聚會，並擔任線上寫作師資。

FLP Taiwan founder YuheRina Gusman is still involved in the group to this day, and serves as one of its online creative writing instructors.

印尼籍的異鄉遊子，齊聚台北車站大廳裡，
慶祝一年一度的印尼開齋節盛會。

To mark the end of Ramadan, Indonesian migrant workers far from home enjoy the customary feast—this time in the concourse of Taipei Railway Station.

　　有一天，一位非常同情老百姓受苦的武士，向國王提出請求說：「不如由我來代替百姓受死吧，但也請您從此以後不要再吃人了。」「區區一個武士，竟然也敢妄想干涉我的決定！」國王怒而拒絕武士的請求。當武士發現國王根本不聽從勸告，他放棄和平訴求，與國王展開激烈的打鬥。搏鬥過程中，濕婆神（Shiva）進入國王的身體中、佛陀（Buddha）進入武士的身體裡各顯神通，誰也贏不了對方，雙方僵持不下。最後，梵天（Brahma）介入打鬥中說：「Bhinneka Tuggal Ika！」（呼籲兩人停戰）因為他們雖然外表長相不同、想法差距頗大，但彼此卻是一體而不可分割的。

　　印尼作家 Mochtar Lubis 以「彩虹下的大地（Land under the Rainbow）」描述印尼，這塊大地擁有諸多珍貴的古老文明、豐富多元的社會風貌，以及老百姓日常生活的智慧。閱讀這些印尼作家的文學作品與和他們間的互動交流，正好打開了一扇台灣人理解與同理的友善窗口。

　　文學作品中所描述的生命、欲望、喜悅與苦難種種，是跨越種族、語言、文化的人類普遍性訴求。也因此，FLP Taiwan 的存在，不只讓在台的印尼移工、留學生有個為自己說故事的個人表達空間，他們筆下所描述的一切，也是人類集體文化意識的一部分；自然，台灣人的創作也是這集體的一部分。一切在這塊土地上的匯集，終將如同神鷹腳下的古老格言所說：異中求同。

2018 年 1 月刊出

Creative interaction

Members also interact via a private group on Facebook, in addition to gatherings and regular writing classes arranged by FLP Taiwan. Justto Lasoo, current head of the Taiwan chapter, and senior members such as YuheRina Gusman and Bunda Umy, set homework for other members to do for practice, and they also review works and share creative writing techniques. Bunda Umy, who has only a high-school education, teaches how to write four-line, rhyming *pantun* verse in the classical Indonesian style. Her own passion for poetry aside, familiarity with this format is also due to the fact that in Southeast Asia students generally learn to write poetry from a young age.

As FLP Taiwan has matured over the years, it has also begun to institute the practice of external interaction that has become a tradition for FLP headquarters in Indonesia. The Taiwan chapter invited the organizers of the Taiwan Literature Award for Migrants (TLAM), a competition for migrant workers writing in their own languages, to Jakarta, where two presentations were held to highlight the Indonesian-language works that won awards from 2014 to 2016, and to show a film about the presentation of the awards, featuring interviews with the winners. While in Jakarta, TLAM participated in the "Taiwan–Indonesia Migrant Workers Literary Forum," together with FLP Taiwan, FLP Jakarta and other Indonesian literary associations. In 2016, FLP Taiwan and 4-Way Voice Culture and Creativity invited Pipiet Senja—dubbed "the mother of migrant worker literature"—to hold a writing workshop in Taiwan.

Seeking unity in diversity

The lower portion of Indonesia's national emblem consists of a scroll gripped by the claws of a legendary Garuda bird, on which appears a phrase in Old Javanese: *Bhinneka Tuggal Ika*—"Out of the Many, One." This is an adage from an ancient myth. It is said that long, long ago there lived a king who devoured one human each day, thereby instilling fear amongst the people unsure who would be next.

One day a warrior, saddened by the plight of the common folk, made a request of the king: "Better that I die on behalf of the people. But I beseech Your Highness to cease this practice henceforth!" Outraged, the monarch refused. "How dare a lowly warrior dream of interfering with the will of the King!" When the warrior realized his advice would not be heeded, he abandoned his peaceful appeal and initiated a fierce fight. During the battle, the Hindu deity Shiva entered the body of the king, while Buddha likewise entered the warrior's. Each demonstrated his prowess to the fullest, but a deadlock ensued. Finally, Brahma intervened: "*Bhinnekha tuggal ika!*" he pronounced, signaling an end to their duel. For although the pair were dissimilar in looks, and the gulf between their mindsets was great, in reality they comprised an indivisible entity.

The various lives, desires, joys and tribulations portrayed in literary works represent a universal appeal that transcends ethnicity, language and culture. Therefore, FLP Taiwan exists not only to provide a space in which Indonesian migrant workers, students and immigrants in Taiwan can tell their own stories; everything they describe when they put pen to paper is also part of human collective cultural awareness. Of course, the creative works of Taiwanese also form part of this collective. Everything coalesces on this soil, echoing the words on the scroll gripped in the Garuda's talons: "Out of the Many, One."

— Published in January 2018

Immigrant Literature in Taiwan

移民工文學在台灣

文・鄧慧純　圖・莊坤儒
Cathy Teng / photos by Chuang Kung-ju / tr. Jonathan Barnard

2015 年 8 月 30 日，在台北市館前路的國立台灣博物館有一場特別的頒獎典禮。第二屆移民工文學獎召集人張正說，只要你會一句東南亞國家的問候語，不管是泰文的「sawa dee-ka」，或是印尼文的「apa kabar」、越南文的「xin chao」、菲律賓語「kamusta」或緬甸文的「mingalarba」，都歡迎來參加。這是一場另類的文學盛宴，會場中聽到的是交雜各國語言的談話，出席者的服飾從越南的奧黛（Ao Dai）到穆斯林女性的頭巾（Hijab），繽紛多彩。這個文學獎參賽文體不限，雖然投稿的文章都需再翻譯成中文，評審才能閱讀，但重要的是，這是為台灣近 50 萬移工、近 20 萬婚姻移民及達 30 萬的新移民二代所舉辦的文學獎，期望藉此讓他們說出自己，更具意義。

//////////////////////////

On August 30, a special ceremony was held at the National Taiwan Museum: the Second Taiwan Literature Award for Migrants. Organizer Chang Cheng said that anyone who could fluently utter a word of wellwishing in a Southeast Asian language—whether the Thai *sawa dee*, the Indonesian *apa kabar*, the Vietnamese *xin chao*, the Tagalog *kumusta* or the Burmese *mingalarba*—was welcome to take part. It was a multilingual literary feast like none other, with a variety of clothing on display too, from the Vietnamese *ao dai* to the *hijab* that is traditional for Muslim women. Submissions for the award weren't restricted in terms of form or genre, but all had to be translated into Chinese so the judges could read them. The prize is directed at Taiwan's nearly 500,000 foreign workers from Southeast Asia, the nearly 200,000 Southeast-Asian women that have married Taiwanese men, and their 300,000 children. It aims to get them to talk about their lives in meaningful ways.

第二屆移民工文學獎作品以印尼入選的篇數最多，獲得首獎的〈寶島框架背後的肖像〉是 Dwiita Vita 寫的移工群像，描寫在台移工的各種遭遇；Keyzia Chan 撰寫獲優選的作品〈WIN〉寫逃跑移工的故事，故事性很強，很吸睛，結局的安排給讀者很大的想像空間。

越南獲選的兩位得獎者都是博士，范雄協以〈母親的遊戲〉獲評審獎，他以實驗性的文學風格、如散文詩般的語言、倒數的時間，寫著遊子的母親無盡期的翹首盼望與等待。另一位博士作者黎黃協以〈夢魅〉寫移工未竟之夢，為移工在台灣無法翻轉的命運覆上一抹淡淡的哀傷。

泰國的安南・徐拉兀（Anan Srilawut）是本屆文學獎最年長的得主，得獎作品〈友誼和音樂之寶藏〉寫的是他自己的故事，在泰國，安南是個樂師；在台灣，他一手操作起重機，一手在鍵盤上敲打出動人的字句。

「寫」出「她們」的故事

獲得首獎的 Dwiita 在雇主家協助家庭照護工作。初見她時，瘦小的身軀，始終平靜的表情，讓人感覺到在她心裡藏有一份很深沉的疲憊，從她娓娓道來的故事中知道，Dwiita 在大學讀的是資訊工程，本應是很好找工作的專業，但迫於經濟因素中輟，出社會就業後，公司又因經濟不景氣倒閉，她只好拋下尚在強褓中的孩子來到台灣工作；然而，兩地婚姻難經考驗，身在印尼的先生另結新歡，Dwiita 選擇結束婚姻，隻身撫養小孩。

在家鄉找不到工作或工資過低是許多移工離鄉赴台的原因，台灣提供了許多工作機會，但每個人的機緣不同。Dwiita 的文章中寫著各種在台灣社會存在的真實：全年沒有休假的辛苦、宗教信仰受管制、受誘於虛擬世界的移工、仲介公司不聞不問與剝削等問題，在文中如實呈現。移工的問題尚待政府自結構面制訂法律才能解決，但 Dwiita 期望透過寫作，說出移工的處境，讓更多人知道

並正視它。得獎與否不是她參加文學獎的目的，而是她相信透過書寫能夠改變些什麼。Dwiita 打算用這次的獎金，在印尼的家鄉成立一間小圖書館，讓附近的孩童們能有機會接觸書籍，徜徉在閱讀的世界中。

Dwiita 的工作合約在明（2016）年 1 月即將結束，她期盼能早日見到久別的小孩與母親，她也希望未來有機會能將在台灣工作的見聞寫成一本書，實現她的作家夢。

尋找與其他移工不同的出路

來自印尼東爪哇的 Keyzia，來台工作除了補貼家中經濟外，年紀輕輕的她一直想著能做些什麼事，讓自己不同於大多數的移工。

在一次機緣下得知開放大學的訊息，徵詢雇主同意後，她報名註冊，主修管理學。「學習永遠不嫌晚」，在印尼只有高中學歷的她，勉力地、每月一次出席實體課程，與老師、同學面對面討論、參與報告，週間則有 3 次夜間網路授課，每次兩小時。然而，除了原本的照護工作外，還有繁重的課業要預習複習。中輟的學生很多，班上人數從 30 人銳減為 15 人，Keyzia 堅持下來，她希望累積管理學的專業，再加上自己工作的存款，未來回印尼後開一家屬於自己的咖啡店。

Keyzia 利用閒餘的時間創作，她也加入「印尼筆社」，在網路上分享創作。這一屆文學獎的獲獎作品〈WIN〉頗獲評審喜愛，這是 Keyzia 第一次投稿也是第一次獲獎，她認為，逃跑移工必定有其難言之隱，她試著把它寫出來，並在故事結尾給了讀者一個開放的想像，餘韻縈繞。

Keyzia 照顧的阿嬤已經八十多歲了，她與阿嬤感情深厚，形同祖孫一般。阿嬤身體不好，需要全天候的貼身照顧，所以 Keyzia 出門一趟不容易，我們利用她課程中的休息時間訪問拍照。下課時間，看見 Keyzia 與同學開心地玩鬧、自拍，不同於照顧長者時的穩重認真，彷彿此時才恢復她二十多歲青春年華該有的笑顏。

身著開放大學黃色制服外套的Keyzia，利用休假到台北市館前路上課。與冰冷的線上課程不同，這裡有老師親自授課，可以參與課堂討論，下課時間與同學聊天笑鬧，「學生」是Keyzia 另一個身分。

//////////////////////////

Wearing the yellow uniform of Indonesia's Universitas Terbuka, Keyzia Chan takes advantage of her days off to attend classes on Guanqian Road in Taipei City. Unlike impersonal online courses, these classes feature teachers in the flesh, who lead class discussions. As she chats and laughs with classmates afterwards, Keyzia looks completely at ease with another of her identities: student.

The Indonesian entries were the most numerous. Dwiita Vita took the top prize for *The Portrait Behind the Formosan Frame*. Keyzia Chan won an honorable mention for *WIN*, which tells the tale of a foreign laborer fleeing her place of employment. The compelling story features an ambiguous ending that leaves a lot to readers' imaginations.

The two Vietnamese winners both have doctorates. Pham Hung-Hiep won the special jury prize for *Mother's Game*. In poetic prose, he describes a mother who eagerly awaits her son's return from living abroad. In *The Dream*, Le Hoang-Hiep, another PhD, writes about the unrealized dreams of migrant workers. It's a poignant and sad look at foreign workers' futile efforts to change their fates.

The Thai writer Anan Srilawut was the oldest prizewinner. He won for the autobiographical *The Treasure Chest of Friendship and Music*. A musician in Thailand, in Taiwan Anan both operates an overhead crane and bangs out moving works on the keyboard.

Writing "their" stories

Dwiita Vita, winner of the top prize, works as a domestic caregiver. Dwiita describes how she studied information engineering at university, but had to drop out and get a job because of financial pressures. Then the company she was working for went bankrupt in the poor economy. She was forced to leave her toddler behind and come to Taiwan to work. Meanwhile, her husband, who remained in Indonesia, fell in love with someone else. Dwiita decided to end the marriage and raise her children on her own.

The inability to find work or earn sufficient wages at home is why many foreign workers leave their home countries to come to Taiwan. Although Taiwan certainly offers jobs, everyone experiences different situations. Dwiita writes about social realities in Taiwan: workers who are cheated by their employers or forced to work long hours, issues connected to days off and religious practice, exploitation

〈母親的遊戲〉──倒數的孤獨

　　獲評審獎的范雄協，1984 年出生於越南河內。他的作品〈母親的遊戲〉以特殊的敘事手法、詩化的散文獲得評審的一致讚賞。作品採取特殊的視角，寫著被遺落在故鄉的人們，他們的思念與孤獨。

　　當代人的孤獨感是范雄協關注的主題。關於思念與孤獨，他有一個範本，范雄協的哥哥早在 1997 年就離家，身為旁觀者的他，有機會觀察母親如何思念離鄉的兄長，在日常的生活作息中如何編織著孤單。孩子在外頭長大，經歷了人生各階段的轉變，母親都不在場，只能憑著想像，倒數著孩子歸來的日子；2004 年換范雄協離家到法國讀書，之後再輾轉到台灣。他在兩年前一個陰雨的午後，想著母親與孤獨，寫下〈母親的遊戲〉。

　　范雄協現為中國文化大學企管學的博士生，雖然研習的是工商管理，但他對文藝創作有著濃厚的興趣，課餘時間會寫詩與短篇小說。問到他喜歡的作家村上春樹，他認為，村上的文章提供讀者無盡的想像空間，而村上書寫的主題，描述 70 ～ 80 年代日本年輕世代的徬徨與不安，正似當前越南的處境，這也是他感興趣的所在。未來他希望能將作品集結成冊出版，目前范雄協正進行一個以當代越南青年世代為主題的書寫計畫，希望完成 20 個短篇故事，〈母親的遊戲〉正是這系列的其中一篇。

　　范雄協與妻子現分隔兩地，他希望早早完成學業，回越南和妻子小孩團聚，結束孤獨的等待。

「嗯，母親即將見到孩子了。還有七天六小時一分。還有七天六小時零分……」范雄協描寫被遺留在故鄉的母親，一分鐘、一小時都成為母親手中的經緯線，編織成名為「孤獨」的作品。

（范雄協提供）

//////////////////

"Oh, Mother is soon to see her child. Just seven days, six hours, and one minute to go. Just seven days and six hours to go...." Pham Hung Hiep describes a mother back home counting down her child's return by the minute and the hour. In a work about loneliness, these marks of time make up the very warp and weft of the character's life. (courtesy of Pham Hung Hiep)

by employment agents.... Although the problems workers face are systemic in nature and will require political and regulatory solutions, Dwiita writes to get more people to confront these issues. She plans on using the prize money to establish a small library in her hometown, giving neighborhood kids a chance to explore the world of reading.

Dwiita's work contract concludes in January of next year, and she is looking forward to reuniting with her children. She also hopes to have an opportunity to turn her experiences in Taiwan into a book so that she can realize her dream of becoming a writer.

Taking a different approach

Keyzia Chan, who hails from East Java, has long been looking to distinguish herself from other foreign workers. With the blessing of her employer, she registered for management classes at Indonesia's Universitas Terbuka, which has classrooms in Taipei.

Added to her work as a caregiver, the coursework isn't easy, but Keyzia is determined. She hopes that she can take the money she's earned at work and the knowledge she's learned in class to open her own coffee shop when she returns to Indonesia.

Keyzia uses her spare time to write. She has joined the Forum Lingkar Pena, an Indonesian writers' association, and she shares her work online. Her submission *WIN* won the prize from the jury comprising children of immigrants. In her view, foreign workers who run from their employers must have reasons for doing so. She tries to capture their complex emotions, however difficult they are to put into words. The ending provides space for readers' imaginations, helping the work resonate in their minds long afterwards.

Due to work reasons, it's not easy for Keyzia to get out, so we took advantage of her breaks between classes to interview her and take her photograph. As she jokes with her classmates and takes selfies, she finally has a chance to behave like the 20-something she is.

Mother's Game: Countdown of loneliness

The winner of the special jury prize, Pham Hung-Hiep, was born in Hanoi in 1984. His work *Mother's Game* is a feat of narrative virtuosity, and its poetic language earned the appreciation of the judges.

The loneliness of contemporary people is a main theme of Pham's work, a theme for which he has a personal frame of reference: In 1997 his older brother left home, giving him an opportunity to look at how his mother dealt with missing her oldest son and coped with the hole his absence left in her life. In 2004 Pham left Vietnam to study in France and then later found his way to Taiwan. Two years ago, on a dark and rainy afternoon, he wrote this poetic meditation on his mother and loneliness.

Pham is a doctoral student in management at Chinese Culture University. He has a great interest in artistic and creative work. In his spare time, he writes poetry and fiction. At some point in the future he hopes to publish a collection of his works. Currently, he has a plan to write a book on the lives of contemporary Vietnamese youth, comprising 20 vignettes of which *Mother's Game* is but one.

Separated from his family, Pham longs to soon finish his studies so that he can end his own loneliness and be reunited with his wife and child.

Dreaming a dream of a foreign land

Le Hoang-Hiep was the winner of the prize awarded by the juvenile jury. Although he studied electrical engineering, he has a strong interest in writing. When asked how he gathers material, Le says that he sometimes translates or interprets for Vietnamese women who have come to Taiwan as foreign workers. He has recorded their stories. He hopes to imitate his favorite author Nguyen Ngoc-Tu, whose works were once banned in Vietnam due to their focus on social issues, such as disparities of wealth. Le believes that drawing attention to these stories can help to improve the lives of foreign workers.

〈夢寐〉——夢中的他鄉之夢

　　獲評審推薦獎的作品〈夢寐〉，作者是黎黃協，大家都叫他阿協，1982 年出生，家鄉在越南平定。阿協的父母都是教師，因此他從小就耳濡目染喜歡閱讀，高中畢業後離家到胡志明市念大學，之後轉赴台灣取得碩士與博士學位。

　　戴副眼鏡的阿協給人感覺斯文而有禮，雖然讀的是電機工程，但提筆寫作是他平時的興趣，從小就有寫日記的習慣，不過以前是寫給自己看，這回他公開給大家看。問到阿協如何收集寫作的素材，他說偶爾會幫助雇主與來台工作的越南女孩翻譯，藉此機會，他記錄了她們的故事，希望仿效他喜愛的作家「阮玉斯」（她的書曾因勇於寫出越南的真實概況與貧富差距等社會問題而被查禁），阿協想，如果能把大家的處境說出來，讓更多人知道，或許移工的現況能有所改善。

　　問阿協為何寫「夢」？他說，這些越南女孩到台灣工作，必定是懷抱一個夢想，希望在台灣能夠美夢成真，但每個人的機運不同，有些人只能在夢境中讓美夢成真。說來頗有夢中夢的味道，而這層巧妙的安排也讓他獲得評審團的青睞。

　　7 年了，阿協已十分適應台灣的生活，上市場買菜都難不倒他。去（2014）年，阿協的寶貝剛出生，現在夫妻倆的生活還繞著這小佛祖轉，所以阿協現階段只能找兼職的工作，等妻子完成學業後，一家子要回到越南找教職工作。回去之前，阿協希望能接家鄉的父母來一趟台灣，看看台灣的美好。

寫作・音樂・起重機

　　「我覺得自己是一棵被連根拔起、移植到遙遠地方的樹。適應新的環境很難，幸運的是，有台灣朋友跟我說話、噓寒問暖。」這是本屆移民工文學獎唯一獲獎的泰國籍安南・徐拉兀的作品〈友誼和音樂之寶藏〉。

　　安南 7 歲喪父，身為家中的長子，孝順的他隨著母親工作養家，生活一直很辛苦。45 歲到

台灣工作，當時，家中一雙子女，女兒 19 歲，兒子 15 歲，都是正花錢的年紀。他說，很感謝有這個機會到台灣來工作，可以有較高的薪資，供家裡蓋新房子，供子女完成學業；而他自己也利用閒暇之餘，修習泰國基督教大學的國際課程，順利的話今（2015）年 11 月就可取得學位，這些都是以前的他無法夢想的願望。

　　工作之餘，安南不愛跟其他工人一起出去玩，而是看書和玩音樂。安南本來就有塗塗寫寫的習慣，來到台灣後，思念家鄉，讓他寫得更勤了；2012 年，安南投稿台北市政府主辦的外籍勞工詩文競賽，獲得詩文組第三名，讓他很受鼓勵，今年從廣播聽到文學獎徵文的消息，安南決定試試看，寫下自己的故事。

　　近期還有另一個徵文比賽要公布，安南希望能夠得獎，他想用獎金買一台 keyboard。多才多藝的安南，精通各種樂器，從吉他到 keyboard 都難不倒他。安南也熱心參與各式義演活動，如教會聚會或是監獄探訪。組樂團是他另一個夢想，安南正嘗試自己譜曲

「如果自己可以從這裡游回家那該有多好呀！」
黎黃協得獎的文中，逃跑的移工小草這樣想著。
而當記者和他來到了彰化的海邊，
海的另一頭連接到阿協越南的家鄉。
和他聊起家鄉的父母，阿協停頓了許久，
落淚了。

"If I could swim back home from here, how awesome would that be!"
In Le Hoang-Hiep's prizewinning work, foreign laborer Thao has this
wish. When our reporter and the author visited the beach in Changhua,
Le looked out across the water toward his home in Vietnam. When
discussing his parents, he choked up, and tears came to his eyes.

He explains that foreign women who come to Taiwan have dreams that they hope will come true here. But everyone has different luck, and some of them can only attain those dreams when they are asleep. There's a bit of a dream-within-a-dream flavor to it, and his deft handling of the material earned him the judges' admiration.

Here for seven years, Le is already quite accustomed to life in Taiwan. His first child was born just last year, and now his life revolves around that "little Buddha." As soon as his wife finishes her studies, the family will return to Vietnam to look for work. Before they return, Le hopes that his parents will come on a visit to see what Taiwan has to offer.

Writing, music, crane

"I feel that I am a tree that has been uprooted and planted in a distant location," reads a passage of *A Treasure Chest of Friendship and Music* by Anan Srilawut, the only Thai winner in this year's awards. "Getting accustomed to a new environment is hard. Fortunately, I have Taiwanese friends who look out for me."

Anan came to Taiwan to work when he was 45, his daughter 19, and his son 15. Both children are at an age when they cost a lot of money. He says that he is grateful for the opportunity to come to Taiwan and make higher wages that his family can use to build a house and pay for the children's educations. And he uses his spare time to take international division classes at the Christian University of Thailand. All of this is beyond what he had previously dreamed possible.

In his spare time Anan reads and plays music. In 2012, he earned third place in a poetry competition for foreign workers sponsored by the Taipei City Government. That encouraged him, so when he heard the call for submissions for the Second Taiwan Literature Awards, he thought he'd try writing his own story.

Soon there's going to be another writing competition, and Anan hopes to win. He wants to use the prize money to buy a keyboard. Multitalented Anan is

寫歌，他說他的家鄉在泰國的東北方一個叫
Roi-Et 的地方，那邊閱讀的風氣不盛，所以他
想用音樂告訴大家他在台灣的故事。

去年，經朋友推薦，安南獲選中央廣播
電臺主辦的「泰國優秀勞工子女來台省親活
動」，兒子獲資助來台與父親相見，加上女兒
專科畢業後到台灣來工作，隔了 3 年，一家
三口在台灣團聚，安南提到這段，還是高興
地抹了抹眼淚。

來台的這些年，雖然二度遭逢家中親人過
世，但安南始終樂觀進取，問他如何面對人
生的磨難？安南沉思了一會，說：「想到還有
兩個孩子，再苦都要撐下去。」

安南吹奏著「khene」，這是泰國東北部特
有的樂器，長長短短的竹管共 16 支，排成兩
排束起，中低的音色略帶哀淒，悠悠地迴盪
在安南的宿舍內，那應該是遊子想家的音符。

更多的故事　期待被說出

其他的入選作品，如菲律賓 Carla F. Padilla
的〈農田彼端〉、印尼 Erin Cipta 的〈江子翠
膽大妄為的變態男〉、Arumi Olive 創作的〈早
晨之前〉，更多的故事、更多的情感散落在台
灣社會、每一個家庭、每一個角落，謝謝他
（她）們願意寫下來與我們分享。

移民工文學獎從第一屆被主辦單位戲稱為
「買塊地」文學獎（因 migrant 發音聽起來像
「買塊地」），篳路藍縷地進行到第二屆，有近
兩百篇的作品參加競賽，寫出他們對台灣的
觀察、在台灣的故事。兩屆移民工文學獎的
得獎作品計畫集結成冊，並已藉由 FlyingV 募
得資金將於近期出版。

雖然主辦單位還志忑著是否續辦第三屆，
但移民工文學獎第一屆評委召集人的陳芳明
老師說：「相信還會繼續辦下去吧！……這
個獎的意義，就是持續讓異鄉人發聲，持續
錘鍊本地人心中的價值與信仰，持續打造多
元、公平、正義的社會。」

2015 年 11 月刊出

proficient at various instruments, from guitar to key-
boards. He also enthusiastically participates in a variety
of public service activities, whether church-sponsored
charity events or prison visits. Another dream of his
is to form a musical group. Anan is trying his hand at
composing music and writing lyrics. He says that in
his hometown of Roi Et in Northwest Thailand, there
isn't a high level of literacy, so he uses music to describe
his life in Taiwan to his friends and family back home.

During the years he's been in Taiwan, two members
of his close family have passed away, but Anan has kept
a positive outlook. When asked how he deals with life's
trials and tribulations, Anan thinks for a moment before saying: "I think about my two children. No matter
how difficult things are, I've got to press on for them."

Anan plays the khene, an instrument unique to
northwestern Thailand. It features 16 bamboo tubes
arranged in two rows, which emit plaintive notes in the
middle and lower registers. A tune echoing in Anan's
dormitory evokes a mood of the homesick wanderer.

More stories to tell

As they experienced birthing pains in their first
year, the Taiwan Literature Awards for Migrants were
jokingly called a phrase in Chinese that sounds like
the English word "migrant" but means "buying a piece
of land." In the second year of the awards, nearly 200
works were submitted that captured their authors'
experiences in Taiwan. The crowdsourcing website
FlyingV has already provided funding for a collection
of the winning works.

Although the sponsor hasn't committed for a third
year, Chen Fang-ming, jury convenor for the first year
of the awards, notes: "I'm confident that we can keep
it going! These awards are highly meaningful both in
providing a platform for immigrant voices and in shaping the values and beliefs of native Taiwanese, so that
we can together build a diverse, fair and just society."

Published in November 2015

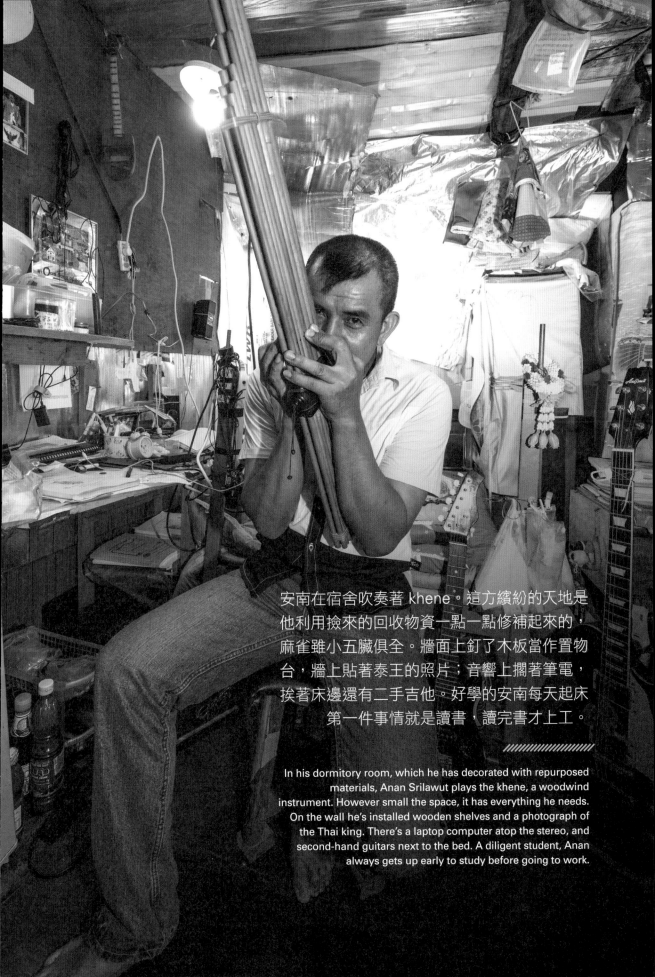

安南在宿舍吹奏著 khene。這方繽紛的天地是他利用撿來的回收物資一點一點修補起來的，麻雀雖小五臟俱全。牆面上釘了木板當作置物台，牆上貼著泰王的照片；音響上擱著筆電，挨著床邊還有二手吉他。好學的安南每天起床第一件事情就是讀書，讀完書才上工。

In his dormitory room, which he has decorated with repurposed materials, Anan Srilawut plays the khene, a woodwind instrument. However small the space, it has everything he needs. On the wall he's installed wooden shelves and a photograph of the Thai king. There's a laptop computer atop the stereo, and second-hand guitars next to the bed. A diligent student, Anan always gets up early to study before going to work.

Southeast Asia Literature Roundtable:
Writers Inspired by Concern for Humanity

東南亞文學圓桌會

生命的關懷，書寫的原點

文・曾蘭淑、武秋香、陳德銘　圖・莊坤儒
Esther Tseng, Vu Thu Huong, Temmy Wiryawan / photos by Chuang Kung-ju / tr. by Bruce Humes

一個靜謐的午後，《台灣光華雜誌》邀請前來參加 2018 東南亞文學論壇的越南作家保寧、印尼作家亞悠・烏塔米，與台灣作家房慧真對談，聊及自己的寫作緣由與對現今政治與社會的觀察，由於各自所處不同的社會與文化脈絡，產生了不同的文學作品，但因著同是書寫對生命的關懷，談話間有著更多瞭解與熟稔，氣氛也熱絡起來。

One peaceful afternoon, *Taiwan Panorama* invited two authors, Bao Ninh from Vietnam and Ayu Utami from Indonesia, to take part in a dialogue with Taiwanese writer Fang Hui-chen at the 2018 Southeast Asian Literature Forum. They discussed the factors that motivate their writing, as well as their observations on current politics and society. Due to the different social and cultural contexts in which they find themselves, they produce distinctive literary works. But because each of them is inspired to write by their concern for humanity, as the conversation delivered a greater sense of mutual understanding and familiarity, the ambience warmed up.

房慧真
Fang Hui-chen | 台灣 Taiwan

////////////////////////

曾擔任《壹週刊》專欄記者，目前為非營利媒體《報導者》的資深記者。著有散文集《單向街》、《小塵埃》等，人物訪談集《像我這樣的一個記者》（2017年鏡週刊十大好書）。〈草莓與灰燼——加害者的日常〉獲得2016年度九歌散文獎。

A former columnist for *Next*, a weekly magazine, and currently senior reporter for the non-profit online magazine *The Reporter*. Her published works include two volumes of essays, *One-way Street* and *Little Dust*, and a collection of interviews, *A Reporter Like Me*, that figured among *Mirror Media Weekly*'s Top Ten Books. Her *Strawberry and Ashes* won Chiuko Publishing's 2016 Essay Award.

保寧
Bao Ninh | 越南 Vietnam

////////////////////////

小說家，首部小說《戰爭的哀傷》（The Sorrow of War，台灣有中文譯本《青春的悲愴》）1990年在越南出版，1994年獲英國獨立報外國小說獎（Independent Foreign Fiction Prize），另有著作《7個小矮人的農場》、《船的封印》、《塞車時的思考》。

His first novel, *The Sorrow of War*, debuted in Vietnam in 1990, and the English edition won the UK-based *Independent* Foreign Fiction Prize in 1994. A Chinese version has been published in Taiwan. His other works include *The Camp of Seven Dwarves*, *A Marker on the Side of the Boat*, and *Rambling While Stuck in Traffic*.

亞悠‧烏塔米
Ayu Utami | 印尼 Indonesia

////////////////////////

曾擔任印尼軍政府時期的新聞記者，1998年處女作《薩滿》被視為促成印尼政治變革的重要作品，並獲得雅加達藝術委員會一等獎，另有劇本著作《蘇西拉的審判》。

A journalist in Indonesia during the period of military rule, her debut novel *Saman*—launched just a few weeks before the fall of Suharto in 1998—is considered to have played an important role in the movement for political change (*Reformasi*) in her country, and won the Jakarta Arts Council's award for Best Novel that year. She also penned the theater script for *Susila's Trial*.

場地提供：思劇場
venue courtesy of Thinker's Theater

光華雜誌：可否談談您對台灣的印象？
Taiwan Panorama: Can you share with us your impressions of Taiwan?

保寧 — Bao Ninh

我去過日本、韓國與東南亞所有國家，唯有台灣是第一次來。在越南時，對台灣的第一個印象是申請台灣簽證很方便，我自己還是屬於免簽的對象。光辦簽證時就讓我覺得台灣和日本、韓國相比，更開放。

來到台灣，我看到許多很現代的地方，甚至不輸給日本，尤其可貴的是台灣還能保留一些古色古香的事物，例如我非常喜歡故宮博物院。台灣給我的感覺是既現代又古典，古今中外的結合。跟台灣人講話雖然語言不通，卻讓我覺得很親切、很溫暖。

Since I arrived in Taiwan, I've encountered many rather modern sights. In this respect, it's not inferior to Japan. What's especially valuable is that things here retain a certain air of antiquity, like the National Palace Museum. Taiwan gives me a sense of both the ancient and the contemporary, Chinese and foreign. Although the Taiwanese and I speak different languages, I feel kindness and warmth.

亞悠‧烏塔米 — Ayu Utami

我以前對台灣的認識僅限於歷史課本與《流星花園》連續劇，對台灣文學從來沒有接觸過。第一次到台灣，讓我感覺這裡很友善、開放、舒適，沒有被排擠的感覺。我這幾天去參觀中正紀念堂、國父紀念館，看到小朋友在跳舞，老人家在練太極拳，覺得氣氛十分平和；到了台北車站，看到印尼移工自在地與朋友聊天，覺得台灣是很容易讓外國人愛上的地方。

This is my first visit, and my feeling is that Taiwan is very friendly, liberal and pleasant. There's no sense of being excluded. When I arrived at Taipei Main Station and saw Indonesian migrant workers chatting with their friends, it struck me: Taiwan is a place that could easily win the affection of foreigners.

房慧真 — Fang Hui-chen

我想說說我與東南亞的關係。我的父親是印尼華僑，1960年來台灣念書後留在台灣。我小學畢業時，父親曾考慮要舉家搬回印尼，我常想，如果我真的回到印尼，今天的我可能是另一個錯身而過的命運。

I'd like to say something about my relationship with Southeast Asia. My father is a Chinese-Indonesian who remained in Taiwan after he began his studies here in 1960. When I completed elementary school, he considered moving the family back to Indonesia. I often reflect on how, if we had really relocated, I might be a very different person today.

可否談談您的「國家」對您的第一本書，帶來何種特殊的影響？

Can you tell us what impact the state of your homeland had on your first book?

保寧 ——————————————————————————— Bao Ninh

　　我 1952 年出生那一天，正好法國人進攻我們的村子，我媽媽告訴我，我是在炸彈聲中出生的。1969 年我入伍，參加「越南人民軍（北越）」的 27 青年旅（27th Youth Brigade），1975 年越戰結束後才退伍，五百多人的部隊只有 10 名士兵存活，我是其中之一。

　　戰爭結束了，雖然說我們是戰勝的一方，但 6 年參戰的經驗幾乎把我摧毀，我每天惡夢連連，連我的父母親看到我，都很害怕。雖然我一直想忘掉戰爭，但戰爭不放過我，因為我不擅於言語，無法訴說出我內心的痛苦。過了 10 年，我才提起勇氣，為了我的民族、我死去的同袍，書寫《戰爭的悲傷》，但其實我的目的是為了書寫和平。

　　對我來說，越戰是僅次於美軍投原子彈在廣島的大悲劇，尤其是越南這麼小的國家，對抗這麼強大的美國。當年人口 4,000 萬的越南，在戰爭中死了 450 萬人，有的家庭 3 個兒子全死了，有的村莊的男人全部戰死，但社會主義的文學作品和報導，卻只會宣傳輝煌與勝利，忽略戰爭帶來的悲劇與傷痛，我認為這樣的行為是對不起人民、對不起祖國。因為暴力如此的可怕，所以人與人之間更要懂得愛護、疼惜。

　　The day I was born in 1952, the French attacked our village. I came into the world amidst the sound of bombs exploding, my mother told me. From 1969 I served in the 27th Youth Brigade of the People's Army of Vietnam. I returned to civilian life in 1975, one of just ten to survive the war out of a force of more than 500.

　　The war was over. We were the victorious side, but undergoing six years of war almost demolished me. Each day brought new nightmares; even my parents feared me. I was keen to forget the war, but it refused to release its grip on me. I was not good with words and could not express the pain deep in my heart. It took me a decade to gather the courage to put *The Sorrow of War* down on paper. War wasn't my subject; I was writing for the sake of peace.

我在印尼強人總統蘇哈托執政末期，擔任新聞記者，由於軍政府箝制言論，要求報社只能刊登政府要刊登的新聞。我與朋友為了爭取新聞自由，創立了「獨立記者聯盟」。由於雜誌社被政府取締而關閉，我的同事坐牢，我上了政府黑名單，求職被所有報社封殺，我改以匿名從事新聞報導。

我的國家經歷被荷蘭、日本殖民的壓迫，蘇哈托軍政府專政 32 年族群的撕裂，印尼人雖然相信「惡有惡報，善有善報」因果論，但這些被政治迫害、人權被踐踏的受難者心聲，卻長期被漠視。我終究發現，新聞報導的寫作風格無法書寫受難者內心深處所遭受的不平，於是我改寫小說。1998 年《薩滿》（Saman）出版後，有許多女性作家與人權作家跟進，也印證了「當新聞沉默，文學就會發聲」這句話。

I was a journalist near the end of the rule of Indonesia's strongman, President Suharto. To resist the military regime's clampdown on speech, which demanded that only pro-government news be published, my friends and I established the Alliance of Independent Journalists.

My country underwent colonization by the Netherlands and Japan, and the dictatorship of Suharto's junta. The voices of many victims who were politically persecuted and whose human rights were trampled upon were long disregarded. When I finally realized that the medium of news reporting could not capture the deep sense of injustice suffered by victims, I switched to writing a novel. After my *Saman* was published in 1998, many female writers and activist-authors followed suit, which confirms the wisdom of the phrase, "When the press is muted, literature finds its voice."

我很同意新聞自由是要冒險達成的。

我想回應 Ayu 的故事。我最近採訪支持黨外雜誌的海王印刷廠負責人，大家知道在 1980 年代的台灣，由於報禁，印刷廠常常要搶在警備總部之前，去印刷廠搶書，包括當初《前進雜誌》要出一萬本二二八事件的專集，警總準備查禁、扣押，接訂單的海王印刷廠不放棄、繼續印，為了躲閉警總的查緝，得把車開進殯儀館，把書藏到六張犁的豬寮，不怕鬼也不怕髒臭，這是台灣爭取新聞自由的一段歷史，Ayu 非常像這些前輩們。

我這一代沒有經歷像保寧般戰爭的離散與饑饉，我當記者時台灣也進入第二次政黨輪替。而我創作的初衷可以說拜台灣書寫部落格風起雲湧之賜，2005 年我被中文研究所期末報告的學術寫作弄得煩躁不堪，因此將我平時的隨筆放到部落格的網路介面上，與網友互動，這些抒發心情的散文隨筆，成為人氣部落格，2007 年集結成我的第一本書《單向街》。

I very much agree that attaining freedom of the press requires taking bold risks.

I'd like to respond to Ayu's story. I recently interviewed Zhang Kunshan, the owner of Haiwang Printing House, a firm that handled underground *dangwai* publications under martial law. Nowadays everyone knows that in the eighties, due to the ban on opposition publications, staff often had to race to remove newly printed matter, such as a 10,000-copy special edition of *Progress* magazine on the February 28 Incident, before the Taiwan Garrison Command could confiscate it. Haiwang planned to continue printing the special edition, so to avoid inspection by the garrison command, printing factory staff transported the magazines to a funeral home, or hid them in a pigsty near Taipei's Liuzhangli—ghosts and stink be damned! This is the history behind Taiwan's battle for freedom of the press. Ayu is very similar to those forebears of ours.

As for my first book, *One-Way Street*, it was inspired by the spirit of Taiwan's rising tide of bold bloggers.

不同社會，相同激烈轉型
Distinct societies, similar transformations

對各位來說，您的國家最近的社會變化，是否影響您的寫作計畫？
Have recent social changes in your country impacted your writing plans?

保寧 ——————————————————————————————————— Bao Ninh

　越南這幾年變化愈來愈快、愈來愈大。一方面發展會帶動經濟發達，但另一方面，價值觀跟著改變；城市進步的同時，出現失序、混亂等問題，以一個作家的角度來看，我覺得滿難過的，但我還是著重寫報導文學。

　In recent years, Vietnam has undergone increasingly quicker and more radical change. On the one hand, development drives economic prosperity; but it also brings problems such as changing mores, urban chaos and a breakdown in social order. From a writer's point of view, I feel rather sad.

房慧真 ——————————————————————————————————— Fang Hui-chen

　台灣社會也是變化很大。我生平第一個工作是到《壹週刊》當記者，工作 4 年，台灣媒體環境歷經激烈的轉變，可以說也反映台灣社會變遷的一面。由於媒體受到資本的箝制、新聞的置入行銷，與一味追求腥色腥，衝點擊率。接著面臨中國資本家欲介入台灣媒體的現象，當時《壹週刊》也面臨相同的威脅，我與同事成立工會，擔任理監事，所幸壹傳媒被中國資本購併案一度喊停，我的新書《像我這樣的一個記者》就提到這個變化。

　Taiwanese society has also changed greatly. My first job ever was as a feature writer for *Next*, a weekly magazine. During my four years there, Taiwan's media environment underwent drastic changes, such as the increasing influence of investors, paid product placement within news, and blind pursuit of scandal and higher click-through rates. This has been followed by the efforts of mainland Chinese capitalists to gain entry to the Taiwanese media scene via investment. My new book, *A Journalist Like Me*, chronicles this transformation.

　　這幾年印尼則是經歷過政治改革，已有新聞自由，但卻有愈來愈多以宗教之名行暴力之實的事件。此外，假新聞充斥媒體，尤其是特定的族群與宗教人士，只選擇自己想聽到的新聞，而不選擇正確、客觀的事實，「獨斷」的風氣改變了原本印尼寬容社會的本質。

　　現在的我認為，有了新聞自由還不夠，人民必須要有「思考的自由」，因此我的下一本書，我想以「critical spiritualism」為主題，希望印尼成為更包容、更寬容的社會。

In recent years, Indonesia has experienced freedom of the press, but nowadays it may be too free. The media is flooded with fake news items, manipulated by certain ethnic groups or religious figures that select solely the news they wish to hear, while ignoring objective facts. This "autocratic" atmosphere is altering the nature of Indonesia's formerly tolerant society.

So I now believe that freedom of the press does not suffice; people must acquire the "freedom to think." For my next project, I intend to write a book around the theme of "critical spiritualism," in the hopes that Indonesia will become a more inclusive and tolerant society.

文學交流，推薦選書
Writers reveal their favorites

▼

保寧 Bao Ninh
亞悠‧烏塔米 Ayu Utami

我們很想更認識台灣，因此可以請她推薦了解台灣文學與歷史的書嗎？

We would like to know more about Taiwan. Could Fang Hui-chen recommend some books that might be helpful in understanding Taiwanese literature and history?

房慧真 ——————————————————————— Fang Hui-chen

　　我首先想推薦齊邦媛的《巨流河》，這本書從外省人的角度，來看台灣外省第二代偏安台灣的時代故事。第二本書是台灣文學之父賴和的《一桿「稱仔」》，他行醫之餘，用漢文書寫在日本長期殖民統治下，台灣底層人民貧困的生活。第三本推薦《呂赫若小說集》，這是書寫 1945 年至「二二八事件」等歷史創傷的故事。第四本是白先勇的《台北人》，作為外省人的第二代在台北生活的故事。第五本是黃春明《蘋果的滋味》，這位代表台灣文學重量級作家透過被美軍撞傷的小人物阿發的故事，呈現台灣鄉土文學的風貌。

　　I'd recommend five books: *The Great Flowing River: A Memoir of China, from Manchuria to Taiwan* by Chi Pang-yuan; *The Steelyard* by Lai Ho, the father of Taiwanese literature; *Collection of Short Stories by Lü Ho-jo*; *Taipei People* by Kenneth Hsien-yung Pai; and *Taste of Apples* by Huang Chun-ming.

房慧真有備而來，也請保寧與亞悠推薦越南與印尼的作品。

Fang Hui-chen evidently came prepared. Now let's invite Bao Ninh and Ayu Utami to recommend works from their own countries.

保寧 ——————————————————————————— Bao Ninh

越南古代文學很受中國文學的影響，很多悠久的作品是用漢文寫的。我本身也很喜歡唐詩。越南作家我覺得可以推薦的有阮輝涉、阮平方，詩人的代表有阮攸。想融入越南文化可以看《金雲翹傳》，連美國兩任總統到越南演說時也會提到幾句《金雲翹傳》裡面的詩詞，很受越南民眾的歡迎。

Two contemporary Vietnamese prose writers worthy of recommendation are Nguyen Huy Thiep and Nguyen Binh Phuong. A representative poet would be Nguyen Du [1765–1820]. For readers who are keen to delve further into traditional Vietnamese culture, I recommend his epic poem *Truyen Kieu*.

亞悠·烏塔米 ——————————————————————— Ayu Utami

我想推薦的印尼作家，包括推動女性權益的一位貴族佳爾丁尼所寫的《佳爾丁尼的信》、安南達·多爾《人類的地土》、阿里·夏班納的《印尼的文化與社會革命》，多哈里的《巴路可之舞孃》，安華的詩《我》。

Indonesian works I'd like to recommend include *Letters of a Javanese Princess* by Raden Adjeng Kartini, a women's rights activist born into an aristocratic family in the then Dutch East Indies; *This Earth of Mankind* by Pramoedya Ananta Toer; *Indonesia: Social and Cultural Revolution* by Sutan Takdir Alisjahbana; Ahmad Tohari's *The Dancer*; and "Me," a poem by Chairil Anwar.

2018 年 6 月刊出 ————————————————————— Published in June 2018

Part *3*

//////////////

新藝向・藝術交織
ARTS

「菲尼」不可：鄒隆娜的電影世界
Rina Tsou's World of Film

影藝・趙德胤：影像敘寫故鄉 成就電影夢想
Midi Z: Taiwan, Cradle of My Cinema

雨過天晴：阮金紅用影像記錄人生
Basking in Sunshine After Rain—Videographer Nguyen Kim Hong

越南安妮：新移民的歌仔戲人生
A New Immigrant Performs on a New Stage

看見天堂鳥的姿態：生命的舞者李庭莉
Passing Down the Legacy of Balinese Dance in Taiwan

Rina Tsou's World of Film

「菲尼」不可

鄒隆娜的電影世界

文・林念慈　圖・林旻萱

Lin Nianci / photos by Lin Min-hsuan / tr. by Geoff Hegarty and Sophia Chen

「拍《阿尼》之前，我去高雄旗津作田野調查，但我迷路了，在那條荒涼的路上，我眼前忽然有一個男人的樣子，他也是自己一個，走在這樣的馬路上，路上什麼人都沒有，只有卡車在他身邊來來去去……」那是在台藝大舉辦的「新南洋影展」映後座談，新銳導演鄒隆娜剛用 23 分鐘的《阿尼》感動所有人，再稍早，她剛跟這部短片一起走過坎城影展的紅毯；紅毯雖長，電影的築夢之旅更長，或許，要追溯到更久更久以前。

////////////////////////

"Before shooting the short film *Arnie*, one day I decided to visit Qijin in Kaohsiung to do some research, but I got lost. On a quiet road, I noticed a man in front of me, also walking alone. There were no other passersby, but there was a bit of traffic on the road...." This is an account by budding film director Rina Tsou, speaking in a forum at the New Southeast Asian Film Festival organized by the National Taiwan University of Arts. The 23-minute film *Arnie* touched the hearts of everyone who saw it at the festival. Shortly before, she had walked the red carpet at the Cannes Film Festival as *Arnie* was selected for the International Critics' Week competition, a parallel section to the main festival. But while the red carpet was long, Tsou's journey into film production has been even longer.

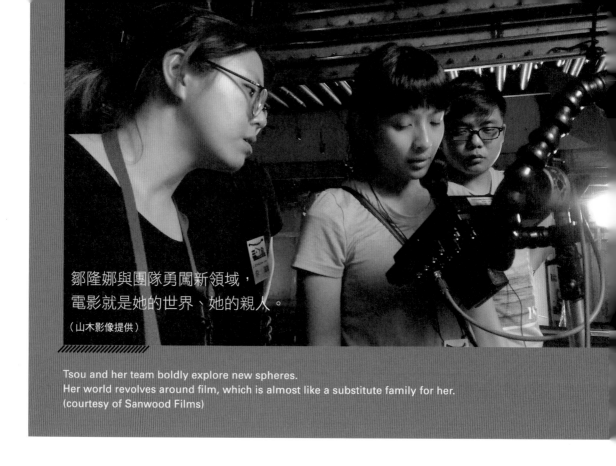

鄒隆娜與團隊勇闖新領域，
電影就是她的世界、她的親人。
（山木影像提供）

Tsou and her team boldly explore new spheres.
Her world revolves around film, which is almost like a substitute family for her.
(courtesy of Sanwood Films)

「小學三年級，我來到台灣，爸爸媽媽老是不在家，HBO 就是我的家人啊！」有雙靈動大眼睛的 Rina，帶點興奮的口吻，完全聽不出身為鑰匙兒童的寂寞：「所以我後來才會那麼喜歡電影！」

那一幕幕「小盒子裡」的人生悲歡，在幼小的鄒隆娜心中埋下種子。

電影就是親人

就讀台大財經系的她，硬是在台藝大轉學考的報名截止日完成手續，並用一個月的時間潛心準備考試，成為電影系的新鮮人；只是一個票戲忽然上了台，聚光燈就在身上，但興奮之餘，無法入戲。

「最可怕的是，我不知道自己要做什麼，我連導演是什麼都不知道。」所以鄒隆娜土法煉鋼，大學四年，什麼位置都去待過，打過燈光，也客串演過朋友的作品，但也因為如此完整的學習經歷，才讓她在拍片的調度上游刃有餘，從容而優雅，才有了後來的《薯片》，而《阿尼》不但獲得矚目，還站上了國際舞台發亮。

在地的異鄉人

出生於台灣，爾後在菲律賓生活，10 歲那年再回到台灣。江西省籍的爸爸、菲律賓籍的媽媽，混合多元文化的生長背景，造就了鄒隆娜豐富的生命經驗，但也給予她無法抹滅的異鄉感。

「《阿尼》不是我的故事，但我們都有在飄零的感覺，所以他才會召喚我；我身上有很多標籤，我覺得我不是一般台灣人，然後我被賦予一個身分，但這個身分不是一個身分。」不是一個完整、確定的身分，始終橫跨在不同種族與語言與文化當中，不斷尋找生命的歸屬感，但怎麼找也找不到。這股異鄉感，是生活裡最細微的部分，可能是旁人一個不經意的眼神，一句隨意脫口而出的辭彙，堆積起來就成了最沉重的影響。

身分認同的自我質詢，根植於個人存在

"I came back to Taiwan after living some years overseas when I was in my third year at elementary school. During my schooldays, my parents were often not at home, so the TV channel HBO became like my family. I think that's why I came to love films so much later on!" Tsou speaks excitedly, her beautiful eyes adding to the expression in her voice. You won't hear any talk of loneliness despite the fact that she was often home alone.

Enthusiasm for film

Tsou began her tertiary studies at the National Taiwan University College of Management, but was determined to move into film studies at the National Taiwan University of Arts (NTUA). With a bit of luck on her side, she was able to apply for the NTUA transfer examination just hours before the deadline. She had spent a full month preparing for the exam, and fortunately was rewarded with success: she joined the Department of Motion Picture at NTUA. Although a film enthusiast since childhood, she had no practical experience of acting, so finding herself in front of the camera being expected to act naturally came as quite a challenge.

So Tsou began her trade at the bottom and tried her hand at all or any roles that presented themselves during her four years at university. She gained experience of lighting, for example, as well as taking acting

「我們的電影故事工作坊」帶領菲國學子進入電影世界，也是鄒隆娜一輩子不願放掉的志業。（鄒隆娜提供）

Ating Pelicula Film Workshop helps Filipino students in Taiwan enter the world of filmmaking, a vocation that Tsou will never relinquish. (courtesy of Rina Tsou)

鄒隆娜鼓勵有類似背景的青年，去創造一個我們要的世界，往更好的方向去努力。（移人網站提供，Asuka Lee 攝）

Tsou encourages youth who share a similar background to her own to create the world they want and find a better way. (photo by Asuka Lee, courtesy of Migrants' Park)

roles in friends' film projects. Such a broad and comprehensive foundation has enabled her to produce films like *Chicharon* and *Arnie*, the latter of which has shown at international film festivals.

Like an outsider

Born in Taiwan but spending her early childhood in the Philippines, Tsou returned to Taiwan at age ten. Her father was from Jiangxi Province in mainland China, and her mother was Filipina, a mixed cultural background that enriched Tsou's young life but also brought feelings of not belonging, of being an outsider.

Her identity seemingly incomplete and uncertain, spanning different ethnicities, languages and cultures, she searched in vain for a sense of belonging in life. Her feeling of being a stranger in a strange land made the smallest occurrences in life, such as unthinking looks or tactless words from other people, build up over time into a heavy burden.

Doubts about her own identity were embedded at the very root of Tsou's individual existence. Her diverse life experience is reminiscent of that of Edward W. Said, an intellectual who was born in Palestine, bore an Arabic family name but an English given name, and went to study in the USA after spending most of his childhood in Cairo. Throughout his life

的本源。鄒隆娜的多元生命經驗，不禁讓人想到薩依德（Edward W. Said）這位當代知識分子，他出生於巴勒斯坦，有著英語名字與阿拉伯姓氏，童年大多在埃及開羅度過，後來負笈美國，終生為身分認同所苦的同時，透過文學評論、文化研究的論述尋找自身定位，大放異彩。生命中的沉重與掙扎，給人許多放棄的理由，但鄒隆娜選擇與薩依德一樣，正視這份包裝醜陋的生命禮物，不斷向內挖掘、向外觀看，將自己的個人議題，轉化為獻給世人的思索與創作。

這種在地、異鄉的調適，與親情之間的拉扯，是鄒隆娜目前最關注的故事；就像 10 歲那年，幼苗已成，她還分不清自己是「出國」還是「回國」，就已經踏上台灣的土地，面對全然不同的教育和生活方式，對她來說是一種生命成長。

她也承認，目前在她的電影中，「跨種族」的議題比例還是偏重，但身為一個電影創作者，她從不局限，更不希望自己的電影充滿控訴，如果有使命感，那都是電影拍成以後的事了，最重要的，還是影片本身的溫度。

不論是何種題材，她最在乎的仍是角色的血肉。一個菲律賓移工，同時也是人子，可能也是一個情竇初開的男孩；即便如《薯片》這樣一部談「認同」的片子，劇中小女孩的心事，也僅是小孩的寂寞，不是國族血淚，她認為因為只有回歸到人與人之間的情感，故事才會動人。

創造一個新的世界

自嘲不算是太典型的新二代，鄒隆娜仍然鼓勵有類似背景的二代青年：「不要自我憐憫，有問題就解決。這社會給我們太多悲情想像，其實有時我們太關注傷口，就看不見自己的強項；去創造一個我們要的世界，往更好的方向去努力，有造福人的能力就要做，不是你有這個問題才要造福人，而是你有能力就要勤快點！」

她舉了一個例子，26 個英文字母，少一個都不好，因為都不完整；當我們自己好了，就要想著別人好不好，能做的，多做一些，這才是一個理想國度。

對鄒隆娜來說，電影就是那個嶄新的世界。這世界又奇幻、又真實，在黑暗之中投下一束光亮，就像電影帶來的影響力，或許還不足以指路，但告訴你：夢想在哪裡，光，就在那裡。

—————————— 2017 年 2 月刊出

鄒隆娜（左）與《阿尼》女主角陳又瑄（右）一同出席第 69 屆坎城影展國際影評人週之夜。（山木影像提供）

Rina Tsou (left) and Chen Yu Hsuan, the female lead from *Arnie*, attend the opening of the International Critics' Week competition, which ran in parallel with the 2016 Cannes Film Festival. (courtesy of Sanwood Films)

《阿尼》用 23 分鐘感動坎城，在國際間發亮，但真實的菲律賓漁工生活，還在海上繼續飄零。（山木影像提供）

The 23-minute short film *Arnie* moved the audience at the Cannes International Film Festival and shone a light on the international stage. But the Filipino fishermen who were the film's subjects are still enduring a lonely life at sea. (courtesy of Sanwood Films)

he was troubled by issues of identity, even as he strove to define his place in the world through his brilliant writings in literary criticism and cultural research. The burdens and struggles of life may give people many reasons to give up, but like Said, Rina Tsou has chosen to look this unattractively packaged gift horse of life in the mouth, constantly delving within it while also looking outward, thus transforming her own individual issues into reflections and creative work that she gives as a gift to the world.

This tension between feelings of fitting in and of being an outsider is a recurrent theme of Tsou's film works. It reflects her own story of being brought to Taiwan at age ten. She was unable to comprehend whether she was going abroad or returning home, and facing a totally different education system and lifestyle in Taiwan forced her to grow up quickly.

But while this issue of interethnic relations is a major focus of Tsou's work, she doesn't limit herself. Most important is the warmth of the story being told.

No matter what the topic, the flesh-and-blood emotions of the characters are always the main focus. *Chicharon*, for example, discusses the theme of identity. While it depicts the loneliness of a little girl, the type of suffering is unrelated to personal identity as a function of race or nationality. Tsou believes that stories based on interpersonal feelings are the most effective way to touch the hearts of an audience.

A new world

Tsou provides encouragement for second-generation migrants who share similar backgrounds: "Society often presents us with great sorrows, but in fact we are sometimes too concerned about our own wounds, and as a result we are unable to realize our own strengths. We need to create the world we desire, and endeavor to work for the better. If you are capable of helping people, then you have a duty to do that, not just because you have the same problem but because you simply want to help. Helping others is a fundamental value as long as we are capable," says Tsou.

For Rina Tsou, the world is both fantastical and real. The influence of a film can be like shining a light in the darkness. The light may not be strong enough to guide you all the way, but it can indicate the direction of your dreams. The light is your guide.

—— Published in February 2017

Midi Z: Taiwan, Cradle of My Cinema

影藝・趙德胤

影像敘寫故鄉 成就電影夢想

文・李湘婷　圖・岸上影像及前景娛樂提供
Lee Hsiang-ting /
photos courtesy of Seashore Image Productions and Flash Forward Entertainment /
tr. by Geof Aberhart

「感謝台灣的栽培！對當時在緬甸的我來說，『能來台灣』是個像中樂透一樣的命運安排。」甫於威尼斯影展獲頒歐洲電影聯盟最佳影片大獎，《再見瓦城》導演趙德胤發文寫下了他對於台灣的感謝。曾以電影《冰毒》代表台灣角逐 2015 年奧斯卡最佳外語片入圍資格，而今再以新片《再見瓦城》入圍 2016 年威尼斯影展正式競賽獲頒大獎，屢次登上國際舞台，領獎時趙德胤總是說，是台灣自由的創作氛圍，給了他拍電影的養分，雖然他原本不是學電影的。

/////////////////////////

"Thank you, Taiwan! For me, being able to come to Taiwan from where I started in Myanmar has been like winning the lottery!" So said Myanmar-born Taiwanese director Midi Z in a social media post after his latest film, *The Road to Mandalay*, took the FEDEORA Award for Best Film at this year's Venice International Film Festival.

After having represented Taiwan in pursuit of an Oscar in 2015 with *Ice Poison*, Midi Z's next feature, *The Road to Mandalay*, was chosen to compete at the 2016 Venice International Film Festival. Every time he has won awards on the international stage, the young director has made it a point to thank Taiwan, remarking that Taiwan's liberal creative environment has done much to nurture his filmmaking despite his having studied design rather than film.

多數作品以緬甸僑民悲歌為題材，導演趙德胤在台灣電影圈已然是一種獨特的識別碼。

2006 年大學畢業製作短片《白鴿》開始，便不斷地以台灣導演身分在國際影展嶄露頭角、獲得注目。當年趙德胤就讀於國立台灣科技大學設計學系，雖不是電影本科系，教授看見他的長才，讓他以影片製拍完成畢業製作，而從此每年至少兩部的短片、紀錄片、長片作品產出，趙德胤從未停下拍片腳步，綿密而計畫性地操練著自己。

為糊口、自學電影

「我曾經用著很土法煉鋼的方法嘗試做電影。」趙德胤回憶起當初開始拍片，其實目的只是為了賺錢。

大學時期獨立接案，拍攝婚禮、畢業典禮，剪接、配樂都靠自己摸索。大四時擔心畢業製作過不了關，可能被趕回緬甸，於是他到中央圖書館與國家圖書館把所有關於電影、導演的書籍借回來看。研究所時期住在研究室，拆掉燈管每天租 DVD 觀摩，甚至連幕後花絮也不曾忽略。為了省錢，不敢跟同學外出玩樂，鑽研電影佔據了大部分課餘時間，當時不覺得這樣的努力有多重要，現在回想起來，發現對於創作上幫助不小。

重要的是在苦練過程中，這位不太有自信的緬甸僑生因此而喜歡上了電影，教授也發現他有天分。

「我不敢講天分這兩個字，但如果跟人家做一樣的影像攝製，我可能比別人好一點點、也比較快、比較舒服，成就感也比較高。」趙德胤說話總是謙和，帶著一點緬甸腔，談到自己時表情靦腆，與他在電影鏡頭中展現的寫實力道很不相同。

畢業製作短片《白鴿》一鳴驚人，得到釜山影展、哥本哈根影展、澳大利亞影展、里昂影展等國際影壇的肯定，趙德胤也因此被廣告公司延攬，工作簽證成為留在台灣的契機，一年之內他不分晝夜地接案，終於賺了錢給老家蓋洋房，為了能繼續留在台灣這個

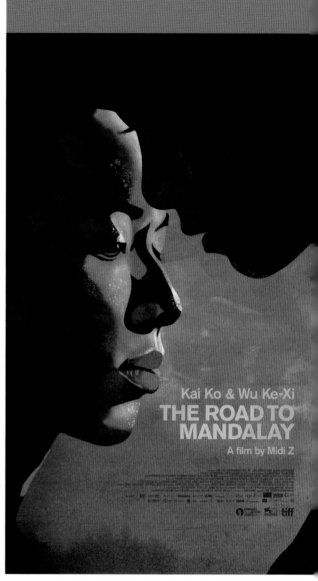

《再見瓦城》海報由好萊塢電影海報設計大師 Akiko Stehrenberger 操刀設計，呈現電影中男女主角不同的愛情觀。

The poster for *The Road to Mandalay* is the work of Hollywood poster designer Akiko Stehrenberger, and reflects the different perspectives on love of the male and female leads.

自由創作的環境，他考上研究所，也同時思考接下來要拍攝什麼樣的題材。

用影像、書寫故鄉

「我應該至少看過上千部電影，因此逐漸懂得一些技法，其中觸動我內心的，通常與我

With many of his films focusing on the tragic plight of Burmese-Chinese, director Midi Z holds a unique place in Taiwan's film world.

Since his design course graduation short *Paloma Blanca* in 2006, Midi Z has been an attention-getter among Taiwan-based directors at film festivals around the world. Since completing college, he has gone on to make at least two films a year—shorts, documentaries, and features—and he shows no signs of slowing down in his ongoing intense and planned efforts to stretch himself.

Learning film for a living

"In the past I used some pretty basic approaches to making films," says Midi Z, recalling his start, when the entire effort was just a way to make some money.

In college, he took on freelance projects, doing filming, editing, and scoring for things like weddings

8 萬美元攝製的《冰毒》，工作團隊只有 7 位，代表台灣角逐 2015 年奧斯卡最佳外語片入圍資格。

Ice Poison, made by a team of only seven people on a budget of just US$80,000, was chosen as Taiwan's entry for the 2015 Academy Award for Best Foreign Language Film.

and graduations. In his senior year, he got worried that his graduation project wouldn't make the grade and he might have to return to his native Myanmar, so he hit the library and borrowed every book he could find on film and directing. After successfully making it through college, Midi Z went on to graduate school, also in design, where he rented DVDs daily, watching everything on the disks down to the behind-the-scenes featurettes. His explorations of film took up most of his free time, and as he fell more deeply in love with the world of cinema, his professors began to recognize that he had a gift.

"I wouldn't presume to say I have a 'gift,' I'm just able to shoot a little better and a little quicker than most, and I get more of a sense of comfort and achievement out of it," says the ever-modest director. As he speaks about himself with a hint of a Burmese accent, Midi Z comes across as quite shy, completely unlike the powerful realism of his films.

His graduation short *Paloma Blanca* received acclaim at film festivals in countries as diverse as South Korea, Australia, Denmark, and France. Thanks to this, Midi Z caught the attention of advertising agencies, earning himself a work permit that let him stay in Taiwan. For a year he worked on projects night and day, eventually earning enough to build a house for his family in Myanmar. Afterwards, to stay on in Taiwan, he tested into graduate school, which was when he began seriously thinking about what he wanted to film next.

Telling tales of home

"I'd watched at least a thousand films by then, so I'd started to pick up a few techniques and begun realizing that what really touched me were stories that related to my own background. That inspired me to start thinking about telling my own story to similarly touch others."

What he most wants to do through his films, Midi Z says, is tell his stories to others, since his own

2016 年以色列南方影展以趙德胤的紀錄片《翡翠之城》為主視覺，整個城鎮四處掛滿印有該片劇照的看板。

The 2016 Cinema South Film Festival in Sderot, Israel, used Midi Z's documentary *City of Jade* as its visual motif. The town was practically full of billboards for the film.

生長背景故事相關，也因為這種觸動，讓我想拍自己的故事去感動別人。」

趙德胤說，他的電影並不是想拍緬甸家鄉的故事，而是希望將自己的故事說給另一群人聽。

因為關於趙德胤的故事，跟生長於台灣土地的你我很不一樣。

祖籍江蘇南京，出生在緬甸東北方靠近中國邊界的城市臘戍，16 歲以前，趙德胤生活於資源匱乏的貧窮環境，權力、財富決定尊卑，現實環境的黑洞讓他想方設法要逃離。

1998 年家裡以一個月的生活費買來台灣學校入學考試報名表，趙德胤從 6,000 個報考者中考取前 50 名，帶著家人籌款半年買的一套西裝與美金 200 元，隻身赴台念書。

為了支付生活費與學費，還要能寄錢回家，半工半讀的日子自他抵達台灣後的第二天就開始。

前輩提攜、感念在心

來台 10 年期間，趙德胤沒有回去過家鄉，2008 年卻在想要「書寫家鄉」的念頭驅使下，趙德胤自己一個人帶著攝影機回到緬甸

background is much different to that of the average Taiwanese.

Midi Z was born and raised in the city of Lashio, near Myanmar's northeastern border with China, to an ethnically Chinese family that traces its origins to the city of Nanjing. Until he was 16, he lived in an area characterized by poverty and a lack of resources. In a world where power and wealth dictate status, life around him was a black hole he desperately wanted to find a way to stay clear of.

In 1998, when Midi Z was 16, his family spent a month's worth of living expenses to sign him up for an entrance test for a Taiwanese school. He tested among the top 50 of the nearly 6,000 applicants, and with US$200 and a suit that cost half a year's family savings, headed to Taiwan alone to study. From his second day in Taiwan, he was already working part-time to support himself.

Help from higher up

For ten years after arriving in Taiwan, Midi Z had not returned to his hometown. In 2008, driven by his desire to tell the stories of his home, he picked up his camera and headed back to Myanmar to start shooting. The next year he was selected for the Golden Horse Film Academy, shooting the short film *Huashin Incident* with renowned director Hou Hsiao-hsien as producer. He went on to become one of Hou's apprentices.

"Mr. Hou told me then that even without resources you can still make films, and that was how he started out himself. He taught me a lot, and his encouragement gave me the courage to shoot a film entirely solo," says Midi Z. In fact, he says, the elder statesmen of Taiwanese cinema have all been more than happy to help out the new generation.

For example, in 2014 Ang Lee braved the cold, wet New York winter to make a special appearance at the premiere of the only Chinese-language film to show at that year's Tribeca Film Festival, Midi Z's *Ice Poison*. After the screening, Lee was effusive in his praise for Midi Z's ability to produce a robust, expressive film dealing with an unusual topic despite a lack of resources and equipment. Lee went on to share his own experiences with him, talking about the different problems a filmmaker faces making a film solo versus making one with a crew of 200. Midi Z also still remembers Lee's assistant telling him that the director had been up all the previous night dealing with meetings, but still insisted on making it to the screening and getting up on stage. He even made time beforehand to share a meal with Midi Z and give him personal encouragement. To this day, Midi Z remains touched and grateful for Lee's support.

趙德胤說侯孝賢、李安都幫助他許多，台灣電影圈前輩非常願意指導後輩。圖為李安出席第 13 屆紐約翠貝卡影展為趙德胤打氣。

Midi Z says that elder statesmen of Taiwanese cinema like Hou Hsiao-hsien and Ang Lee have been more than happy to give advice to newcomers like himself. This photo shows Lee at the 2014 Tribeca Film Festival giving words of encouragement to Midi Z.

拍攝，隔年他入選金馬電影學院主創學員，在侯孝賢的監製下，拍攝了《華新街記事》電影短片，成為侯導門下子弟。

「侯導當時跟我說，沒有資源也能拍片，當年他自己也是如此，因此教了我很多，有他的鼓勵，給了我一個人也能拍電影的勇氣。」趙德胤感謝地說，台灣電影圈的前輩都很願意提攜後輩。

李安導演曾在 2014 年特地冒著溼冷的冬雨，赴紐約出席唯一入圍翠貝卡電影節的華語電影《冰毒》首映會，映後他盛讚趙德胤能以極其克難的器材與資源，拍出結構完整、議題獨特、表達清晰的電影，他還以自身經驗告訴趙德胤，一個人拍片與 200 人拍片會遇到的困難差異。趙德胤猶記得李安的助理告訴他，李安導演前一夜通宵開會未休息，仍堅持趕赴會場站台，甚至提早抽出時間希望與趙德胤吃頓飯，當面給他鼓勵打氣，當年的這些感動，至今讓他點滴在心。

2010 年買了 3 張機票，帶著一台攝影機，就跟製片、收音 3 人完成首部劇情長片《歸來的人》，真實呈現緬甸人的生活，一舉入圍釜山影展和鹿特丹影展老虎獎，前往鹿特丹影展前，趙德胤正式取得中華民國身分證。

2012 年第二部電影《窮人。榴槤。麻藥。偷渡客》則獲鹿特丹影展 HBF 電影基金贊助計畫補助。2013 年底，趙德胤帶著 7 人團隊深入中緬邊境，以 10 天時間拍完第三部劇情長片《冰毒》，獲選第 64 屆柏林影展電影大觀單元，並於愛丁堡國際影展獲得最佳影片獎，和瑞典影展及台北電影節最佳導演獎，代表台灣參加 2015 年第 87 屆奧斯卡金像獎最佳外語片，最後雖未獲提名，但實力已不容小覷了。

身兼編劇、導演、攝影、製作人，一萬美金就能拍出一部長片，期間還完成《挖玉石的人》與《翡翠之城》兩部紀錄片，記錄分隔 20 年大哥採礦的故事，趙德胤說，前幾部劇情皆與家人、朋友有關，是自己熟悉的情感，是不得不講出來的故事，「對我來說，不先拍這些，拍不了別的，即使《再見瓦城》也是我姊

《再見瓦城》是趙德胤從獨立製片轉為商業作品的首部長片，故事講述海外華人的台灣夢。

The *Road to Mandalay* is Midi Z's move from indie film to the commercial mainstream and tells the tale of two ethnic Chinese in Myanmar and their "Taiwan dream."

姊的故事，她比我大 12 歲，劇情講述她們那一輩的人，以及現在東南亞華人的台灣夢。」

拉長戰線、做大市場

趙德胤的電影有種張力，直視小人物挑戰命運，急切想抓住機會以脫貧、致富的現實，長鏡頭下親人的悲傷絕望，以及人、事的被宰割性，形成獨特電影語彙，吸引了全世界影評的關注。

趙德胤眼中，電影是純然的創作，對他而言沒有任何政治目的與社會包袱，他說自己

In 2010, Midi Z again picked up his camera to shoot his first feature-length film, *Return to Burma*, working alongside a producer and a sound mixer. The film, depicting the realities of life in Myanmar, was nominated for the New Currents Award at the Busan International Film Festival and won the Tiger Award at the International Film Festival Rotterdam. Just before heading to the latter festival, Midi Z formally became a citizen of the Republic of China.

His second feature, 2012's *Poor Folk*, even received sponsorship from the International Film Festival Rotterdam's Hubert Bals Fund. In late 2013, Midi Z and a team of seven spent ten days in the China–Myanmar border region shooting his third feature film, *Ice Poison*. In 2014 the film was screened in the Panorama section of the Berlin International Film Festival, won Best International Feature Film at the Edinburgh International Film Festival, and won Best Director at both the Peace & Love Film Festival in Sweden and Taiwan's Taipei Film Festival. It was also selected to represent Taiwan in the Best Foreign Language Film category at the 2015 Academy Awards. While it wasn't nominated for an Oscar in the end, all of this is a powerful sign that Midi Z has become a force to be reckoned with.

While making *Ice Poison* on a budget of only US$10,000 and serving as writer, director, cameraman, and producer, Midi Z also completed two documentaries, *Jade Miners* and *City of Jade*, which tell the stories of Burmese jade miners, and in particular

沒有義務要為緬甸的弱勢講話，也不是由他講述了就能有所改變，他的電影來自於很個人的觀察與表達，「我沒有創作上的包袱，也沒有資源上的限制，更沒有設定觀眾目的，只覺得想要把這些故事講出來才舒暢，是一種藝術家創作發洩抒發的概念。」

而我們從另外一個角度反視，也因為這些電影，觀影者認識了趙德胤。

《再見瓦城》將近四千萬的製作成本，是由法、德、緬甸等國投資，故事本身涉及全球關注的經濟難民議題，引起國際銷售與發行商的投資興趣。這次的製作團隊人員多達200位，是趙德胤第一次挑戰大製作劇情長片，相較於近年國片市場不景氣，許多導演籌資困難，拍攝計畫延宕，向來不以資源設限作品格局的趙德胤，反向將投資分散於國際舞台，踩穩步伐把市場做大。

5年前便開始撰寫《再見瓦城》劇本，由於非電影劇本專科出身，信心不足，謙虛面對戰場卻從不怯戰的趙德胤，於是計畫性將劇本拿去投全世界重要的劇本比賽，一方面期望賺獎金挹注於拍攝，另一個原因，是藉此了解在全世界評審眼中，這個故事能否被理解、認同。

「《再見瓦城》光是劇本就易稿了12次，」趙德胤回想起易稿過程，因此結識許多評審，也得到面對國際創投的機會，他親自到國際市場找尋資金，身兼製片也學習發行，面對創投時還要能「賣」自己的作品，以強悍的精神與理智的分析，想辦法讓自己的作品有一天被實踐，如今作品再次獲獎，他感動地說：「這樣的鼓勵讓我多了自信，激勵著我在電影路上繼續走下去。」

電影不是夢、而是實踐

趙德胤今（2016）年33歲，為電影跑過四十幾個國家，一百多場國際影展，許多國家還為他這位年輕導演舉辦作品展，而他從不以此為傲，私下生活仍與常人一般，沒有名車華服，不拍戲時為自己煮飯，每日如常地看企畫案、看劇本。受訪隔日，他即將飛

趙德胤再次站上威尼斯紅毯，他的電影從台灣出發，敘寫故鄉的故事，發光於世界舞台。
（左至右／男主角柯震東、女主角吳可熙、趙德胤）

Midi Z has once again taken to the red carpet at the Venice International Film Festival. His films have started in Taiwan, told tales of his home in Myanmar, and drawn attention on the world stage. From left to right: lead actor Kai Ko, lead actress Wu Ke-xi, and director Midi Z.

到威尼斯參加《再見瓦城》全球首映，擔心英文不夠好，提醒自己別忘記帶翻譯機，電影是他每天的生活日常，而不是一個大夢。

「我很少說電影是一個夢，這不太真實，對我來說電影是一種實踐，有很多故事與很多計畫一步一步去實踐，愈做才會愈好。」趙德胤說，他隨時都準備好，回到一個人拍電影的模式，台灣的自由帶給他無限的創作靈感，而台灣的電影產業也因為這位異鄉導演而有了更開闊的格局，趙德胤始終相信，自己對電影的誠意與付出，不會因製作規格而受限，只要是情感真實的影像，最終都將會被看見。

—— 2016 年 10 月刊出

of his own elder brother, who had left the family some 20 years earlier to work in the mines. "Personally, I feel that if I hadn't made these first, I wouldn't have been able to make anything else. Even *The Road to Mandalay* is the story of my sister, who's 12 years older than me, her generation, and the 'Taiwan dream' of so many ethnic Chinese in Southeast Asia."

The bigger picture

Midi Z's films have a kind of tension in how they look directly at the challenges facing ordinary people desperate for a way out of poverty. With his long takes, their desperation and oppression at the hands of people and circumstances become a cinematic vocabulary, and this has caught the eye of critics around the world.

In Midi Z's eyes, films are simply creations, with no particular political or social pretense. He says he feels no duty to speak for the underprivileged of Myanmar, nor does he feel that just by telling his stories he will somehow change everything. His films come simply from his personal observations and ideas; "I don't try and dress up my films, I just want to tell these stories and get them off my chest. I'm simply an artist venting his emotions."

From our position as outsiders looking in, these films also help us get to know Midi Z.

The Road to Mandalay cost nearly NT$40 million to make, with investors from France, Germany, and Myanmar helping foot the bill. The film's story is focused on something the world is concerned with—economic refugees—and as such attracted considerable attention and investment from distributors and buyers on an international level. The film is also Midi Z's first attempt at a large-scale feature production, and in an age when Taiwanese filmmakers often struggle with a stagnant market and have trouble attracting funds, Midi Z finds himself no longer struggling with limited resources, while the international nature of his investors has also helped him get a foothold in a larger market.

When he began writing the script for *The Road to Mandalay* five years ago, not having a professional background in film meant Midi Z felt somewhat lacking in confidence, but he was nonetheless determined to see things through. He submitted his script to major script competitions around the world, going through some 12 drafts and getting suggestions from a range of judges, as well as finding more opportunities for international investment. As both director and producer, he learned about distribution and how to sell his films to potential investors. Approaching it all with a strong will and clear-headed analysis, he slowly found ways to make his idea into reality. As his latest work has started racking up recognition, he has remarked that such encouragement is a huge boost to his confidence, and helps keep him moving on his journey through film.

More than just a dream

At 33 years old, Midi Z has traveled with his films to more than 100 film festivals in over 40 countries, with several countries even putting on special screenings of his works. However, he hasn't let all this go to his head. In private, Midi Z is an ordinary person, with things like reading proposals and scripts just his everyday work rather than some grand dream.

"I don't really talk about film as being a dream, that's not realistic. To me, film is a practical pursuit, with all kinds of things that need doing and plans that need making. I just take everything one step at a time, getting better with experience," he says. At any moment, he could go back to his old one-man model. The freedom of Taiwan, he says, has given him near limitless creative inspiration, and his passion and personal investment in film aren't restricted by the scope of any given production. As long as the images feel real, feel true, then ultimately they will be seen.

Published in October 2016

Basking in Sunshine After Rain
—Videographer Nguyen Kim Hong

雨過天晴
阮金紅用影像記錄人生

文‧鄧慧純　圖‧阮金紅提供
Cathy Teng / photos courtesy of Nguyen Kim Hong /
tr. by Jonathan Barnard

下午 3 點，嘉義民雄的黃昏市場正開張，阮金紅頭戴遮陽帽，手持攝影機，今天要記錄同是來自越南的姊妹阮蓓海的故事，阮金紅以中文、閩南語、越南語 3 聲道並用，像朋友般地和受訪者打招呼。經歷家暴、失婚，如今她是一位紀錄片導演，也是首位獲得「雲門流浪者計畫」資助的新住民。

///////////////////////////

It's three in the afternoon and Chiayi's Minxiong evening market is just opening. Nguyen Kim Hong is wearing a hat to shade herself from the sun. Today she wants to record the story of Nguyen Thi Be Hai, another woman who hails from Vietnam. Nguyen Kim Hong speaks Vietnamese, Mandarin, and Taiwanese, and she greets her interviewee as she would a friend. A victim of domestic violence and a divorcee, she is today a director of documentaries and the first "new immigrant" to receive a Cloud Gate Wanderer grant.

阮金紅的親和力與同理心，
能夠卸下受訪者的心防，
建立信任感。
圖為她與受訪者阮蓓海互動的情形。

（林格立攝）

Nguyen's warmth and empathy enable her to gain her subjects' trust
and get them to open their hearts.
The photo shows her interacting with Nguyen Thi Be Hai,
a subject of one of her documentaries. (photo by Jimmy Lin)

　　阮金紅來自越南同塔省，家中除了務農外，還經營農作物的買賣，經濟狀況還算過得去，但父母的工作很辛苦，為了幫家裡減輕負擔，阮金紅讀到國小五年級就休學了，一個人撐起田裡的工作。她一心一意努力工作幫助家裡經濟，從沒有想過自己，沒買過一件新衣，住家隔壁的雜貨店，二十多年來，從沒賺過阮金紅的錢。

破碎的異國婚姻

　　阮金紅家裡有9個兄弟姊妹，但家族中重男輕女的觀念頗重，認真單純的她得不到家族親戚的喜愛，因而起了離家的念頭。聽說同鄉有人嫁到台灣，生活過得不錯，透過仲介，阮金紅談定了自己的婚姻，21歲那年到台灣來，懵懵懂懂地開始她峰迴路轉的人生。

　　嫁到台灣後，阮金紅的生活卻非她想像：丈夫賭博、欠債、家暴、被夫家親戚欺負、恐嚇威脅，如同社會版新聞的內容；這段婚姻維持了8年，她自認在婚姻中努力過，盡力做個好太太、好媳婦了，但始終不被前夫家族接納，所以她死了心，勇敢地結束了婚姻，走出自己的路。

雨停了，太陽會出來

　　離婚後，阮金紅隻身帶著小孩，打工賺錢，生活極其困頓，有時候一天只有一個便當，還不時遭受來自前夫的恐嚇；走出那段

《失婚記》入選第 15 屆台北電影節紀錄片獎項，阮金紅（右）自當屆台北電影獎主席張艾嘉手中接過入選證書。

Out/Marriage was nominated for the best documentary prize at the 2013 Taipei Film Festival. The photo shows Nguyen (right) accepting a certificate of nomination from the festival's chair, Sylvia Chang.

Nguyen Kim Hong comes from Dong Thap Province in Vietnam, where her family were farmers and agricultural produce traders. They were making ends meet, but to help lighten the load on the family, Nguyen dropped out of school after completing fifth grade and went to work in the fields.

Broken transnational marriage

Nguyen has nine siblings, but the male chauvinism and patriarchal attitudes run pretty deep in her family. Innocent, hardworking Nguyen didn't feel valued by her family members, and her frustrations pushed her to think about leaving home. She heard that other women in the village who had moved to

Taiwan as "immigrant brides" were doing well there. Through an agent, she negotiated her own marriage. At 21 and somewhat clueless, she traveled to Taiwan, embarking on a journey that would take her through many more twists and turns of fate.

Married and living in Taiwan, Nguyen's life was far from what she had imagined. Her husband gambled, fell into debt, and beat her. The marriage lasted eight years. She firmly believes that she worked at the marriage and did all she could to be a good wife and daughter-in-law. But she was never truly accepted by her husband's family, so she gave up and boldly ended the marriage to make a life on her own.

Here comes the sun

After getting divorced, Nguyen had to care for her child as a single parent and work to make ends meet. Her life was difficult. Sometimes she could only eat one meal a day. At one point she had thoughts of suicide but felt that just as she had fallen, she could also pull herself up. She thus slowly got on her feet, attending self-help courses. She also volunteered for the Changhua New Immigrants Association, giving it her all.

She met her current husband Tsai Tsung-lung at a film seminar. Both divorcees, they are able to support each other in their lives. Nguyen says that unlike her former husband, Tsai was willing to help her out, even though he wasn't then family. After a few months the two of them decided to get together. Meeting Tsai she regards as a gift from Heaven. It prompts her to repeat her favorite Vietnamese saying: "After rain, the sun comes out." And right now she is basking in the sunshine.

Using video to tell stories

Tsai is an assistant professor of communications at National Chung Cheng University, and it is thanks to him that Nguyen began to film *Out/Marriage*. Nguyen says that she has from time to time discovered that old friends have divorced as well. Their stories prompted her to make the documentary.

陰影花了很長的時間，也曾有過輕生的念頭，但阮金紅覺得在哪邊跌倒，就應該在哪裡站起來。女兒是支撐她的力量，她整理自己，慢慢把心安定下來，參加自我成長課程，並在彰化縣新移民協會擔任志工，能力所及地貢獻自己的力量。

和現任的丈夫蔡崇隆是在一次影片座談會上邂逅的，她笑說當初認識蔡崇隆時，感覺他的行徑像個同志；蔡崇隆說：「剛認識金紅的那陣子她的狀況很差，都不會笑。」同是離過婚的人，他們在生活上相互扶持。阮金紅說，對比她前夫，蔡崇隆與她非親非故，卻願意伸出援手幫她，要她先暫停工作，把身體養好。幾個月後兩個人決定在一起。認識蔡崇隆，是老天爺送她的禮物，阮金紅說越南有一句諺語：「雨停了，太陽會出來。」而她現在正沐浴在陽光中。

用影像說故事

蔡崇隆是中正大學傳播學系的助理教授，是個長年專注新住民議題的紀錄片導演，拍攝過移民新娘三部曲：《我的強娜威》、《黑仔討老婆》、《中國新娘在台灣》。蔡崇隆引領阮金紅進入攝影之門，剛開始時，她愛拿著攝影機記錄生活片段，包括社團姊妹的聚會。問她怎麼開始拍攝《失婚記》，她說一切並非計畫中，是偶然發現昔日好友有一、兩位姊妹離婚了，才啟發阮金紅拍攝《失婚記》。

《失婚記》劇情源於她自己的經驗，影片中的主角均在婚姻中挫敗而歸。蔡崇隆說：「將攝影機交給金紅，是因為性別、語言優勢再加上本身的遭遇，金紅更容易讓受訪者打開心門。」她把自己的故事也放進去，游移在導演與被記錄者的身分中，影片中與4位姊妹的生活互動、真情流露的鏡頭更是男性導演無法捕抓到的畫面。因為社會的刻板印象，新住民的失婚問題常被歸因於女方，所以阮金紅想透過鏡頭扭轉大眾對於買賣婚姻的看法，她說：「我不是愛錢，我只是要幸福。」

現在阮金紅與蔡崇隆正進行《可愛陌生人》的後製作業，故事敘述逃跑移工的故事，越南的不肖業者與仲介抽取了高額的仲介費，所以逃跑移工以越南最多，他們超時工作賺取的微薄工資無法負擔生活開銷，不得已只能當非法勞工。在拍攝的過程中，有移工被遣返了，阮金紅為此承受了許多莫須有的流言蜚語，一度失去了動力，停擺了1年，但後續她仍打起精神，回越南追蹤遭返移工的近況。為了守住與移工們的信賴關係，這部影片將不公開發行，未來也只打算在影展或學校中放映，這是阮金紅與蔡崇隆的堅持。

進階而圓滿的生命

拍攝《失婚記》需要經費，蔡崇隆鼓勵她申請雲門的「流浪者計畫」，於是阮金紅自己寫了企畫書投案，作PPT，參加人生第一次的面試。面試的時間很短，讓她一度以為沒機會了，卻意外收到入選的通知信。面試委員之一蔣勳說，這些人都是台灣孩子的母親，理當受到應有的重視，至少要讓每個都活得不委屈。阮金紅素來對自己缺乏自信，但雲門給了她不只是補助的經費，更是自信心的建立，她是首位獲得「雲門流浪者計畫」資助的新住民。阮金紅說以前在越南時，沒有機會旅遊，也不瞭解自己的國家，因為雲門的支持，讓她有機會回國流浪，一張機票支助她飛到越南，跑了很多地方。

拍攝紀錄片更讓她遭逢許多危險與考驗，要學習跟受訪者溝通、面對群眾、建立關係、取得信任；途中曾有受訪主角退出，還要承受

阮金紅在攝影機後靜靜地關注拍攝受訪者的生活樣態。

Behind the camera, Nguyen quietly focuses on the lives of her subjects.

Out/Marriage is informed by Nguyen's own experiences. Like her, the leading characters have experienced a failed marriage. Tsai says that he gave the camera to Nguyen because she would—as a result of her gender, her language abilities and her own personal history—be better able to get her subjects to open up. She put her own story into the film as well. The point of view shifts between the director and her interviewees. The film follows the interactions and heartfelt revelations of four women, and there are many scenes that a male director simply wouldn't have been able to capture. Because of ethnic stereotypes in society, when marriages between immigrant women and Taiwanese men fail, most blame the women. Consequently, Nguyen hopes to use the camera to change how people think about these "mail-order brides." "I didn't come here because I wanted money," she says. "What I wanted was to be happy."

Lovely Strangers is a video that Nguyen and Tsai worked on together. It describes Vietnamese migrant workers who have illegally changed jobs while in Taiwan. Unscrupulous Vietnamese middlemen took large introduction fees from them. Despite working overtime, their earnings were not enough to support themselves, so eventually they had no choice but to leave their designated workplaces for other employment. During shooting, some of the workers were deported. As a consequence, Nguyen was the subject of a lot of unwarranted gossip. The experience was draining and caused her to suspend shooting for a year. Eventually, she got her mojo back and once again began to investigate the situations of deported workers. In order to preserve the trust of these migrant workers, the film hasn't been publicly released, and they plan to screen it only at schools and at film festivals. They're quite insistent about that.

A progressive and fulfilling life

Shooting *Out/Marriage* required outlays of money, and Tsai encouraged Nguyen to apply for a Cloud Gate Wanderer grant. She drew up her own proposal, created a

來自四面八方的誤解與流言。阮金紅沒想過她的人生會走到這般光景，從前她是個很要強的女生，總是一個人、悶悶的，沒有可以傾訴的對象；遇到蔡崇隆後，雖然骨子裡還是住著那個很有想法的女孩，但現在的她，線條柔和了，更懂得生活，懂得對自己好。

採訪當天，我們請阮金紅穿上越南國服拍照，蔡崇隆在一旁用手機側拍記錄，他說金紅以前少有機會拍照，現在要幫她多拍一些留作紀念。每隔一段時間，阮金紅會沖洗精選的照片做成紙本相本，要等老了一起看照片，回憶兩人的甜蜜時光。阮金紅用手框出一個愛心，要送給蔡崇隆，這時的她笑得幸福又開心。

更多更多想做的事

除了執導演筒，阮金紅還多方擴展她的嘗試，她學開車接送先生、小孩，分擔舟車勞頓的辛苦；擔任公共電視《我在台灣你好嗎》的主持人，跨海追尋新住民朋友的人生故事；在國小推廣新住民母語教育，自己擬課綱，教小朋友唱越南童謠；還策展「雲林新移民／工影展」。她用「異國大家庭」的社團名義深入社

從家暴、失婚的陰影中走出後，身著越南國服的阮金紅自信又亮眼。（林格立攝）

Having endured dark days of divorce after falling victim to domestic abuse, Nguyen Kim Hong, seen here in a traditional Vietnamese *ao dai*, has emerged bright eyed and brimming with self-confidence. (photo by Jimmy Lin)

阮金紅（左2）與蔡崇隆一同策展「雲林新移民／工影展」。開幕當天，她和女兒身著越南傳統服飾，阮金紅的父親剛好來台灣短住，留下一家人的團圓照。

Nguyen (second from left) and her husband Tsai Tsung-lung together curated a film festival in Yunlin focusing on migrant workers. At its opening, she and her daughter wore traditional Vietnamese *ao dai*. Her father happened to be in Taiwan for a visit, so they were able to take a family photo as a keepsake of the occasion.

區舉辦活動，藉由小型社區能親身與長者們交流，傳達她們的關心。阮金紅想做的事情還很多，想出書、寫姊妹的故事、持續拍片，她也持續把自己的社會觀察作成短篇的公民報導，放上 PeoPo 公民新聞，跟大家分享。

阮金紅為其他尚在顛簸路途中的新住民打氣，即使遭遇挫折，請大家謹記千萬不要放棄追求幸福的權利，「這是老天爺給的人生課題，相信最後一定會看到陽光。」這是她以過來人的身分殷殷的叮囑。

—— 2016 年 4 月刊出

PowerPoint presentation, and went to the first interview of her life. Nguyen has always lacked self-confidence, and Cloud Gate not only gave her a grant—it also greatly boosted her self-esteem by awarding her the first Wanderer grant ever given to a "new immigrant."

Shooting documentaries has been challenging for Nguyen. She has had to learn how to communicate with her subjects, face large groups of people, make connections, and build trust. In the course of her work, leading subjects of her documentaries have pulled out, and she has had to suffer through all manner of misunderstandings and unfounded rumors. She had never expected that her life would lead in this direction. She used to be a very competitive woman, always alone and ruminating with no-one to confide in. But the new Nguyen, since she met Tsai, is gentler, more understanding about life, and better able to cut herself some slack.

On the day we interviewed Nguyen, we asked her to wear a traditional *ao dai* for the photo shoot. Off to the side, Tsai documented the whole thing, taking photos with his cell phone. He said that when he first met Nguyen, she was in bad shape and never laughed. Now she's all smiles. He wants to shoot more photographs of her to hold on to. Nguyen frequently has photos printed and puts them into albums. She says that this way when they get older they can look back on the good times they've had together. Nguyen forms a heart shape with her hands and makes a gesture of giving the heart to Tsai. At this point she laughs with carefree joy.

So much more to do

Apart from working as a director, Nguyen is trying different things. To take some of the load off her husband, she is learning to drive. She is a host of the public television show *Far and Away* and goes overseas to track down the backstories of the "new immigrants" she interviews. She is designing a curriculum for teaching Southeast-Asian "mother tongues" to the children of immigrants in Taiwan's schools, as well as teaching children to sing Vietnamese folk songs. She has helped to curate a migrant workers' film festival in Yunlin. Under the auspices of an organization serving immigrants, she goes into communities to hold activities that allow her to personally communicate with the elders there and convey their concerns. Nguyen says there is so much she wants to do. She wants to go on making documentaries and to write a book that tells immigrant women's stories. And she's putting short clips of her observations onto PeoPo, a citizen journalism website affiliated with public television, so as to share them with other people.

As for those immigrants still having a rough go of it, encountering setbacks and frustrations, Nguyen asks them simply not to give up their right to happiness. "This is a life lesson that Heaven is giving you. Trust that you will eventually see sunny days." This earnest exhortation has roots in Nguyen's own experiences.

———— Published in April 2016

「雲門流浪者計畫」支助阮金紅（右2）赴越南拍攝《失婚記》，她是該計畫第一位獲選的新住民。

A Cloud Gate Wanderer grant helped support Nguyen as she went to Vietnam to shoot *Out/Marriage*. She is the first "new immigrant" to win one of these grants.

A New Immigrant Performs on a New Stage

越南安妮

新移民的歌仔戲人生

文・劉婑楓　圖・莊坤儒

Liu Yingfeng / photos by Chuang Kung-ju / tr. by Jonathan Barnard

本名阮氏映的安妮，正在舞台上吟唱歌仔戲小調，紮實的表演身
段、流利的台語，任誰也猜不出她來自越南。

2005 年，一場在嘉義的馬戲團表演，讓安妮從越南遠道來到台
灣。如今的她，依舊在舞台上閃耀，只是這回她的身分不再是越南
國家馬戲團的團員，而成了傳承三代的新麗美歌劇團的當家花旦。

////////////////////////////

Nguyen Ngoc Anh, or Annie as she is more commonly called, is
up on stage singing a part in a Taiwanese opera in a minor key.
With her excellent command of the postures of Taiwanese Opera
and her fluent Taiwanese, no one would ever guess that she was
originally from Vietnam.

Ten years ago, a circus performance in Chiayi brought Annie to Taiwan
for the first time. Today, at 29, she is just as radiant on stage as ever,
but now, instead of performing with a circus troupe from Vietnam, she
is performing *huadan* (vivacious young female) roles for the Xin Li-
Mei Taiwanese Opera troupe, which has existed for three generations.

戴上頭飾、畫上眼妝，
安妮和先生張芳遠為了午後即將開演的
「扮仙戲」，加緊著裝打扮，
小冊子裡，全是安妮為了記住台詞，
一字一句以越文標註的筆記（下）。

Both in makeup, Annie and her
husband Zhang Fangyuan (top) are
busy preparing to play immortals
of Chinese myth in a matinee
performance. Her notebook (left) is
full of notes in Vietnamese to help
her remember her lines.

嘉義水得寺供桌擺滿供品，準備謝神。廟埕前，新麗美歌劇團的戲台準備就緒，這是戲班3日來奔波台中、嘉義表演後的最後一場。

正午當頭，烈日毒辣，地面熱氣讓後台燠熱難當。新麗美歌劇搭好的戲棚正靜待良辰吉時，後台的團員加緊梳妝，絲毫不得閒。幾個充作梳妝台、寫著團員名字的整理箱上，赫然出現一個充滿異國風情的字樣「安妮」。

這是越南新移民阮氏映的名字，因為「映」的越文發音就像「安妮」，10歲入選越南國家馬戲團的她，便以此為名。2005年，這個名字跟著主人阮氏映來到台灣後，一直沿用至今。幾年來，家人和親朋好友已經習慣「安妮、安妮」喚她，而在來到台灣前，這個名字已經跟著她，站在馬戲團的舞台上騰空、翻越多年。

離鄉背井的馬戲團人生

抓緊上台前的空檔，安妮滑開手機裡畫質模糊的照片，彷彿回到了10歲進入國家馬戲團初次練習下腰、拉腿的時光。

安妮的家鄉位於越南中北部的清化。某天，父親在電視上看到國家馬戲團甄選團員的廣告，一時興起要家裡的小孩嘗試看看，後來因為排行老大的姊姊功課成績太好、沒有興趣，弟弟年紀太小不符報名資格，滿足父親願望的任務，落到了從小愛玩、愛跳舞、個性活潑的安妮身上。

經過三輪評選，年僅10歲的安妮從激烈的競爭中脫穎而出，成為同期最年輕的入選者，開始越南國家馬戲團員的生活。

「下腰、拉筋、平衡感，什麼都要學啊。」安妮說。最初對城市花花世界的好奇，隨即被訓練的辛苦取代。遠從家鄉隻身來到河內的安妮，平日的生活只靠著團裡的一位阿姨照料，日子的難過辛苦沒有家人朋友可以傾吐。來到馬戲團的第一年，安妮總是哭著想家。

正想放棄時，剛好團裡有人退團，表演時少了一位團員，馬戲團要求安妮替補上場，年僅11歲的她打破了經過3年培訓才能上台

At noon, with the scorching sun overhead, the heat is hard to bear. In Xin Li-Mei's performance tent, the cast is backstage busily dressing and applying makeup. A few boxes bearing the names of troupe members have been arranged to serve as vanities. Among them, one sticks out for its distinctly foreign-sounding name: Annie.

The name belongs to Nguyen Ngoc Anh, a Vietnamese "new immigrant" who has married a Taiwanese. The Vietnamese "Anh" sounds a lot like "Annie," so she adopted Annie as her name when she joined a circus at the age of ten. The name came with her to Taiwan when she moved here in 2005, and she's continued to use it ever since. Her family and friends are accustomed to calling "Annie, Annie" to get her attention, but before she came to Taiwan the name was already following her as she soared through the air and performed back flips at the National Circus of Vietnam.

The itinerant life of a circus performer

Taking advantage of some free time before a performance, Annie looks at a blurry photograph on her cell phone. It transports her back to the age of ten, when she left home for the circus for the first time, and began practicing bends and stretches.

Annie hails from Thanh Hoa in northern Vietnam. One day her father saw a television commercial announcing auditions for the National Circus of Vietnam and immediately started hoping that one of his children would try out. A playful, extraverted lover of dance, Annie was the one to satisfy her father's wishes.

After three rounds of highly competitive tryouts, Annie was selected, becoming the youngest member of the circus. "Bends, stretches, a sense of balance—I had to learn everything," Annie says. Her original curiosity about life in the city was replaced with the hardship of training. During her first year at the circus, homesick Annie was frequently reduced to tears.

Just when she was ready to give up on her training, someone retired, and the performing circus was short one person. The circus wanted Annie to fill

表演的慣例，成了最年輕的一員，跟著前輩海內外四處表演。

遠渡重洋來台，唱起歌仔戲

炫麗的馬戲團舞台，讓安妮從故鄉踏上首都河內，看見了都市的繁華，更讓她遠從越南來到台灣，展開了另一段的戲劇人生。

2005 年，19 歲的安妮跟著馬戲團來到嘉義藝都表演村，展開一年的表演。雜耍、後空翻、高空單人特技……等高難度技巧的表演，總是引得觀眾一陣驚呼。而當時的安妮並不曉得，未來的公公張金湖在舞台下早已相中她，希望找來熟人牽線，介紹給兒子張芳遠認識。

家中 3 代都是歌仔戲班的張芳遠，當時正在軍中服役，聽聞父親有意幫忙牽紅線。年紀尚輕的他本來一度有些排斥，直到見到安妮的單純認真，決定展開追求。回憶起初交往時，總是說著破碎的中、英文，加上搭配肢體動作才懂得彼此意思的光景，兩人都笑了。

嫁來台灣後，忙著適應新生活、照顧出生的女兒，國台語聽說程度都還不好的安妮，「以為頂多就是幫忙戲班打雜、或是翻翻觔斗、跑龍套。」但後來戲班人手不足，只會零星國語的安妮，只好硬著頭皮上台。考慮到她的台語不流利，戲班導演特地替安妮安排了丑角角色，負責串場、炒熱氣氛，台詞說錯了也不要緊。

短短 5 句的台詞，卻讓她吃足苦頭。為了初登場的表演，聽不懂台語的安妮先是請先生教學，再用越文逐字逐句標記發音，「他說一句，我講一句，就像鸚鵡學舌一樣。」但因為全是硬背下來的，「我還是緊張到腦袋一片空白，全都忘光了！」安妮說。

隨著安妮的台語愈說愈好，5 年前，從戲班退休的資深演員相中她的表演潛力，特地邀請安妮擔任戲裡「女媧」一角。

猶豫再三的她，想到過去每次克服挑戰後表現更上一層的經歷，決定答應。安妮雖然有過表演經驗，比起別人更有舞台魅力、身

段柔軟，但歌仔戲得說口白、吟曲調，台上表演講究舉手投足的「腳步手路」更是絲毫馬虎不得。

更難的是，野台演出時間不固定，安妮得在短短一週內學會整套戲路，身旁的先生、導演、戲班的資深前輩，全成了她的老師，「只要不會就問，」她說，儘管對自己首次擔綱主角的演出評價不差，但第二回上台，「好不容易記下的的台詞又全忘光了。」

從前安妮因為不懂台語，只能強記而無法臨場反應的表演困境，已不成問題。現在台語說得流利的她，還能跟著一起編台詞、想劇本。

苦練台語，「吃苦當吃補」

但初來乍到時，安妮曾因為不諳台語鬧過不少笑話。正當她回想過去的「血淚史」時，旁人就已率先爆料，安妮昨日才剛把友人孫子「保陸」的姓名，誤聽為「豆乳」；此外，因為搞不清台語發音的抑揚頓挫，把「聖旨」誤說成「槍子」的搞笑例子更是不勝枚舉。

in, and she became its youngest member, traveling abroad and all over Vietnam to perform.

Learning Taiwanese

The bright stage lights of the circus brought Annie from a small town in northern Vietnam to the splendorous capital of Hanoi, and then carried her even farther, to Taiwan, where she has embarked on a new life, working in another performing art.

In 2005, Annie, then 19, arrived with the circus at the now-defunct Yito Show Village in Chiayi, for a year-long stay. Vaudeville routines, back flips, high-wire and trapeze acts... she did them all. The difficult feats of derring-do always earned nice rounds of applause. At the time Annie was unaware that her future father-in-law Zhang Jinhu had seen her perform and was pulling strings with an acquaintance to arrange a meeting with his son, Zhang Fangyuan.

Fangyuan, the third generation of his family to perform Taiwanese Opera, was serving in the military, but he got wind that his father was arranging a meeting with a potential bride. Still quite young, Fangyuan was resistant to the idea—up until he laid eyes on Annie and saw how innocent and earnest she was. Then he decided to make a proposal.

Upon moving to Taiwan as a bride, Annie bus-ily adapted to her new life and to taking care of her newborn daughter. With very limited Mandarin and Taiwanese, Annie thought that the most she could do for the troupe was "perform odd jobs or perhaps a few somersaults or small roles." But the troupe encountered a shortage of performers, so Annie, despite the language gap, had to steel herself to get up on stage and perform.

Just uttering five lines proved to be difficult. To prepare for her first performance, Annie went to her husband for lessons and used the Vietnamese alphabet to create approximate sounds. "He'd say a line and then I'd parrot it." But because it was all memorized cold, with no true understanding, once she actually got up on stage, "My mind went blank, and I forgot everything!"

Annie's Taiwanese improved, and five years ago, when a retiring member of the company spotted her performance potential, they specially invited Annie to play the role of Nüwa, the creator of human civilization in Chinese mythology.

She had a lot of performing experience, and possessed great stage charm and a limber body, but for Taiwanese Opera you've got to be able to recite lengthy passages and sing. The stylized opera poses must also be fully mastered.

Then there are the difficulties created by the lack of a regular schedule. Annie had to learn her part in

10 歲開始苦練馬戲團特技的安妮，過去曾是越南國家馬戲團的台柱。（左圖）

一場在嘉義的表演，讓安妮從越南來到台灣與先生張芳遠結識相戀，搖身一變成了歌仔戲演員。（下圖，安妮提供）

When she was ten Annie began training hard at the National Circus of Vietnam (facing page), and she ended up a star performer there. A performance in Chiayi provided an opportunity for Annie and her future husband Zhang Fangyuan (right) to get to know each other and fall in love. One thing led to another, and she's now a Taiwanese Opera performer. (photo at right courtesy of Annie)

有時台詞說錯了，若剛好遇上台下觀眾只有三三兩兩，也就罷了，但若遇上爆滿觀眾，難免惹來一陣訕笑揶揄。「聽到有人在笑，就會難過，有時甚至氣到不想演了。」安妮說。

好在小小年紀就離鄉背井、獨自生活的安妮，早已練就一身面對陌生環境的適應能力，就算遇到挫折，活潑開朗的她，也能馬上收拾好情緒。

從未想過成為歌仔戲演員的安妮坦言，戲班生活並不輕鬆。有著淡旺季之分的野台歌仔戲，忙碌起來常是一整個月不間斷的連續演出，固定中午、晚上兩場表演結束後，戲班就得趕赴下個目的地。

若幸運的話，表演地點就在嘉義附近，大夥兒還能抽空回家睡覺，但多數時候是戲團連夜趕車，橫跨縣市間的奔波。等到搭好戲棚可以入睡時，往往已經是凌晨時分。這樣的生活，安妮卻不以為苦。「吃苦當作吃補。」她用台語說。

跟著戲班南征北討，不少地方的鄉親都認識了安妮，每每演出還會熱情送來紅包、水果，甚至指明非她演出不可。「就是要聽到我的越南腔啊！」安妮說。超乎預期的觀眾反應，讓她感到「揪甘心耶。」

2005 年與先生張芳遠結婚，安妮的故事引起各界矚目，「越南孫翠鳳」……，媒體為她冠上許多稱號，但不演戲的時候，安妮的日子是平平淡淡地過著。

有時趁著浮生半日閒一覺到午後；有時是陪著張芳遠騎著重機，與朋友跑遍台灣各地遊山玩水；或是煮幾道越南料理懷念家鄉；再不然就是點開 YouTube，看著歌仔戲影片，學習身段、口條，練習基本功；或是帶著女兒拜訪來到台灣表演的越南國家馬戲團舊識，讓孩子了解媽媽過去的生活……。

今（2015）年安妮在台灣的生活即將邁入第 10 年，貼在後台梳妝箱的照片，還是嬰兒時期的女兒，如今也已開始在台上表演。

回想當年，當安妮告知父親自己即將嫁來台灣，愛女心切的父親曾悶悶不樂。這幾年安妮的父親終於卸下了擔心，「因為他看到我現在的生活過得不錯啊！」安妮說。

———— 2015 年 10 月刊出

just a week. Her husband, as well as the troupe's director and senior performers, all became her instructors.

Annie understood very little Taiwanese back then, so she had to memorize everything and was unable to react in the moment. But she has come to speak Taiwanese fluently, with less of an accent than her Mandarin. She even works with other members of the troupe in developing scenarios and writing scripts.

Annie, who had never imagined that she'd be singing Taiwanese Opera, acknowledges there's nothing easy about life in a Taiwanese Opera troupe. Things really ratchet up during the peak season, when they may be busily performing without a break for an entire month. They'll have set performances at noon and in the evening, and then afterwards have to move on to their next location.

If she's lucky, the performance locations will be near to Chiayi, so that she can find some time to go home and rest. But most often they'll have to drive to the site of their next performance overnight, scurrying from one county or municipality to another. Typically, it's the wee hours of the morning before

the theater tent is erected and they can go to sleep. But she doesn't regard the lifestyle as one of hardship. "Rather than causing me suffering," she says in Taiwanese, "it's making me stronger."

As she has traveled with the troupe, she has attained quite a following, and often receives red envelopes and fruit in appreciation. Many say that they won't watch if she's not performing. "They want to hear my Vietnamese accent," Annie says. She finds herself "truly moved" by the response, which has exceeded all expectations.

Since she married her husband Zhang Fangyuan in 2005, Annie's story has garnered a lot of attention, and the media has crowned her with all kind of titles, including the "Vietnamese Sun Tsui-feng" (after the most famous Taiwanese Opera diva). But this is how she spends her days off:

Sometimes after the troupe has performed for the better part of a month without a break, she takes advantage of a free day to sleep until the afternoon. Sometimes she gets behind Zhang Fangyuan for a spin on his motorcycle, or joins her friends on outings to the mountains or the shore. Otherwise, she might cook some of her favorite Vietnamese dishes or watch some Taiwanese Opera videos on YouTube to study postures and phrasing, thus bolstering her foundation in the art's basics. She might even take her daughter to watch performances of the National Circus of Vietnam when it visits Taiwan, so that her child will gain an understanding about her mother's life....

This year is Annie's tenth in Taiwan, and that daughter whose baby photos grace Annie's makeup table is herself already beginning to perform.

Annie recalls that when she told her own father that she was marrying a Taiwanese and moving here permanently, her father, who adores her, was sad. But in recent years he has come to peace with her decision, Annie says, "Because he sees that things are going pretty well for me!"

— Published in October 2015

一如兒時站在華麗的馬戲團舞台，自信地翻滾飛躍，如今的安妮則在歌仔戲台上，吟唱出屬於她的戲劇人生新篇章。

As a child, Annie was doing back flips and leaping through the air in the circus. Today, as a Taiwanese Opera diva, she is writing a new chapter in her life as a performing artist.

心南向・一家人 *123*
Bonds of Friendship, Bonds of Love—Taiwan and Southeast Asia

Passing Down the Legacy of Balinese Dance in Taiwan

看見天堂鳥的姿態

生命的舞者李庭莉

文‧鄧慧純　圖‧金宏澔

Cathy Teng / photos by Chin Hung-hao / tr. by Jonathan Barnard

2015 年 6 月，以亞洲多元藝術與文化為特色館藏的故宮南院發表了一支宣傳短片，拍攝亞洲各區域極富特色的傳統舞者表演。當中有一抹漂亮的身影，金色錦緞緊裹上身，配上紅裙白紗巾、優雅細膩的舞姿，她是印尼的代表，是來自峇里島的舞者──李庭莉。

////////////////////////

In June of 2015 the Southern Branch of the National Palace Museum, which has a special focus on the glorious and multifaceted diversity of Asian art and culture, released a short promotional film featuring performances of unique forms of dance from various Asian locales. There was one particularly beautiful dancer whose upper body was wrapped in a tight-fitting golden brocade garment, matched with a red skirt and white scarf. She moved with great elegance and delicacy. She was the film's representative of Indonesia, the Balinese dancer Ni Ketut Juni Artini.

李庭莉的印尼名是 Ni Ketut Juni Artini，中文名是先生李培慶用她印尼名的諧音（Artini）取的，Juni 指六月出生，Ketut 代表排行第 4。李庭莉來自一個大家庭，兄弟姊妹共 12 人，她是家中最小的女兒。

為愛遠嫁台灣

李庭莉與先生是在峇里島認識的，李培慶年輕時在島上經商，住處與庭莉家為鄰，近水樓台的追求李庭莉。李庭莉心中對他雖有好感，卻從沒想過要與外國人交往，再加上是家中的么女，家人更捨不得讓她遠嫁他鄉。最後，李培慶在李庭莉生日時，送上 99 朵玫瑰擄獲芳心，她才點頭答應在一起。兩年後，兩人攜手步入婚姻，原本計畫婚後在峇里島定居生子，但先生是家中獨子，公婆希望兒子能回台灣，李庭莉也不忍先生為難，才踏上新旅程來到台灣。

個性開朗的李庭莉喜歡接觸人群，再加上峇里島的觀光氛圍，與人互動係屬稀鬆平常；但她 23 歲來台後，語言不通、文化、食物都不適應，再加上當時台灣的新住民人數還很少，每回出門常被誤認是來台工作的移工或是買賣婚姻，無心的語言傷害造成她心中的陰影，讓李庭莉足不出戶長達 13 年，這段經歷至今想起仍讓她難忍傷心，最終，是舞蹈讓她重拾快樂與自信，讓她重新面對人群。

再次起舞，重拾自信

峇里島人無論是祭祀儀式、婚喪嫁娶或是生辰慶典都離不開舞蹈，當地的女孩通常從 5 歲開始習舞，母親是李庭莉的舞蹈啟蒙老師，李庭莉一直記著孩提時候，在母親哼唱的歌聲中、滿天星斗的穹蒼下，眾人一起跳舞的美好時光。

但到台灣之後，李庭莉卻忘了跳舞的快樂，忙碌在柴米油鹽的雜務中，直到好友邀約參加高雄市新移民家庭服務中心的聚會，加入印尼姊妹會，她才走出家門參與人群；

穿上舞衣，盤起髮髻，頭飾雞蛋花，相隔十多年，母女倆再次共舞。（李庭莉提供）

Wearing their dancing outfits, with frangipani flowers in their made-up hair, mother and daughter have reunited after more than a decade to dance together once again. (courtesy of Ni Ketut Juni Artini)

她在那裡找到歸屬感，「高雄新移民家庭服務中心就是我在台灣的娘家。」李庭莉說。

印尼的好姊妹知道庭莉是個專業的峇里島舞者，鼓勵她發揮自己的專長，讓更多人看見。她鼓起勇氣，再次站上舞台表演，昔日那個自信又美麗的庭莉重生了。塵封已久的美好回憶被喚起，更讓她發現自己想做的事，獲得家人同意後，李庭莉投身峇里島文化的推廣，全台各地的邀約表演都盡力參加。她還把家裡的地下室改裝為舞蹈教室，開班授課，只要是對峇里島舞蹈有興趣的朋友都傾囊相授。

母女一同練舞，峇里島的舞蹈代
代相傳，延續三世代。
Mother and daughter practice
Balinese dance traditions that
have been passed down from
generation to generation. Just
as Juni learned these dances
from her mother, so too has
she taught them to her own
daughter.

Married and living in Taiwan, "Artini" was trans-literated to create her Chinese name, Ting-li. (Her husband is surnamed Lee, so she is Lee Ting-li.) "Juni," which she prefers to go by, refers to her birth in June, and "Ketut" describes her place as the fourth child in the family. She comes from a truly large family with 12 siblings in all, and she is the youngest daughter.

To Taiwan for love

Juni met her husband Lee Pei-ching in Bali. In his younger days, Lee ran a business on the island. Juni was a neighbor, and he was smitten by her. Although Juni liked him, she had never considered having a relationship with a foreigner. What's more, she was the family's youngest daughter, a fact that made her parents just that much more reluctant to see her carried off to a foreign land. In the end, Lee delivered 99 roses on Juni's birthday, and she finally agreed to marry him. The original plan was to live in Bali, but Lee was an only son, and his parents insisted that he should come back to Taiwan. It would cause Juni to shift tracks in life.

When she first came to Taiwan, she faced a language barrier and wasn't used to the culture or the food. What's more, unintended hurtful comments by some people she encountered bothered her deeply. Consequently, she barely stepped outside her home for 13 years. Memories of this period of her life still cause her pain today. Ultimately, it was dancing again that gave her back her joy and confidence and allowed her once more to face crowds.

Dancing restores self-esteem

During her first decade in Taiwan, Juni kept herself busy at home. It wasn't until a good friend invited her to join a sisterhood of Indonesian immigrant women that she finally ventured outside and started interacting with people. She found a sense of belonging there.

李佳玲自國中起便向母親習舞，
現已可與李庭莉一同登台表演。

Lee Chia-ling has been studying dance
with her mother since she was a student
in junior high school.
Today they perform together.

絕美舞姿中的豐富內涵

在課堂上，李庭莉是個嚴格的老師，她高標準地要求學員每個動作都要準確到位。李庭莉說：「峇里島的傳統舞蹈是代代相承，每個舞碼有規定的動作與服裝。」她從舞者的站姿、S型的身體曲線及眼神如何懾人，每個動作都嚴格地叮囑，期望學員能呈現峇里島舞蹈的絕美。

初學峇里島的舞蹈，難在音樂與動作的配合，傳統音樂的節奏拍子不明顯，舞蹈動作是由音樂來決定，聽著鼓聲節拍擺頭，眼睛、手指、脖子、腳部移動的音樂都不一樣，李庭莉從小耳濡目染聽慣了旋律，她聽著音樂，身體已經記憶了所有動作而律動，

但對初學者來說，數了拍子就會落了動作，所以學習的方法無二，就是反覆地熟悉音樂，讓舞蹈融入身體為止。

李庭莉在服裝上也下了重本，峇里島傳統舞蹈的舞衣多以紅色為底，上面飾以金箔圖案，還有頭冠、項鍊、手環、臂飾等配件，不同的舞碼搭配不同的服裝，再加上表演人數，治裝費的開銷所費不貲。但為了讓表演更出色，她都親自赴峇里島烏布傳統市集採購服飾，更顯出李庭莉為推廣峇里島文化的用心。

李庭莉更希望社會大眾能更認識峇里島舞蹈的內涵，如最能展現女性的優雅氣質的雷貢舞，是峇里島舞蹈的基礎，其他的舞碼都

峇里島傳統舞蹈的服飾以紅色為底，金箔為紋，華麗至極。

Traditionally, Balinese dancers wear richly colorful red garments ornamented with gold leaf. They're extremely beautiful.

Her Indonesian "sisters" knew that she was an expert dancer, so they encouraged her to show her talents to more people. When she gathered her courage to get back up on stage, that Juni of the past, confident and beautiful, was reborn. With the consent of her family, Juni threw herself into promotion of Balinese culture and began to accept invitations to perform throughout Taiwan. She even turned her basement into a dance studio, where she teaches classes. She will teach anyone with an interest in Balinese dance.

The meaning behind beautiful poses

Juni is a strict teacher. She has high standards and expects her students to learn proper movements. The tradition of Balinese dance has been passed down from generation to generation. Every individual dance has its own choreography and costumes. Juni pays strict attention to posture, the body's curvature while in motion, and the expressiveness of the eyes. She strictly critiques every gesture in the hope that students can capture the stunning beauty of the genre.

Beginners find it difficult to synchronize their movements to the music. Traditional Balinese music doesn't have a clear beat, but the choreography nonetheless follows the music, as one moves one's head to the sound of the drum. There are different musical cues to trigger a variety of gestures with the eyes, the fingers, the neck, and the feet. From a young age, Juni grew accustomed to these melodies and movements. When she hears the music, her body automatically responds to its rhythms. But beginners, struggling to count out a beat, won't move correctly. The only way to learn is to play the music over and over so that the dancer eventually becomes fully immersed and at one with it.

Juni hopes that the general public will gain a greater understanding of the meaning behind Balinese dance. *Legong* dance, which is the foundation of all Balinese dance, is concerned with conveying the quintessence of feminine elegance. Everything else in the Balinese dance repertoire extends from that. According to tradition, only prepubescent girls could perform *legong*, and they could perform it only at the royal court. But with political reforms and the development of tourism, these restrictions no longer hold.

是從雷貢舞的基礎動作上衍生而來的。傳統的雷貢舞要求由初經前的處女來擔任，並只在皇族宮廷中演出；現在因為政治體系改制了，加上觀光的發展，已去除這些限制，而是藉著推廣讓更多人能學習這優美的舞姿。李庭莉希望台灣人能更深入去瞭解峇里島的文化，用眼、用心去體會峇里島傳統舞蹈的動人之處。

舞蹈生命的傳承

李庭莉在台灣舞出了名聲，獲得各大媒體的報導，其中，公共電視赴李庭莉峇里島的老家採訪，安排她們母女倆再次共舞，兩人的情感在相視的眼神中流轉，這一幕感動了許多觀眾。李庭莉說起那次經驗既難過又興奮，媽媽已近 90 歲了，這可能是最後一次母女共舞，想起媽媽當初一直不希望她遠嫁台灣，對此始終深感內疚。

李庭莉一身優美的舞藝與身段，是媽媽為她建立了舞蹈的基礎，讓她體驗了跳舞的快樂。而在台灣，她也把這份技藝傳承給她的女兒——李佳玲。李佳玲從國中開始正式學舞，遺傳自媽媽的舞蹈天分，她的眼神與動作到位極了。李佳玲說，國小的時候還有點排斥自己的身分，但長大後體認自己也有一半源自母親峇里島的血統，進而認同並喜歡上母親的文化。李佳玲現在就讀義守大學觀光系，在學校參加熱舞社，未來可結合所學與舞蹈專長為就業做準備，是個極有想法的女孩，多元文化的交融在新台灣之子身上更見優勢。

課業之餘，李佳玲陪媽媽到各處表演；看著舞台上母女表演的身影，李庭莉的臉上除了專業舞者的自信外，還有身為母親的驕傲，女兒認同自己的文化，更是她無比的快樂。

生命的舞者

「舞蹈」成為李庭莉融入台灣社會的方式，也為她找到生活的新動力。李庭莉說如果她在峇里島結婚生子也可能像媽媽一樣少有跳

李庭莉堅毅的眼神，散發出屬於自己的美麗與自信。
Ni Ketut Juni Artini's determined gaze expresses a unique beauty and self-confidence.

舞的機會而「息舞」了，反而因為嫁到台灣，讓她在婚後仍能保有跳舞的興趣，能繼續跳舞的她現在很幸福。

李庭莉的努力讓她榮獲 2014 新住民家庭楷模獎，母女倆當天穿上峇里島的傳統服飾自馬英九總統手中接過獎牌，一路的付出讓她被更多人看見。在台灣舞出天堂鳥的姿態，沉浸在最愛的舞蹈中，生命的舞者——李庭莉是那般的耀眼奪目，讓人移不開視線。

———————— 2016 年 4 月刊出

Juni also hopes that Taiwanese will delve deeper into Balinese culture, seeing with their eyes and with their hearts what is so captivating about traditional Balinese dance.

Passing down living dance

In Taiwan Juni has gained renown for her dancing and has been the subject of major media reports. In particular, Taiwan's Public Television Service has sent her back to her old home in Bali on assignment, arranging to have her dance with her mother. The mother and daughter conveyed their deep love for each other through their expressive glances. Many viewers found these scenes deeply moving. Juni says that the experience was both difficult and exciting for her. Her mother is almost 90, and the program may well have been the last time that mother and daughter ever dance together. Her mother had been dead set against her move to Taiwan years ago, and Juni will always feel a deep sense of guilt about that.

Juni's mastery of dance was fostered at a basic level by her mother. It was she who gave Juni an understanding of the joy that is the essence of dance. And in Taiwan Juni has passed this cultural inheritance along to her own daughter Lee Chia-ling. Chia-ling started studying dance in junior high school. Having inherited her mother's talent for dance, her motions and eye movements are already quite refined. She explains that when she was in elementary school, she felt socially inferior. But as she grew up she came to understand that half of her blood was Balinese, and she began to identify with and value her mother's culture. She is now studying tourism at I-Shou University, where she is active in the dance club. In the future she hopes to find a career that brings together her course of study and her dance expertise. With strong-minded women such as her, it would appear that the transmission of cultural diversity will only grow stronger in Taiwan's next generation.

Outside of university, Chia-ling performs with her mother in various venues. When mother and daughter perform together, you can see in Juni's face not only the confidence of a professional dancer, but also a mother's pride that her daughter is identifying with her culture. For Juni, nothing compares to it.

The dance of life

Dance became a way for Juni to become part of Taiwan society, and has given her life new motivation. Juni says that if she had stayed in Bali and raised her children there, she might have stopped dancing, just as her own mother did. It may well be that it is only because she moved to Taiwan that she continued with dance performance—and she feels very blessed that she has.

In 2014 Juni's diligence and immersion in the world of dance earned her a government award given to "new immigrants" of distinction. The commendation brought more attention to her contributions as a dancer. In the dance of life, Juni is a brilliant performer, as striking as the birds of paradise that are so often subjects of Balinese dance.

——— Published in April 2016

Part 4

/////////////

新商機・產業開創
ENTREPRENEURSHIP

「印」是要去：台商探見印度內需
Taiwanese Businesses Eye India's Domestic Market

布局東協新商機：台商搶搭泰國 4.0 列車
Next Stop, ASEAN Opportunities! Taiwanese Companies Board the Thailand 4.0 Train

新創產業走出台灣：搶攻印尼內需市場
Beyond Taiwan: Realizing Entrepreneurial Dreams in Indonesia

農業領軍：綠金生技創新局
Green Gold: Farming Enterprises Take Root

特別篇 93 師咖啡：延續泰北孤軍的故事
93Army Coffee: Granddaughter of a Forgotten Army

Taiwanese Businesses
Eye India's Domestic Market

「印」是要去

台商探見印度內需

文‧鄧慧純　圖‧莊坤儒

Cathy Teng / photos by Chuang Kung-ju / tr. by Scott Williams

在 2014 年柯喬然就一個人頂著鋼盔，直闖當地羽球市場，為「勝利體育」插旗印度；王雨農以最貼近印度生活的方式，要以台灣甜點征服印度人的胃，為多元的印度再添一味；「漢你中文」的閔幼林早在 2006 年就看到印度市場的藍海，從華語教學起家至今（2018）已 11 年，斐然有成。

//////////////////////

Joe Ko went to India in 2014 to help Victor Rackets break into the country's domestic badminton market. Hugo Wang is nibbling away at India's snack foods market by introducing Taiwanese treats to Indian palates. Cannie Min saw opportunities in India in 2006, and has enjoyed great success with her Chinese language training business in the years since.

印度，這近年崛起中的神祕國度，擁有各國覬覦的 13 億人口市場；但踏進印度的日常，諸多超出常理的不可思議，也讓人瞠目結舌。

為了到古爾岡拜會全球第二大羽球運動品牌「勝利體育」在印度分公司的主管柯喬然，我們搭捷運一路向南直達 HUDA City Centre。正值通勤時間，人潮比台灣跨年還誇張，也沒有先下後上的規矩，閘門一開，幾名印度男子齊聲喊了「one two three」，我們像被大浪沖上岸的魚隻，被推進車廂，卡在人群中動彈不得。這是我們對印度 13 億人口體感的初體驗。

不明原因的，我們在 Sultanpur 站被趕下車，眼看採訪時間已近，立馬轉搭 Uber 赴約。剛起步沒多久，司機卻在路旁一間破舊的小屋停下，一問方知，從德里到古爾岡已跨進哈里亞納州境內，跨州的營業用車要先繳納稅金才能通行。沒有任何現代科技，諸如 ETC 之類代勞，純人工的工序，司機慢條斯理地排隊。在 21 世紀的現代，再一次讓我們對印度感到無止境的驚奇。

當我們千辛萬苦抵達勝利體育，喘吁吁地告訴柯喬然這段經歷，他卻像是武俠小說中入定的老僧露出笑意，微微頷首：「沒事，不要急，印度就是這樣的。」

柯喬然：先來再說，且戰且走

柯喬然到印度拓展市場已經三年多了，他對印度的林林總總已是處之泰然。

早年勝利體育的產品委託印度代理商銷售，但業績始終不見好轉。2014 年，印度政局大變，印度人民黨勝選，大家高度期待莫迪主政後將帶領印度大步向前。柯喬然同年

柯喬然（左二）隻身到印度開發市場，「先來再說，且戰且走」是他的策略。勝利體育與當地協會、教練配合，贊助比賽、蓋球場，深入各城鎮。

Joe Ko (second from left) went to India to grow his company's sales. His strategy was to "get here, then work it out on the fly." Victor Rackets is working with local badminton coaches and associations, sponsoring matches, and building courts to establish itself across India.

到印度出差，感受到當時社會信心爆棚的氛圍，於是跟台北總部報告，決定中止與原代理商的合作關係，「印度市場既大且好，那我自己來做就好了。」他說。

於是，柯喬然隻身到印度蹲點，「先來再說，且戰且走」。住在印度的屋子，吃當地的咖哩，學習他們的語言，觀察人民的每天日常生活。唯有這樣地深入在地，才能了解到這個不拿筷子的國家思維有多麼不同。他舉例說，印度人的家庭觀念重，不願離家寄居工廠宿舍，因此設廠地點要慎選，否則將影響招工情形。要了解當地稅法、供電情況、哪邊適合圈地設廠，這些投資的 ABC，都是要實際踏入當地才能了解。

實際深入當地生活，是成功的第一步，第二步是找到對的人。柯喬然邀請前代理商

India's economy has taken flight in recent years, but its much-coveted 1.3-billion-person market presents mindboggling barriers to entry.

Victor Rackets, the world's number-two manufacturer of badminton equipment, has its Indian offices in Gurgaon, 30 kilometers southwest of New Delhi. We decide to take the Delhi Metro there to see Joe Ko, the company's managing director in India. When the train arrives at the platform and the doors open, a few young Indian men shout "one, two, three" in unison. We have our first experience of India's unfathomably large population as we are borne into the carriage by a suddenly surging wave of humanity and find ourselves effectively pinioned by the crowd of commuters.

When later compelled to leave the train for reasons that weren't entirely clear, we arrange an Uber to continue our trip. Shortly after we climb aboard, our driver halts outside a shabby little building where drivers of business vehicles must line up to pay a tax at what turns out to be a state border. Absent any automation at all, the process is managed entirely by hand, leaving us flabbergasted again by 21st-century India.

When we finally arrive at Victor's offices and breathlessly relate our experience to Ko, he smiles like a monk in a martial arts novel. Nodding his head slightly, he says, "Don't worry about it. That's just the way it is in India."

Joe Ko: Figuring it out on the fly

Having worked in India for more than three years, Ko is unfazed by its quirks.

Victor used to operate its India business through

負責勝利的業務經理，加入印度分公司的行列。對的人到位了，使他能在短時間內與全印度的市場、球界接觸，建立合作關係。

在印度，勝利體育同樣遇到它最大的競爭對手——日本的 YONEX，印度各地協會仍為其壟斷。面對勁敵，柯喬然只能耐心等待換約的時機點，與各地的協會溝通遊說，全印度約有 32 個地方協會，勝利體育目前已經談下三、四個地方協會的贊助；藉由贊助球員、舉辦比賽，提供當地協會另一個選擇。

勝利體育也深入各城鎮的體育用品社，與當地協會、教練配合，贊助比賽，提供產品試用，並藉此推廣產品。柯喬然說，這樣的銷售模式等於是需要無數的灘頭堡，壞處是慢，好處是很踏實。

一步一腳印，柯喬然有信心 2017 年可以挑戰 1 億盧比的營業額門檻，雖然他的競爭對手已樹立了至少 30 億盧比營業額的高牆。但若不是柯喬然在當年勇敢地、什麼都不管、頂著一頂鋼盔就衝過來，沒有蹲這 3 年的馬步，是不可能有這漂亮的營業數字，柯喬然略帶驕傲地說。

王雨農：善用地緣人脈，抓準在地口味

位在南德里拉札柏拿加（Lajpat Nagar）中央市場區，一間不大的店面，門口掛著「泰姬之月」四個漢字，店內藏著一間金黃色調的和室，室內畫上印度人喜愛、象徵吉祥的孔雀。老闆用來自台灣的臺華窯瓷器招待客人品茶，自家產品的包裝用上粉紅、寶藍、

印度的樣貌複雜，傳統的、摩登的都有，要滿足這多元的市場，得實際深入當地才能了解。

India is a complex place that mixes tradition and modernity. Before you can even begin to meet the needs of its diverse market, you must first immerse yourself in the country.

an agent, but its sales were stagnant. Ko happened to visit India in 2014, a year in which it underwent a major political shift, and found the nation bursting with confidence. After he reported this to Victor's Taipei head office, the company decided to terminate its relationship with its Indian agent and open its own office there. "India is a good market, and they decided I could handle it myself," says Ko.

So he set up shop, figuring he'd work things out on the fly. He lived in an Indian building, ate the local food, learned the language, observed how people went about their everyday lives, and immersed himself in the local culture, all to get a grip on the ABCs of investing—taxes, the electricity supply, good spots to set up a factory and hire workers—as they applied to India.

Once Ko had done that, he had to find the right person to work with. He asked the individual who had handled Victor's business at its former agency to join the branch office, and, with the right person in place, was able to build relationships in the Indian badminton community and market very quickly.

In India, Victor again encountered its biggest competitor, Japan's Yonex. Facing such a formidable rival, Ko could only talk to local associations while waiting for contracts to come up for renewal. Victor has so far negotiated sponsorship arrangements with three or four local associations and established itself with sporting goods stores in a number of cities and towns.

Ko is building Victor's India business one step at a time, and is confident that 2017 sales will top Rs100 million. True, his competitor already has annual India sales of at least Rs3 billion, but Ko is proud to point out that if he hadn't leapt into the fray three years ago, Victor wouldn't have reached this milestone.

Hugo Wang: Tailoring flavors to local tastes

Hugo Wang's food store Moon of Taj has a small storefront in the central market district of Lajpat Nagar, South Delhi, that blends Indian style with Taiwanese elements: tucked away inside the store is a gold-colored room with a raised floor, one wall decorated with a painting of peacocks, which Indians regard as auspicious; visitors are greeted with tea served in cups made by Taiwan's Tai-Hwa Pottery; and the store's own products are wrapped in eye-catching pink, sapphire blue, and violet packaging.

Hugo Wang established the Moon of Taj brand in India. Born in 1981 to a family that owns a well-known *baozi* shop in Jinshan on Taiwan's north coast, he has been around the food processing business since he was a boy. His personal work history is interesting as well, including stints in traditional manufacturing, and electronics, as well as food processing. He began competing with Indians in 2006 while working for a Japanese firm. "I recognized

紫羅蘭等鮮豔的顏色妝點，整個空間台灣元素與印度風格，混搭得一片祥和。

「泰姬之月」是來自台灣的王雨農在印度的基地。1981年次的王雨農，出身新北市金山王家，食品加工是他從小耳濡目染的日常。他的工作資歷也傲人，跨足傳統、電子產業、食品加工等產業，在日商公司的經歷，讓他早在2006年就跟印度人交手，知曉印度人的想法與行為模式和台灣截然不同，「我那時候就知道說這個國家很有挑戰性，但是商機在那兒，你不能不密切關注這個國家。」王雨農說。

不僅於此，他當年在英國曼徹斯特讀書時以交換學生的身分進入印度管理學院阿默達巴德分校（IIM Ahmedabad）學習，可說是台灣第一人。印度管理學院是孕育管理人才的搖籃，阿默達巴德分校更是管理學院之首。因為這個機緣，讓他對印度有不一樣的印象，認識了不同階層的印度人士，建立當地人脈。2016年，莫迪政府號召「印度創業，印度崛起」計畫（Startup India，Stand-Up India），鼓勵青年創業投資，王雨農就決定到印度市場試身手。

甜品是印度生活中不可或缺的品項，尤其在各式的節慶祭典中。王雨農以甜品為切入點，把自己專長的食品加工生產流程搬到印度去，不僅申請印度的國家安全標章，更從商標、產品包裝、店面設計，整體打造品牌精神。品牌從滿月時的泰姬瑪拉陵獲得靈感，以「泰姬之月 Moon of Taj」取得印度人的認同，用「Taiwan Sweets‧Indian Heart」為標語，把台灣的糕點介紹給印度。

如何抓住印度人的胃？王雨農開玩笑地說：「印度人的味覺敏感度比我們少一半。」他嘗試按照印度口味開發拿鐵奶油口味，嚐起來有如我們熟悉的酥油餡，這也是印度人熟悉的傳統味道，十分受當地人喜愛。當然也有失敗的產品，綠茶芒果的品項就因印度人認定綠茶是藥的一種，而停產了。食材的使用習慣也不一樣，紅豆在印度被視為咖哩的佐料，因此台灣傳統糕點大量使用的紅豆沙，印度人幾乎無法接受。

隨著新時代健康趨勢，王雨農也朝向提供印度人喜愛、但少油少糖的產品，用優質的原料進行加工，使甜點在健康和口感之間達到完美的平衡。

泰姬之月目前鎖定印度在地的婚宴市場，公司還在新創階段，未來還會轉型，目標是創造出「台灣印度化口味」的甜點。這個挑戰真的很大，但看見市場，王雨農會繼續努力下去。

閔幼林：看見市場，取得先機

時間回到11年前，閔幼林憶起當時的印度，只有一間印度人開設的華文補習班，「一個沒有市場的市場，才是真的市場。」於是她在印度下了錨，開始深耕這塊台灣少人觸及的藍海。

王雨農把自己放到印度的市場擂台，
用「泰姬之月」為品牌，
要與世界各地的高手一較高下。

Hugo Wang was attracted to the Indian market by the opportunity to compete head to head with some of the world's best and brightest with his Moon of Taj brand.

even then that the country would be challenging. But the tremendous business opportunities it offers demand your attention nonetheless."

Later he entered the Indian Institute of Management Ahmedabad (IIMA) as its first exchange student from Taiwan. The experience would give him a different impression of India, introduce him to members of its higher social strata, and enable him to build a local network. When Indian prime minister Narendra Modi's government launched its Startup India and Stand-Up India programs in 2016, Wang decided to give the Indian market a try.

Sweet snacks are an essential part of life in India, especially around holidays, so Wang took his experience in food processing and manufacturing to India, and set about designing the logo, packaging, and storefront for his new sweet snacks company. Drawing inspiration from the look of the Taj Mahal in the light of the full moon, he named his brand "Moon of Taj," introducing Taiwanese cakes to India with the tagline "Taiwan Sweets – Indian Heart."

How did he interest Indian palates? He started by developing a latte-flavored treat with the kind of butter filling common in Taiwan. Indians loved the flavor, which was already familiar to them.

However, as people have become more interested in healthier eating, Wang has moved towards products containing less fat and sugar, but still delivering flavors that Indians love. His use of high-quality ingredients ensures that his products perfectly balance healthfulness and taste.

Moon of Taj currently serves India's wedding-banquet market, but it is still innovating. The challenges are great, but Wang plans to continue to diligently pursue the Indian market's outstanding opportunities.

初期以貿易為主，閔幼林也兼教華語。因為 1962 年爆發的中印戰爭，中印關係僵滯，在印度少有華文的母語人士。看見市場，她從商務華語入手，剛開始雖只有個位數的學生，但多是企業老闆或執行長。待了兩年多，明明看見有市場，卻不見起色，帶去的資金也燒完了，她為印度先打一個逗號，返國思索，是否還要繼續下去。

朋友說：「頭都已經洗下去了，要不要再撐一下呢？」她想了想，跟家人借了錢，約定再給自己兩年的時間。這一趟回到印度，除了華語教學本業，她也與印籍合夥人成立梵天旅遊，擴展旅遊版圖。

2012 年，閔幼林才有固定的辦公場所與教室，在此之前，她都是背著教材、教具，四處上課。5 年前才買了行李箱，之前都是一只背包走天下。

一切的辛苦被她以「忘記了」輕描淡寫地帶過，在印度創業的諸多不便，閔幼林笑說就「見招拆招」。印度的改變，閔幼林也看在眼裡；她剛到印度時，人口結構的金字塔呈沙漏型，上層和底層階級居多，但十年後，中產階級邊增，消費市場興起，印證了她當初所見的藍海。

然而，在政府「新南向政策」喊得震天價響的同時，多數台商對印度 13 億的市場仍望之卻步。為此，已在印度走踏多年的閔幼林，有一點氣憤，又有一點擔心，日韓各國皆已深耕印度市場三十多年，台商願意眼睜睜地錯失嗎？進入印度市場雖然有難度，但不能因為市場開拓困難就裹足不前。「身為一個企業主，你的產品很好，難不成就因為那個地方不方便，便放棄去拓展商機嗎？」她反問。

閔幼林早早在印度下了錨，
深耕這塊台灣少人觸及的藍海。

When Cannie Min arrived in India
more than a decade ago,
she was one of very few Taiwanese businesspeople
endeavoring to put down roots in its market.

印度中產階級遽增，消費市場興起，印證了閔幼林當初所見的藍海。
The growth of India's middle class and the rise of its consumer market validate Cannie Min's early optimism.

Cannie Min: A first mover

Cannie Min recalls a time 11 years ago when there was only one private-sector Chinese language school in Delhi, which was Indian-owned. "The only true market is one in which there is no market," says Min, who decided to take her chances in the "blue ocean" of the Indian market where there were very few other Taiwanese.

In her early years there, she was involved in the import–export business while also teaching business-oriented Mandarin language classes. Two years in, she knew there was a market for her language venture, but it hadn't taken off and she had burned through all of her capital.

A friend told her, "You're already in this deep. Why not try a little longer?" Min thought it over, borrowed some money from her family, and gave herself two more years. During this period, she also founded a travel agency, Companion Travels, with an Indian partner.

It wasn't until 2012 that Min had her own office and classroom. Before that, she taught all over, carrying her teaching materials with her. She didn't even buy a suitcase until five years ago—she used to travel with just a backpack.

She downplays the hard times with an "I don't remember," and laughs that she had "countermoves" for all of the difficulties associated with starting a business in India. She's also seen the changes in the country at first hand, noting that when she first arrived, the population skewed towards the top and bottom of the social ladder. A decade later, both the middle class and the consumer market have grown, validating her initial optimistic view of the market's opportunities.

But even with Taiwan's rollout of the New Southbound Policy, many Taiwanese businesses have hesitated to move into the huge Indian market, one in which Japanese and Korean businesses have been

2014 年她開始回台灣開分享會，分享她的故事與經歷，也招募有興趣到印度教書的華語老師。2016 年，她成立福昕國際有限公司，要把自己 11 年來的親身經驗傳承。同是身為中小企業主的她，建議台灣業者當邀集上下游廠商，大家一起來，才能發揮產業鏈的綜效。而且這個 13 億人口、22 種語言的市場當然不容易打下，也不易短期回收，一切就端看企業主的決心了。

「印」是要去

柯喬然為自己在印度市場開發的前景感到興奮，在印度，他有很大的發揮空間，希望在 2020 年能挑戰 40% 的市場佔有率，他說：「這是在台灣無法實現，也是許多行銷人夢寐以求的市場。」

王雨農響應莫迪的政策，把自己放到印度的市場擂台，要與世界各地的高手一較高下，他知道這條路會走得孤獨且辛苦，但王雨農說：「我們就先蹲在這邊吧！」他的成功，還在等待中。

倦了台灣一陳不變的日子，不甘於安逸的閔幼林，選擇出走到台灣人較少看上眼的印度。11 年來，她成功在印度生存，公司現在已有獲利，但畢竟是一個教育事業，需要時間深耕、觀察，閔幼林自言：「我認為我現在是半成功。」

美國詩人 Robert Frost 曾寫下：「Two roads diverged in a wood, and I— / I took the one less traveled by, / And that has made all the difference.」（林中有兩條岔路，而我，選了那條較少人走的路，而這，也展開了我截然不同的人生。）

企業爭先西進或往華僑資源豐沛的東南亞發展時，有人選擇了較少人走過的路；雖然孤單，儘管困難，但經歷了迥然不同的風景，也成了人生轉變的起點，在他們身上，我們見證了。

putting down roots for more than 30 years. Difficult though the market is, Min wonders why an entrepreneur with a good product would let a few hurdles keep them from pursuing opportunities there.

Min began returning to Taiwan in 2014 to share her story and experience with others, and to recruit Taiwanese interested in teaching Chinese in India. In 2016, she established FUCE Consulting to pass on her 11 years of experience in the country. Speaking as a fellow small business operator, Min urges Taiwanese companies not to try to go it alone because the market is just too big. Instead, she advises them to work together to develop production chains there.

An Indian presence is essential

Joe Ko found excitement and the space to advance his career in India, where he hopes his company can achieve a 40% market share by 2020. He says, "That's something that couldn't happen in Taiwan. India has the kind of market that salesmen dream about."

Hugo Wang responded to Prime Minister Modi's policies by diving into the Indian market, where he can compete head to head with some of the world's best. He knows his path is a lonely one, but success beckons.

Never satisfied with taking the easy way, Cannie Min chose to leave Taiwan for India. Eleven years later, she has built a profitable business there. Min says, "I think I'm halfway to success."

The American poet Robert Frost famously wrote: "Two roads diverged in a wood, and I— / I took the one less traveled by, / And that has made all the difference."

The road less traveled by may be lonely and difficult, but it is flanked by vastly different scenery and may well bring you to a turning point in your life, as it has for these three individuals.

2018 年 2 月刊出 ——— Published in February 2018

13 億人口、22 種官方語言、多元種族，以及宗教複雜的印度，是一個值得深耕的市場。

With a population of 1.3 billion and 22 different official languages, India's ethnically and religiously diverse market offers a host of opportunities to Taiwanese businesses.

Next Stop, ASEAN Opportunities!
Taiwanese Companies Board the Thailand 4.0 Train

布局東協新商機
台商搶搭泰國4.0列車

文・蘇俐穎　圖・林格立
Lynn Su / photos by Jimmy Lin / tr. by Scott Williams

在東協經濟共同體中一向舉足輕重的泰國，2017 年 2 月總理帕拉育（Prayuth Chan-ocha）宣布啟動「泰國 4.0」（Thailand 4.0）經濟改革計畫，包含擘劃發展 5+5 目標產業、建設海陸空等交通硬體設施、打造東部經濟走廊（Eastern Economic Corridor，簡稱 EEC），並提供各種租稅優惠吸引外資投入等措施，全力推動泰國經濟升級轉型。

/////////////////////////

In February 2017, Thai prime minister Prayuth Chan-ocha announced the "Thailand 4.0" economic reform program, which focuses on boosting five established industries, developing five new ones, building transportation infrastructure, and creating the Eastern Economic Corridor (EEC). An influential member of ASEAN, Thailand is also planning a variety of tax incentives to attract foreign investment as part of this all-out effort to transform and upgrade its economy.

台商布局泰國，最早可上溯至日治時期，1990 年代經濟起飛，台商大舉湧入。如今，台商在泰人數約有 15 萬人，是僅次於美、日的外資投資第三大國，其中又以中小型企業經營的代工製造業為最大宗。近年，時逢泰政府推動泰國 4.0，勢必迎來下一波的南向熱潮。

傳統製造業積極推動升級轉型

1972 年創立於台灣，1988 年移師泰國的第一琺瑯，即是製造業裡的中堅代表。

董事長劉樹添回首當時的創業路，當時毅然決然帶著 1 億元到泰國投資，初期卻因著語言隔閡，管理不易，產品損壞率高居不下，事業一度跌落谷底。直到偶然靈光乍現，到機場舉牌尋找曾在台灣工作，由台返泰的泰籍勞工，邀請對方到廠工作，藉此找到合適的人才，事業才漸上軌道。

第一琺瑯目前以生產茶壺、鍋具為主，又以其壺身無接縫、一體成型的技術獨步於琺瑯市場，包含知名餐廚品牌 Le Creuset 都是他們的客戶。然而，劉樹添談到，過去因著泰國土地、人力成本較低廉，加上貿易條件較佳等，他才將工廠遷至泰國，但泰國工資相較初到之時已成長約 5 倍，近年漲幅也相當穩定，昔日以壓低生產成本換取利潤的策略，顯然不再適用。

曾胼手胝足在異鄉打下一片天的劉樹添，辛苦逾 40 載，如今已將事業交由第二代經營。有鑑於市場條件不可同日而語，因此，第一琺瑯正積極與工業技術研究院、中國生產力中心等研究單位合作，希望藉由導入智慧機械，提高生產效率與產品附加價值，同時著手打造企業品牌，開發建材、家飾、禮品等琺瑯相關產品，嘗試由代工製造走向自有品牌之路。

數位時代的危機與轉機

第一琺瑯的案例，可視為反映全球市場變化的一幀小影。

由於科技的日新月異，帶來生活樣貌的演進，全球市場也因應改變。泰國外國商會聯合總會主席康樹德指出，交通上的變革，好比高鐵的普及，不僅造成物流加速，人流與金流也同時發生。由於人會逐高薪移動，對企業而言，意味著再也沒有廉價勞工可言，人力短缺的情況下，採用智慧製造已然刻不容緩；加上資通訊技術的純熟與大數據的產生，面對將來的數據科技（Data Technology，簡稱 DT）時代，能懂得善用數據科技，才能在商場上立於不敗之地。

「國際市場愈來愈像在同一個平台上。」康樹德一針見血地說：「加上貿易的自由化、平等化，變成同一個市場，競爭是很大的，大家的生意模式都在改變。」在這樣的背景下，除了要以國際市場的格局來作運籌與布局，因應 DT 時代的來臨，大企業多已積極投入創新研發，以中小企業為主的台商，亦不能自外。

也由於過去台商多為國際知名品牌捉刀，面臨當前危機，創新研發除了有助於擺脫「做得多，賺得少」的困境，不啻為提昇企業競爭力的一大轉機。

以「泰國4.0」對接「5+2產業創新計畫」

此時展開的泰國 4.0 經濟改革計畫，恰猶如一輛急速前進的發展列車，如何搶搭上車，趁勢起飛，更攸關未來存亡的關鍵。

一般常聞的「工業 4.0」，僅聚焦於工業發展。由於急於擺脫「中低收入陷阱」，泰國 4.0 除了將科技創新視為帶動整體經濟發展的主要驅動力，也以橫跨未來 20 年的時間軸，

第一琺瑯董事長劉樹添南向創業，
以獨家技術受到國際品牌青睞。

Liu Shu-tien, president of First Enamel Industrial Corporation, established a Southeast-Asian subsidiary that is sought out by major international brands for its in-house technology.

Taiwanese business investment in Thailand dates back to when Taiwan was under Japanese rule (1895–1945), but surged when Taiwan's economy boomed in the 1990s. Taiwanese businesses currently employ some 150,000 Taiwanese in Thailand, and are the third-leading inward investors in the country behind only American and Japanese companies. Most of these Taiwanese own or work for small or medium-sized enterprises in the OEM business.

Transforming traditional industries

Established in Taiwan in 1972, First Enamel Industrial Corporation opened its Thai subsidiary, Thai First Enamel, in 1988, and is in many ways representative of Taiwanese manufacturers in the country.

Thai First Enamel primarily produces teapots and cookware. Unrivaled for its seamless teapot manufacturing technology, its clients include the internationally renowned kitchenware brand Le Creuset. Company president Liu Shu-tien says that he moved his factory to Thailand to take advantage of its lower land and labor costs, and its more advantageous terms of trade, but labor costs in the country have quintupled since he arrived. While wage growth has been stable in recent years, the company's old strategy of profiting from low costs is no longer viable.

Liu worked his fingers to the bone for more than 40 years building his business abroad, and has now turned its operations over to the next generation. Market conditions aren't what they used to be, so the company has partnered with two Taiwan-based research groups, the Industrial Technology Research Institute (ITRI) and the China Productivity Center, in hopes of providing efficient production and value-added products to smart-device makers. It is also developing enameled construction materials,

盤整工業、農業、服務業、觀光業等不同產業，提出宏觀性的國家發展興圖。

而對於台灣來說，這樣的發展策略，無疑提供了雙邊交流合作的機會，也與我國政府目前推動的「5+2產業創新計畫」與「新南向政策」不謀而合。

好比泰國4.0中全力扶植的5+5目標產業，代表現有產業的「新世代汽車」、「智能電子」、「醫療健康旅遊」、「農業與生物科技」、「未來糧食」，以及未來產業的「機器人」、「醫療中心」、「航空與物流」、「生物燃料與生物化學」、「數位經濟＋大數據」等；對照5+2提出的「智慧機械」、「亞洲‧矽谷」、「綠能科技」、「生醫產業」、「新農業」、「國防產業」、「循環經濟」，處處皆有呼應。

因此，由泰國4.0出發，尋求與5+2產業創新計畫的謀合之處，將會是未來台泰經貿合作的主要戰略方向。駐泰國台北經濟文化辦事處代表童振源表示，在這樣的前提之下，2017年6月，台灣工業技術研究院與泰國國

家科學院已簽署合作備忘錄，資訊工業策進會也指派1位專員定期赴泰出差，希望藉此分享彼此的科技實力。

亟待升級轉型的台商，2017年9月，也由泰國台灣商會聯合總會主導，駐泰國台北經濟文化辦事處從旁協助，成立「泰國台灣高科技中心」。以此為平台，延攬約210位在國情研析、智慧製造、資料經濟等不同領域的專家學者，除了舉辦相關講座，也形成跨國的產官學研鏈結，積極協助台商升級轉型。

前進泰國，東協市場關鍵樞紐

泰國4.0進行得如火如荼，不僅台商躍躍欲試，國際業主也正摩拳擦掌。作為台商第二代，赴泰已有38年的康樹德談到，過去來泰投資的台商，多是看準這裡低廉的生產成本，因此形成「兩頭在外」的情況，先從國外進口原料，加工生產以後再全數外銷出口。但國際大廠則是瞄準東協十國的廣大市場與經濟發展的多元性，尤其泰國在旅遊服務、觀光醫療、

曼谷是國際級都會，「不來不知道，來了你就會愛上她。」康樹德表示。
Stanley Kang says that Bangkok is an international city that you can't help but fall in love with.

泰國外國商會聯合總會主席康樹德看好新生代台商，能以數據科技發揮創新能量。

Stanley Kang, chairman of the Joint Foreign Chambers of Commerce in Thailand, believes the new generation of Taiwanese businesses in Thailand will use data technology to innovate.

home furnishings, and gifts as a means of transitioning away from its original OEM business model and building its own enterprise brand.

Crises and turning points

First Enamel's story is emblematic of the changes taking place in the global marketplace.

Rapid technological progress has driven an evolution in lifestyles, and in global markets. Stanley Kang, chairman of the Joint Foreign Chambers of Commerce in Thailand, says that the transportation revolution has not only accelerated the movement of goods, but also of people and capital. The fact that people can now easily relocate in pursuit of salaries means that

businesses no longer have access to cheap labor. This lack of manpower is compelling companies to shift quickly to smart manufacturing. With the concurrent arrival of big data and advanced information and communications technologies, we are entering an age in which the successful application of data technology is becoming essential to business success.

"The international market is becoming more and more unified," says Kang. "The liberalization and equalization of trade is turning it into a single market. As a result, competition is stiff and everyone's business models are in flux." These days, Taiwan's SMEs not only have to take the global market into consideration when planning and deploying resources, but must also adapt to the data-tech age in the same way that larger corporations do: by actively pursuing innovative R&D.

4.0 and 5+2

The Thailand 4.0 plan now getting under way is pulling away like a high-speed development train. Finding a way to climb aboard will be crucial to many companies' survival.

Unlike the much talked about "Industry 4.0" model, the Thai plan focuses on more than just industrial development. Thailand has decided that technological innovation should be an important driver of its overall development as it seeks to escape the "middle income trap." But its national development plan also aims to grow its manufacturing, agricultural, service and tourism industries over the next 20 years.

This development strategy provides Taiwan with opportunities for bilateral exchange and cooperation, and accords with our own government's promotion of its 5+2 Industrial Innovation Plan and its New Southbound Policy.

Finding areas in which Thailand 4.0 aligns with the 5+2 Industrial Innovation Plan will be a key focus of future Thai–Taiwan trade cooperation. Tung Chen-yuan, who serves as Taiwan's representative at

文化創意產業，發展均相當蓬勃，台商不妨善用獨門的 knowhow，從中尋求商機。

不過，面對東協 6 億 4,000 萬人口的廣大市場，康樹德也建議，泰國在風俗民情、歷史發展，以及地理位置上，都擁有高度優勢，可作為台商布局海外市場的據點。

一來，由於泰國是小乘佛教國家，民情溫和、包容度高；二來，在歷史上，泰國也是東南亞國家中，唯一不曾受列強殖民、也未遭兩次世界大戰戰火波及的國家，政治態度中立，猶如歐洲的比利時、盧森堡，甚至吸引不少國際重要組織，如聯合國在此設立辦事處。

加上泰國毗鄰寮國、柬埔寨、緬甸，免除與中國、印度等大國直接接壤的壓力，也是東協國家的中心與歐亞重要的轉運樞紐，更是中國發展「一帶一路」時，通往「海上絲綢之路」時必經的重要門戶。

此外，若以曼谷為輻輳點，1 個小時的飛行距離，即可抵達北東協國家（泰國、緬甸、寮國、越南、柬埔寨）的主要城市；2 個小時的飛行距離，可觸及中國西南的廣西、雲南與新加坡等地；3 個小時的飛行距離，連同台灣、印尼雅加達都在覆蓋範圍之內，交通相當便捷。

劉樹添也回憶道，在進軍泰國以前，他先前往印尼投資設廠，卻因當地排華嚴重，生意上雖能獲利，但由於安全缺乏保障，心境始終惴惴不安，最後才選擇移至泰國，從此落地生根。他笑道：「台商在泰國的滿意度高達 95%。」

走出台灣，善用變形蟲優勢

台灣小國寡民，本土企業時常面臨內需市場有限的困境，也因著如此，必需要放眼國際，才能持續成長。康樹德提及，台灣有著獨特的歷史背景，歷經日治時期、美援時代、兩蔣時期等不同年代，使得台人的處事性格，擁有高度的彈性。

他說：「我們的容忍度最高、適應力最強，就像變形蟲，跟誰在一起都能活。」這樣的特

駐泰國台北經濟文化辦事處代表童振源積極推動各項台泰交流平台，協助台商產業升級轉型。

Tung Chen-yuan, Taiwan's representative at the Taipei Economic & Cultural Office (TECO) in Thailand, is working to promote platforms for Thai–Taiwanese exchange that can help Taiwanese companies transform and upgrade.

性，成為台商斡旋於美、日、中等大國之間的關鍵優勢，也因此搶得不少商機，好比泰國 Toyota 汽車的零件，七成以上是由台商與日商合作製造。

而站在產業結構轉型的關鍵時刻，「過去，我們曾以 MIT 讓全世界認識台灣，現在，我們更要作出價值，才不會只是成為『台勞』，以價值為基礎，讓全世界看到台灣。」康樹德說。

———————— 2018 年 7 月刊出

the Taipei Economic & Cultural Office (TECO) in Thailand, says that this focus led ITRI to sign a memorandum of understanding with Thailand's National Science and Technology Development Agency in June of 2017, and the Institute for Information Industry to send a specialist on regular visits to Thailand to share technological expertise.

Taiwanese businesses in urgent need of transformation established the "Taiwan Hi-Tech Center in Thailand" in September 2017 with assistance from the Thai–Taiwan Business Association and TECO. The center then recruited some 210 experts in country analysis, smart manufacturing, data economics and other fields to give lectures and create an international research chain bringing together industry, government and academia, in order to help Taiwanese firms upgrade.

A key ASEAN hub

Thailand 4.0 could take off very quickly, and Taiwanese businesses aren't the only ones eager to become involved. Business leaders from around the world are rubbing their hands in anticipation. Stanley Kang, a second-generation Taiwanese businessperson who has been in Thailand for 38 years, says that most of the Taiwanese firms that invested in Thailand in the past were doing so to take advantage of low production costs, but the big international corporations investing nowadays are focused on ASEAN's huge ten-nation market and Thailand's diverse economy, especially its highly developed travel services, medical tourism, and creative and cultural industries. He argues that Taiwanese firms might as well put their own unique knowhow to use in finding business opportunities.

Kang notes that Thailand's customs, history and location provide advantages to Taiwanese companies hoping to use the nation as a base of operations from which they can develop ASEAN's market of 640 million consumers.

First, Thailand is a largely Hinayana Buddhist nation with a gentle and tolerant people. Second, Thailand is the only Southeast-Asian nation not to have been colonized by the Great Powers and was also relatively unscathed by World War II. Moreover, the country's political stance is moderate.

In addition, unlike its neighbors Laos, Cambodia and Myanmar, it doesn't face border pressure from China or India. It is also central to ASEAN as an important transshipment hub for Europe and Asia. Finally, ships traveling the Maritime Silk Road portion of China's "One Belt, One Road Initiative" will certainly pass through its harbors.

Expanding beyond Taiwan

The fact that Taiwan is a small nation in terms of both land area and population limits the size of our domestic market, which can pose problems for domestic businesses—if they wish to grow, they have to look beyond our island. Kang says that Taiwan's unique history, which includes a period of Japanese rule, a period of material support from the United States, and the era of the two Presidents Chiang, has made us very flexible in our approach to dealing with challenges.

He argues, "We are highly tolerant and adaptable. We're like amoebas: we can live with anybody." This trait gives Taiwanese a key advantage when mediating between larger nations such as the US, Japan and mainland China, one that generates many business opportunities. The fact that more than 70% of the components used by Toyota Motor Thailand are jointly manufactured by Taiwanese companies in partnership with Japanese firms is a case in point.

Reflecting on this period of transformation in the industrial chain, Kang says: "We used the 'Made in Taiwan' label to make the world aware of us. Now, we need to create value. We don't want the world to think of us merely as 'Taiwanese labor.' We need to make it see us as producers of value."

Published in July 2018

新創產業走出台灣

搶攻印尼內需市場

文‧劉嫈楓　圖‧林旻萱

Liu Yingfeng / photos by Lin Min-hsuan / tr. by Bruce Humes

沿路塞車、百貨林立是不少人造訪印尼雅加達留下的第一印象。近年來，雅加達街上景象有了些許改變，除了公共建設如火如荼地興建，身穿制服外套，沿街穿梭於大街小巷的 Go-jek、Grab 則是一例。

與 Uber 共享經濟相仿，乘客只需透過 APP 定位所在地與目的地，加入 Go-jek、Grab 等平台等共享服務的摩托車司機，便會循線上門，將民眾載往目的地。

近年在台灣快速竄起，擁有不少用戶的蝦皮拍賣，同樣也進駐印尼，攻佔機場通往市區的沿途大型 T 字廣告看板；面對日益興盛的創業風氣，印尼證券交易所也成立創業育成加速器 IDX INCUBATOR，協助創業者。

////////////////////////

Traffic-clogged roads and ubiquitous department stores comprise the initial impressions of many a visitor to Indonesia's Jakarta. But the capital's street scene has undergone a subtle change in recent years. Besides eye-catching public construction projects, fully uniformed Go-Jek and Grab drivers now shuttle among the boulevards and alleyways.

Similar to hailing an Uber in today's sharing economy, passengers need only confirm their location and destination via an app, and a motorcycle driver who has joined one of the shared transport service platforms such as Go-Jek or Grab will pick them up onsite and deliver them to their desired destination.

The Shopee online shopping platform, which sprang up in Taiwan in recent years and has attracted many users, has also stationed itself in Indonesia, and now occupies the giant T-shaped billboards alongside the highway between the airport and the city center. Recognizing the increasingly dynamic entrepreneurial atmosphere, in order to lend a hand to startup founders, the Indonesian Stock Exchange has also established the IDX Incubator.

只需透過 APP 定位，共享服務的摩托車司機便會將民眾載往目的地。

Just identify your location via an app, and a shared-ride motorcycle driver arrives to deliver you to your desired destination.

繼新加坡後，台灣紫牛創業協會帶領StyleUp、UChange2、果物配、萊爾思等5組新創團隊展開創業培訓之旅，也在9月來到第二站：印尼雅加達。

台灣紫牛創業協會公關經理王子豪表示，此趟培訓行程停留新加坡時，已拜會Facebook、Airbnb、紅杉資本等廠商，停留雅加達期間，也預計和電商龍頭阿里巴巴、獵豹移動等電商企業進行會面。此次脫穎而出參與行程的創業者，多是電商領域的佼佼者。創辦人出身於時尚媒體圈的StyleUp，則為用戶提供穿搭後台服務；而果物配則是替生活忙碌的消費者搭配果物，直送家中；萊爾思則是著重於線上長照復健。

5組團隊都是首次抵達印尼考察，極為興奮。除了龐大的市場商機，印尼活躍的新創氛圍更充滿吸引力。

王子豪表示，此次行程，也曾屬意前往泰國，比起新加玻、泰國，印尼是全然不同的國家。眾多生活的不便，反倒促使新創服務的興起。例如，因為現有交通線路、公共運輸不完善而興起的Go-Jek、Grab共享摩托車，就是典型的創業模式。

儘管此次為初步考察，「如何因應印尼消費文化，挑選適合的切入主題，是多數新創團隊觀察的重點。」王子豪說。

台灣經驗，全數捨棄

看好東南亞市場，EZTABLE今（2017）年年初，就將總部遷往雅加達，落地生根。

「選擇走出台灣，本就是在規畫之內。」EZTABLE執行長陳翰林說。2008年回國創辦EZTABLE後，憑藉網路定位系統的創新服務，快速崛起。創辦至今，隨著公司業績的成長，EZTABLE公司股東也已含跨日本、香港等地的投資者，陳翰林也從創辦人進一步轉化為專業經理人。儘管EZTABLE台灣業務今年保持50%的成長速度，仍決心要向外尋求海外市場，為公司尋求獲利機會。

前進東南亞前，陳翰林也曾赴中國考察。

EZTABLE執行長陳翰林將總部遷往雅加達，推出「aFamily」全新品牌。

（下圖EZTABLE提供）

////////////////////////

Eztable CEO Alex Chen relocated his headquarters to Jakarta and launched a totally new brand, "aFamily." (photo below courtesy of Eztable)

多年觀察下來，陳翰林認為，中國大陸、日韓以及東南亞市場，競爭局面如同三國鼎立。

他分析，中國大陸市場如同魏國，腹地廣大，資源豐富，兵強馬壯。而日韓則如同吳國，地處偏安，自成一格；而比起吳魏，東南亞市場則如同蜀國，開發較落後，但易守難攻，要通吃東南亞很難，當地超過10個國家，各國語言、宗教文化差異大，卻是重要的市場。

2年前，EZTABLE即已著手布局東南亞市場，卻始終有如隔層面紗，經過今年扎根數個月的觀察，陳翰林對印尼消費市場也有了更多的掌握。

陳翰林表示，印尼中產階級正在崛起，民眾購物已從過去滿足民生需求，轉而講求品牌價值。如今的印尼，如同七〇年代的台

Following a previous trip to Singapore, in September Taiwan-based PurpleCow Startup Association led a new team of five Taiwanese startups, including StyleUp, UChange2, Fruitpay and Liors, to the second stop on its "Entrepreneur Training Tour": Jakarta.

During the Singapore trip, the trainees called on firms such as Facebook, Airbnb and Sequoia Capital, says PurpleCow's public relations manager Eddie Wang, and were expecting to visit with others such as e-commerce industry leader Alibaba and software developer Cheetah Mobile in Jakarta. Outstanding entrepreneurs participating in this itinerary are mainly players in online business.

Members of the five startups were all in Indonesia for the first time, and were very excited about it. In ad-dition to its huge market potential, they were attracted by the country's dynamic entrepreneurial ambience.

PurpleCow originally considered including Thailand in the itinerary for this trip, explains Eddie Wang, but by comparison to both Singapore and Thailand, Indonesia is a totally different country. Ironically, the many inconvenient aspects of life there actually stimulate the emergence of innovative services. For example, less-than-ideal road and rail networks and poor public transport have given rise to the ride-sharing motorcycles of Go-Jek and Grab, a classic startup business model.

Although this is a preliminary study trip, "The points to watch for most of the startups are how to accommodate Indonesian consumer culture, and how to select appropriate themes for market entry," says Wang.

雅加達商場林立，每到假日就會湧進大批人潮。
On weekends and holidays, Jakarta's ubiquitous malls are packed with visitors.

灣，抑或中國大陸於 2000 年前後快速成長的時期，此階段是社會爆發最為快速的階段。不同於台灣、日本、韓國等市場相形成熟，消費者走向分眾。擁有國際光環的品牌，仍是印尼消費者鍾愛的選擇。

除了持續成長的中產階級人數，另一項普見於多數東南亞國家的現象，則是民眾及時享樂的消費習慣。因此，每到發薪日，百貨賣場就會湧進大批人潮，不到幾日，民眾口

袋見空後，便有如潮水般快速退去。「大起大落的消費在印尼極為常見。換言之，民眾多數都是衝動型消費。」陳翰林說。

然而，EZTABLE 主打的網路訂位服務，在不時興訂位的印尼，推展不如預期。陳翰林表示，印尼民眾尚未養成訂位習慣，即使到了餐廳客滿，也隨時有替代選項可以取代，不僅消費者沒有訂位習慣，餐廳業者也不習慣顧客訂位。

一般企業，將國內模式挪植到海外市場的經營模式，也被陳翰林捨棄，全數砍掉重練。日前，陳翰林率領團隊，針對印尼市場的特性，推出「aFamily」全新品牌，為餐廳業者提供會員管理平台，透過會員資料的整合收集，舉辦線上線下的行銷活動，鼓勵民眾消費，塑造品牌認同感。

不論在台灣提供的網路訂位服務，抑或目前針對印尼推出會員管理服務，都連結消費者與餐廳。如此的客戶經營有其必要，尤其現今網路發展，已如中國網路大亨馬雲所言，進入「新零售時代」。數位網路、線下實體的分野已非重點，更重要的是為客戶提供解決方案。

EZTABLE 是少數以實際行動進駐印尼的業者，外界雖看好印尼，然而真正進駐的企業並不多，觀望氛圍仍濃厚。「語言文化、法規制度，都是挑戰。」近年來協助台灣企業進駐印尼的 Rocketindo 創辦人劉士豪說。

Rocketindo，加速起飛

創辦於 2016 年的 Rocketindo，主要為有意進軍印尼的台商企業提供相關服務，除了代辦進駐一切相關稅務、行政手續，也為有意進軍的電商提供線上線下的服務。

Rocketindo 一條龍式的服務模式，全和 5 年前初到印尼創業的失敗經驗有關。2012 年，劉士豪和太太在台灣已擁有高薪穩定的工作，在岳父的建議下，劉士豪決定前往印尼創業。然而，劉士豪投入的礦業貿易生意，在不諳投資環境，又誤信合作夥伴的情況

Discarding the "Taiwan Experience"

Optimistic about the Southeast-Asian market, in early 2017 Eztable—an online restaurant reservation platform—relocated its headquarters to Jakarta, where it intends to put down roots.

"Choosing to expand overseas has been part of the plan from the word go," says Eztable CEO Alex Chen, who returned to Taiwan and set up the firm in 2008 after studying and working in the US. The new platform rose rapidly thanks to the innovative services offered by its network positioning system. As sales have grown, shareholders have widened to include investors from places such as Hong Kong and Japan. Chen has also evolved from founder to professional manager. Although Eztable's Taiwan revenues have recorded 50% growth this year, he is still determined to seek opportunities overseas.

Before deciding to enter the Southeast-Asian market, Chen also went to China for onsite study. After several years of observation, he sees a triangular competitive situation similar to that of ancient China's Three Kingdoms period, in which the modern-day players are Taiwan, Southeast Asia and mainland China.

According to his analysis, the mainland market is like the state of Wei, with its broad hinterland, rich resources and robust military; Korea and Japan are the state of Wu, content with their current territory and self-contained; while in contrast to Wei and Wu, Southeast Asia's market resembles the state of Shu, underdeveloped but easily defended. It would be difficult to swallow the region whole, given that it comprises more than ten countries, all of which possess distinct cultures, religions and languages. But they represent important markets nonetheless.

Eztable actually began positioning itself within the Southeast-Asian market two years previously, but did so in a veiled manner. Thanks to several months of onsite observation this year, Chen has a better handle on Indonesia's consumer marketplace.

Indonesia's middle class is just now emerging, says Chen, and people are transitioning from shopping for basics, to a new emphasis on brand value. Similarly to periods of rapid growth that occurred in Taiwan in the 1970s and mainland China around year 2000, Indonesia is undergoing a phase of explosive expansion.

Eztable's main service—online restaurant booking—is not a popular practice in Indonesia, and progress has fallen short of expectations. Chen says that people are not accustomed to booking a table, and even if they arrive to find an establishment full, they always have other options at hand. It is not only consumers who don't normally reserve a seat; even restaurateurs themselves are not accustomed to accepting reservations.

Typically, a firm will transplant its domestic model to its overseas operations, but Chen completely

印尼活躍的新創氛圍與龐大的市場商機，對有意前往的投資者來說充滿吸引力。

Indonesia's dynamic entrepreneurial ambience and huge market potential hold great attraction for investors willing to make the move.

n Global Indonesia

Rocketindo 創辦人劉士豪。
Rocketindo founder Daniel Liu.

下，慘賠新台幣 2,000 萬。劉士豪的親身經歷，也是多數台商進入印尼市場所面臨的最大困境。因此，Rocketindo 成立當下，就把公司定位為育成加速器。

劉士豪提醒，無論新創、傳統產業，語言文化與找尋合作伙伴，都是跨入印尼市場必須克服的挑戰。不論新創抑或零售業，不同於製造產業只需控制製程成本，認識印尼當地消費市場文化更為重要。

劉士豪舉例，不熟悉當地文化的人總以為印尼氣候炎熱，民眾慣以穿著短衣短褲，殊不知，由於氣候炎熱，多數時候人們都是在開著空調的空間辦公，四處可見的百貨商場，室內也都極為低溫；受到回教傳統文化影響，穿著相形保守，短袖衣著並不如預期熱銷。「如果不理解當地文化，就可能犯下錯

誤。」劉士豪說。

除了理解誤區，台灣企業的品牌力也讓進入印尼市場的台灣企業走得辛苦。面對消費市場，企業品牌力就變得極為關鍵。歐美的品牌早已走向全世界，行銷效果不在話下，尤其品牌行銷背後，不僅是產品的銷售，更是一連串文化轟炸下的成效。對比之下，除了幾年前，台灣偶像劇《流星花園》紅遍印尼外，再也沒有戲劇出現類似影響力，當地消費者留下的台灣印象自然不多。

「想在印尼成功，除了落地生根親身體會，更重要的是必須調整心態，過往在三、五年內就急於看到投資回收的思維得要改變。」劉士豪說。

——— 2017 年 11 月刊出

rejected this approach and started from scratch. He recently led a team to Indonesia, specifically targeting its distinctive market, and launched "aFamily," a totally new brand. It provides restaurant owners with a membership management platform, through which, by collecting and integrating membership data, they can organize online and offline marketing activities to encourage consumption and brand recognition.

Whether by providing booking services in Taiwan, or by targeting membership management services for Indonesia, in both cases Chen aims to connect consumers and restaurants. There is a real need for such client management, especially given the current state of development of the Internet, which has entered the era of "New Retail," as China's Internet mogul Jack Ma puts it. The distinction between physical and virtual commerce is no longer a focal point; providing customer solutions is now key.

Eztable is one of a small number of firms that have taken practical steps to enter the Indonesian market. Although the outside world is optimistic about the country, actual participants are still few as a wait-and-see approach dominates. "Language, culture and the regulatory system are all challenges," says Rocketindo founder Daniel Liu, whose firm has helped Taiwan enterprises get a foothold in the Indonesian market in recent years.

Rocketindo: Accelerated takeoff

Founded in 2016, Rocketindo mainly provides services for Taiwanese firms intending to enter the Indonesian market. In addition to serving as an agent for all related tax and administrative procedures, Rocketindo also provides online and offline services for firms targeting e-commerce.

Rocketindo's one-stop service model is intimately connected with Liu's startup failure when he first came to Indonesia five years ago. In 2012, Liu and his wife had steady, high-paying jobs in Taiwan, but at the suggestion of his father-in-law, Liu decided to open a business in Indonesia. Liu was unfamiliar with the sector in which he invested—the mining business—and coupled with misplaced faith in his partner, he suffered a staggering loss of NT$20 million. The biggest challenge facing most other Taiwan businesses as they prepare to make their own entry mirrors Liu's earlier experience in an alien investment environment. Therefore, when Liu established Rocketindo, he positioned it as a "startup accelerator."

Liu points out that regardless of whether one is working in a new or a traditional industry, the challenges of dealing with an unfamiliar language and culture, or of seeking a partner, are ones that must be overcome by all in order to get a foot in the Indonesian market. But unlike in manufacturing, where controlling the costs of the production process is sufficient, in newfangled or retail industries, familiarizing oneself with Indonesia's consumer market culture is even more crucial.

Market misreadings aside, the weak international profile of Taiwanese brands has also hobbled Taiwan firms as they seek to gain a foothold in Indonesia. When dealing with a consumer market, the strength of one's corporate brand name is critical. European and American brands long ago established themselves globally. Their marketing is indeed potent, especially because their brand marketing is not simply about product sales; it benefits from the effect of a series of "cultural bombing campaigns." With the exception of *Meteor Garden*, a Taiwan-made, manga-inspired teen idol drama that took Indonesia by storm a few years back, no Taiwanese drama screened there since has had the same impact. Naturally, local consumers thus have a relatively faint impression of things Taiwanese.

"To succeed in Indonesia, as well as being hands-on and putting down roots, even more importantly you must adjust your mindset," says Daniel Liu. "The customary expectation of a rapid return on investment—in say three or five years—must change."

Published in November 2017

Green Gold:
Farming Enterprises Take Root

農業領軍
綠金生技創新局

文・鄧慧純　圖・林格立
Cathy Teng / photos by Jimmy Lin / tr. by Scott Williams

提到農業，它或許不如科技產業的光鮮亮麗，卻是一個國家的根本。台灣擁有世界一流的農業技術，育種改良與病蟲害防治獨步全球；同時，台灣的農業經驗亦曾協助許多國家解決糧食問題。在今日倡議台灣與東南亞各國的雙向交往，農業更可是門好生意，是從「土地扎根」的新南向。

/////////////////////////

Agriculture may not be as flashy an industry as tech, but no nation survives without it. Taiwan's own world-class agricultural technology includes many crop varieties that deliver improved yields and pest resistance. We have also drawn on our deep well of agricultural experience to help many nations resolve problems involving their staple crops.
Taiwan's agricultural prowess could prove helpful in rooting the stronger bilateral ties we are now seeking to establish with the nations of Southeast Asia.

馬來西亞柔佛州新山市的全宇生技控股有限公司辦公室，順著樓梯而上，依序可以看到三幅畫作，一幅是大象帶著小象在殺戮戰場上，四周黃土飛揚，小象怯生生地藏身在大象的身後。第二幅畫作小象已經成長，在藍天綠地下，並立在大象身旁。第三幅則是已歷經風霜的成象，臉上的皺紋是歲月的勳章，眼神流露著生命的智慧。

彭士豪用這三幅畫作比擬他與父親一同在馬來西亞創業的過程。

拿督彭士豪——創造肥料的附加價值

1997年，年僅23歲的彭士豪追隨父親的腳步到了馬來西亞，父親投資的木材加工廠卻經歷金融風暴，讓他體認到原料導向、又是單一客戶的生意，容易受到景氣波及。考量當時台灣的優勢產業：電子業和農業，彭士豪決定在農業領域一較高下。

馬來西亞是農業大國，其農業強在量化管理；台灣農業則因土地面積有限而發展出精緻農業，兩者各有其利弊。彭士豪取其長，避其短，將馬來西亞的大型農作與台灣精緻農業與生物科技結合，開始他的創業之路。

農業經營的六大要素是品種、氣候、土壤、管理、病蟲害控制及肥料。彭士豪從肥料切入，初期藉由台灣農業相關單位的協助，再加上他自己苦讀自修。中研院院士楊秋忠的《土壤與肥料》是他當初入門的聖經，他捧著書，一步一腳印的實際操作。彭士豪苦笑地說：「現在想起來有點可怕，一邊做一邊學，代表著你已經做了才學，就像頭洗下去，沒得回頭了。真是初生之犢不畏虎。」萬事起頭難，再加上彭士豪又從電機工程專業180度地轉到農業領域。在農學專業上，他要補修的學分包括生物科技、土壤學、作物營養學、病蟲害防治等，幾乎等同是一名農學院的學生。他靠著勤勉與努力，一路苦心研究，再加上田間實作的實驗，逐漸將產品從純有機肥料定位修正為結合微生物、化學、有機的功能性肥料。

什麼是功能性肥料？彭士豪以手機作業系統做比喻，肥料就像一個Android系統，把各種細菌、微生物放進去，它們就好比是各類型的app，可以發揮不同的功能；傳統的肥料只有滋養的功能，而彭士豪結合有機質與真菌，把肥料功能化、智慧化。

「其實我們是把生物科技運用在傳統產業上。」彭士豪解釋道。肥料人人都可以做，但是經過特殊功能的處理，讓肥料功能化，產品的價格自然增值。他比喻說，地上的泥土人們踩了都嫌髒，但當把它捏成碗，就可賣到碗的價錢，裝了黃金就變成聚寶盆。就像

大象帶著小象在殺戮戰場上，四周黃土飛揚，小象怯生生的藏身在大象的身後。彭士豪以此畫作比擬他與父親一同在馬來西亞創業的過程。

A frightened elephant calf hides behind an adult elephant on a dusty battlefield. Tony Peng says the painting represents the early part of his and his father's entrepreneurial experience in Malaysia.

全宇的化學有機肥料除在大馬擁有
八成的市佔率，也外銷東協多國。

ACBT's chemical–organic fertilizers account for 80% of the Malaysian market; they are also exported to many other ASEAN nations.

Visitors to the offices of the All Cosmos Bio-Tech Holding Corporation (ACBT) in Johor Bahru, the capital of the Malaysian state of Johor, are greeted by three large paintings as they make their way up the stairs. In the first, a frightened elephant calf hides behind an adult elephant in the midst of a dusty, bloody battlefield. In the second, the calf, now grown, stands shoulder to shoulder with the adult elephant. The third depicts the face of an adult elephant, its aged skin wrinkled and its spirit suffused with the wisdom it has acquired over its long life.

Company chairman Tony Peng says the paintings represent his and his father's entrepreneurial journey in Malaysia.

Tony Peng: Adding value to fertilizer

Tony Peng was just 23 when he moved to Malaysia with his father in 1997. After weighing opportunities related to what were then Taiwan's two dominant industries—electronics and agriculture—Peng decided to seek his fortune in the latter.

Malaysia is an agricultural powerhouse with a farming sector that excels at running large-scale operations. In contrast, Taiwan's small geographic footprint has encouraged it to focus on precision agriculture. Peng's business began as an effort to apply Taiwanese precision agriculture and biotechnology to Malaysian-style large-scale farming, to maximize the strengths and minimize the weaknesses of both approaches.

他把抗病的微生物放到肥料裡，就可以把肥料當藥品販售。

全宇從 2001 年創立，到 2008 年才損益平衡，如今已是亞洲最大的化學有機肥料工廠，在大馬擁有八成以上的市佔率，產品不僅得到馬來西亞政府官方如油棕局、橡膠局、胡椒局等多個單位認證，並外銷到菲律賓、印尼等國。2009 年馬來西亞皇室授予彭士豪「拿督」封號（對國家有特殊貢獻者之授銜），並委任他為綠色農業科技顧問。2010 年，彭士豪更獲選為中華民國海外華人創業楷模。而當年彭士豪當作教科書的《土壤與肥料》已發行第九版，楊秋忠邀請彭士豪代言，對他來說，更是無比的驕傲。

彭士豪的言談中，隱隱藏著一股傲氣，那是他貨真價實的努力與實力。他創造了功能性肥料的附加價值，也看見產業的未來性。話語間他不經意地透露近期正執行的新計畫，卻又像個小男孩一般賣關子，等我們下回造訪再揭曉，但他的聲音壓抑不住雀躍地

說：「我現在的心情就像我當年創業一樣。」更讓人期待他的新版圖。

拿督黃耀佳──生產好食物

從建築承包商到經營吉隆坡最高的旋轉餐廳，華裔企業家黃耀佳近年又有一個嶄新的投入──農業。

踏入各產業的機緣，黃耀佳都說是一種福報。小時家裡貧困，9 歲在餐廳工作，讓他對餐飲業略有所知，怎知 40 年後讓他有機會取得吉隆坡塔旋轉餐廳的經營權。「人生是被準備好的」，他又強調一次，因為承包養殖中心的工程，讓他踏入生態養殖的領域。

「除了獲利之外，我覺得最重要的是提供好的食品給更多人，這也是未來所有人都應該去參與的事情。」於是黃耀佳捲起褲管，穿起雨鞋，開始投入生態養殖的行列。利用循環水養殖魚苗，不僅確保水質，同時減少耗水；培植菌跟藻類做為魚苗的食物，他說這樣雖然增加繁複的工序，但卻較環保且健康。他

Running a farm requires juggling six key elements: crops, climate, soil, management, pest and disease control, and fertilizers. Peng began with fertilizers, first seeking assistance from relevant agencies and organizations in Taiwan, then applying his own hard-won knowledge to refining what he learned from them. He had a lot to learn and studied his then bible—Academia Sinica scientist Young Chiu-chung's *Soil and Fertilizer*—from cover to cover. He also studied biotech, soil science, crop nutrition and pest control, in effect working through a university-level course of study on his own. Peng diligently applied himself to his textbooks and also carried out experiments in the field, meanwhile slowly shifting his product line away from purely organic fertilizers to "functional fertilizers" containing organic, chemical, and microbial elements.

What is a "functional fertilizer?" Peng compares it to the Android smartphone ecosystem, explaining that his fertilizer includes a variety of microbes and fungi, which extend its functionality in much the way that apps extend a phone operating system's functionality. Spelling his analogy out further, he says that supplementing a nutrient-only traditional fertilizer with organic matter and fungi results in a smarter and more functional fertilizer.

"What we're doing is applying biotechnology to traditional agriculture," continues Peng, explaining that while anyone can make fertilizer, his company's unique processing adds value to its products.

Founded in 2001, ACBT didn't break even until 2008, but has since gone on to become Asia's largest chemical–organic fertilizer maker, with more than 80% of the Malaysian market. Its products have not only been certified by the Malaysian government's palm oil, rubber, and pepper boards, but are also exported to the Philippines and Indonesia. In 2009, one of Malaysia's sultans awarded Peng the honorific title of "Dato'" for his contributions to the Malaysian state and designated him a consultant on green agriculture. Taiwan, meanwhile, named Peng an overseas model entrepreneur in 2010.

Peng's words mask his pride in achievements gained through genuine hard work and strength of character. The value-added he has created with his functional fertilizers also points to the future of the industry.

Wong Yew Kai: Producing good food

Wong Yew Kai has worked as a building contractor and as the manager of Kuala Lumpur's tallest revolving restaurant, but he has struck out in a completely new direction in recent years: farming.

全宇生技控股有限公司是亞洲最大的化學有機肥料廠。

（全宇生技提供）

All Cosmos Bio-Tech Holdings is Asia's largest manufacturer of chemical–organic fertilizer. (courtesy of ACBT)

準備了 400 英畝的地打造海洋生態產業園，以養殖食用魚，如金目鱸、吳郭魚等為主，計畫今年就可以啟動落實了。

黃耀佳跟台灣的機緣則起因於他的農田果園。馬來西亞雖是農業大國，但大多種植如油棕樹、橡膠等經濟作物，食品則大量依賴國外進口。因此，他想從糧食作物著手，種植地瓜跟鳳梨。原本到台灣尋求合作夥伴，沒找到，卻從台灣帶回社會企業的概念。

和台灣一樣，大馬也面臨了農村人口外移，勞動力不足的問題。為此，黃耀佳的一方田地打算用契作的方式運作，除了可協助當地馬來人就業，也吸引年輕人回鄉。再結合台灣的食品加工與品牌經營專業，他還要把新加坡納進來，透過新加坡在國際貿易的優勢，結合多方的實力，把產品賣到全世界。

「誰不想吃好的東西？所以市場一定有。」黃耀佳肯定地說。但再細究他務農背後的原因，「看著農作物或魚苗長大，會讓人很開心，這是農業很吸引人的地方。」但這份原始的快樂卻讓太多的外務與社會壓力剝奪了。他想讓更多人從農業裡找到新的生活方式，從過程中生產好的食物，提供給更多的人，黃耀佳充滿希望地表示。

黃耀佳還有自己的農業理論，他號召五種人來參與農業：有影響力的人（如政府，提出農業政策）、有錢的人（如企業家）、年輕有熱忱的人（才能做得長久）、有知識的人（才能做得好）和有需要的人。雖然許多人都認為農業是個高風險的產業，但黃耀佳認為台灣的精緻農業再加上大馬環境的優勢，整合資源、創造多贏局面，正是時機。

農業新南向

糧食議題是人類面臨的巨大考驗，台灣農業多年積累的專業技術與經驗能為世界做些什麼？台灣農業如何於國際市場維持競爭力？在全球經濟區域化的下一階段，台灣農業如何再發揮所長，開創新局？「新南向政策」著眼於與東南亞各國資源共享與深化雙

"It's important to me that my company doesn't just make money, but also produces good-quality food for more people to eat. I think that's something everyone should get involved in." To that end, Wong rolled up his trouser legs, pulled on his rain boots, and joined the ranks of those engaged in eco-friendly aquaculture. He raises fish in recycled water to reduce his consumption of water and guarantee its quality. He also grows fungi and algae to feed his fry even though it means more work for him, explaining that it is healthier and more environmentally friendly.

Wong's connection to Taiwan originated with his orchards. While Malaysia is a major agricultural producer, the country is dependent upon food imports because most of its farmers focus on cash crops like palm oil and rubber. Seeking to address that shortfall, Wong began growing food crops, starting with pineapple and papaya. He traveled to Taiwan intending to find a partner for that venture. Though the trip failed in that respect, it did introduce him to the concept of a social enterprise.

Just as in Taiwan, Malaysia's agricultural communities have been suffering from a "labor drain" as residents have moved away in search of work. Wong decided to attempt to counter this trend by contracting out the cultivation of a large tract of land to local farmers, which he felt would create business and job opportunities for locals and draw some young people back to the community. Having gone on to apply Taiwanese food processing and brand management expertise to the venture, he now wants to take advantage of Singapore's international trade expertise. Wong hopes that drawing on the combined strengths of Malaysia, Taiwan and Singapore will enable him to sell his products around the world.

"Everyone wants to eat good things, so there has to be a market," says Wong. He adds, "It's also a joy to watch crops and fish grow and mature. It's that experience that draws people to farming." Social

拿督黃耀佳攝於他經營的
吉隆坡旋轉餐廳，
窗外可一窺國油雙峰塔與吉隆坡市。

//////////////////////////////

Dato' Wong Yew Kai stands in the Kuala Lumpur
revolving restaurant he once managed, the city and its
famous Petronas Towers visible outside the windows.

黃耀佳從漁場的基地建設、技術引進、
到現場養殖和市場推廣，皆親力親為不假人手。
（黃耀佳提供）

From importing technology and constructing
an aquaculture facility to raising fish and developing
a market for them, Wong Yew Kai has built
his business with his own two hands.
(courtesy of Wong Yew Kai)

邊合作，創造互惠雙贏，或許可為此提供新的思考方向。

黃耀佳表示，馬來西亞的天然資源與台灣的精緻農業技術可以合作互補，極有發展潛能。彭士豪說，台灣政府一直惦記著在國外發展的台僑，大家都記在心裡，所以新南向絕對是一個對的方向。彭士豪也說：「台灣現在有很好的技術，但未在國外市場磨合過，尚未切合國際市場需求。」黃耀佳數次造訪台灣，他發現台灣的小農礙於資金及人力等因素，走出台灣有一定的困難；同時過多同質性的商品，使得台灣農業不易找到具代表性的品牌。

因此，黃耀佳建議台灣業者可先從一個小項目開始，與東南亞真誠合作，在過程中互助學習，成就雙贏。台灣與大馬具有合作潛力，肯定也是好夥伴。

彭士豪期勉台灣人把自己當作國際居民，而不是地方居民。戰場不一定要在台灣，但走到哪都是台灣人。他說，許多台商在國外多年的努力已在當地卡位成功，取得先機；他樂意協助台灣的農業、生技企業到大馬合作，結成夥伴關係。

回顧歷史，台灣不僅以農立國，更是一個海洋國家。海洋居民本當面向海洋，以國際為市場，向世界遠颺，這是本分，也是天分。

2017 年 2 月刊出

pressures and other matters can eat away at this primeval joy, which is why Wong hopes not just to make money but to enable people to develop a new way of life while continuing to farm and produce good food for more people.

Many people see farming as a high-risk industry, but Wong believes that by combining Taiwanese precision agriculture techniques with Malaysia's environmental advantages, he can integrate resources and create a win-win situation.

New southbound agriculture

Food is enormously important to humanity. What can the agricultural technology and experience Taiwan has acquired over the years do for the world? How can Taiwanese agriculture remain competitive in the international market? How can Taiwan's agricultural sector continue to build on its strengths and resituate itself as the global economy splits into regional blocks? The New Southbound Policy, which aims to strengthen Taiwan's sharing of resources and deepen its relationships with Southeast-Asian nations to the benefit of all, may offer a fresh perspective on these questions.

Wong Yew Kai believes that Malaysia's natural resources and Taiwan's precision agriculture technology can complement one another and, together, have tremendous potential for development. Tony Peng says that the ROC government's concern for Taiwanese who work and do business abroad, and the latter's concern for Taiwan, makes the New Southbound Policy the perfect way to strengthen ties between Taiwan and Southeast Asia.

But how will Taiwanese agriculture further develop its strengths under the New Southbound Policy? Where will it find foreign partners?

Wong recommends that Taiwanese businesses start small and engage in genuine cooperation with Southeast-Asian partners. He believes that in this way both partners will learn from one another and enjoy mutual success. Wong is convinced that Taiwan and Malaysia have the potential to work together, and that they can become good partners.

For his part, Peng encourages Taiwanese to regard themselves as citizens of the world rather than of a particular location. Noting that there are already Taiwanese all over the world, he argues that Taiwanese needn't limit themselves to pursuing their fortunes in Taiwan. He observes further that many Taiwanese businesses have, through years of hard work, already gained opportunities, established niches, and achieved success around the globe. Peng adds that he would be happy to help Taiwanese farmers and biotech firms come to Malaysia, and to partner with them there.

Taiwan's history makes plain that the island wasn't built exclusively on farming, and that it owes even more to its maritime endeavors. It is only natural that people who live on an island look to the sea and take the whole world as their market. This is Taiwan's role and its natural gift.

— Published in Februrary 2017

配合微生物菌養殖長大的金目鱸魚苗——超級金瓜仔肉的成色。（黃耀佳提供）

Asian sea bass fry raised on microorganisms are as golden as pumpkin flesh. (courtesy of Wong Yew Kai)

93Army Coffee:
Granddaughter of a Forgotten Army

93 師咖啡

延續泰北孤軍的故事

文·龍珮寧　圖·林旻萱
Lung Pei-ning / photos by Lin Min-hsuan / tr. by Robert Green

台灣作家柏楊創作的戰爭小說，在 1990 年改編成同名電影《異域》與李立劭導演的紀錄片《那山人　這山事》，正都訴說著這群近凋零、漸被遺忘「泰北孤軍」故事。

2017 年 5 月 18 日的午後，正逢台北市萬安演習，警報聲響起前，一群咖啡愛好者早已齊聚在一起，參與「泰北咖啡分享會」，一邊喝著來自泰北「93師莊園」有機種植的手沖咖啡，一邊聽著主辦人、孤軍第三代沈培詩分享土地認同的故事。

The *Alien Realm*, a war novel by Taiwan-based author Bo Yang, its 1990 film adaptation *A Home Too Far*, and the documentary *Stranger in the Mountains* by Taiwanese director Lee Li-shao, all tell the story of Nationalist soldiers stranded in northern Thailand at the end of the Chinese Civil War, a generation that is nearly extinct and slowly fading from memory.

On the afternoon of May 18th, a group of coffee lovers gather at a venue in Taipei to sample coffee from northern Thailand. They sip organic pour-over coffee from the 93Army Coffee Plantation while listening to Liz Shen, founder of a coffee shop in Bangkok, talk about her sense of local identity. She is the granddaughter of one of the soldiers from that stranded Chinese army.

國共內戰期間，國民政府軍隊從雲南一路顛沛流離撤守到泰緬邊境，成為泰北孤軍。（圖為當時的指揮官沈加恩（中）、副參謀長瞿述城（左）、政戰主任魯大湛（右），沈培詩提供）

During the Chinese Civil War some of the Nationalist forces retreated over the borders of Thailand and Burma and became a forgotten army. Pictured here are Commander Shen Jia'en (middle), Deputy Chief of Staff Qu Shucheng (left), and Political Warfare Director Lu Dazhan (right). (courtesy of Liz Shen)

沈培詩，來自泰國北部清萊省帕黨村（Phatang），她是泰北孤軍第三代。

現年 27 歲的她，總是穿著象徵軍人的綠色上衣，配戴的手飾則是能為她帶來「幸運」的藍色大眼睛圖騰。身形嬌小、及肩髮型、說著流利中文的她，在台灣求學期間，曾毛遂自薦在學校附近的「老柴咖啡館」工讀，從最基本的服務、認識咖啡及沖泡技術開始學習。返泰後，在曼谷市以家鄉生產的咖啡豆品牌開設「93Army Coffee」（93 師咖啡店），用咖啡香延續這段泰北孤軍的故事。

泰北種咖啡　孤軍蛻變的故事

「93Army Coffee」位於曼谷大學、地鐵站（BTS）「Ekkamai」附近，遊客循著咖啡馨香推門而入，充滿軍事風及工業風設計的環境映入眼簾，店內的軍事文物布置，宛如走進泰北孤軍的歷史長廊。

點杯手沖溫熱咖啡，店內文宣品及布置正帶領每位遊客從感官到知覺，從每口流入味蕾的咖啡重新閱讀這段漸逝的國共內戰與泰北孤軍史。

「93 師」對現今大多數人而言是陌生的名詞，即便是外國遊客看到店名時，也常會好奇並提高音量地詢問：「93Army? What?!」

「93 師」咖啡的商標是國民政府革命軍第 93 師指揮官「沈加恩」的肖像，1949 年國共內戰期間，部分國民政府軍輾轉從雲南翻山越嶺，一路顛沛流離撤守到泰緬邊境，今常以「泰北孤軍」稱之。直至 1970 年，93 師軍隊協助泰軍討伐泰共（泰國的共產黨）以保護泰北地區，於此獲得泰國身分得以安心居留於泰北。止戰後，他們從拿槍打仗的軍人，轉變為改拿鋤頭耕地的農人。

泰北素有「金三角」之稱，曾是提煉鴉片原料的罌粟花種植地，然而，罌粟花不僅重創泰國國際形象，也影響當地環境的水土保持。1969 年前泰皇蒲美蓬陛下來到泰北地區視察，成立「泰國皇家計畫基金會」（Thailand Royal Project Foundation）。

Liz Shen (Thai name Chamaiporn Charoentangsombut) hails from the village of Pha Tang in northern Thailand's Chiang Rai Province.

Twenty-seven-year-old Shen is fond of wearing army-green shirts and eyeball finger rings that she believes bring her good luck. Petite with shoulder-length hair, she speaks Chinese fluently. While studying in Taiwan, she worked part-time at the Lao Chai Café House near her university. She learned the basics of serving coffee, from the beans to brewing techniques. After returning to Thailand, she opened 93Army Coffee, which serves coffee made from beans grown in her hometown, allowing her to keep alive the story of the lost Chinese army through the aroma of coffee.

Hometown coffee and a community's evolving story

Visitors to 93Army Coffee, located near Bangkok University, are drawn in by the aroma of brewing coffee. A martial atmosphere permeates the industrial-style space. It is decorated with military memorabilia, making visitors feel like they have entered an exhibit on the history of the abandoned Nationalist soldiers.

The name often piques the curiosity of foreign visitors, who pipe up and ask, "93Army? What?!"

The logo for 93Army Coffee is an image of Shen Jia'en, a commander of the 93rd Division of the National Revolutionary Army of the Republic of China. In 1949, at the end of the Chinese Civil War, remnants of the NRA made an arduous journey through the mountains in China's Yunnan Province and crossed into Thailand and Burma, after which they became known as the "lost army." Up to 1970 the 93rd Division helped Thai forces suppress a communist insurgency and protect northern Thailand. In return the Nationalist soldiers were granted Thai citizenship and were able to peacefully settle in the north. After the conflict, they put down their arms and settled down to farm in the area.

沈培詩帶著 93 師咖啡豆來台舉辦泰北咖啡分享會。
Liz Shen brought 93Army coffee beans to Taiwan for a coffee tasting event.

蒲美蓬陛下啟動「皇家計畫」（Royal Project）並與「中華民國國軍退除役官兵輔導委員會」（退輔會）、「財團法人國際合作發展基金會」（國合會）農業技術團合作至今，提供泰北當地居民農業技術協助，藉由種植高經濟價值的農作物取代罌粟花。如今只要是「皇家計畫」的農產品都深受泰國人民及國際旅客好評。

沈培詩的父親、泰北孤軍第二代「沈慶復」曾來台灣接受中學及大學教育，畢業後回到泰北家鄉種植高經濟價值的農作物，直到 2009 年引進咖啡苗並以沈加恩之名成立「93 師咖啡莊園」，開啟與咖啡的不解之緣。

看似高經濟價值的咖啡豆，在收成後透過中盤商低價收購，賣到市場，沈慶復當時只知種植技術，連一杯都沒有喝過，對於「咖啡」是什麼更是一竅不通，而這也是許多咖啡農的情況——喝不起一杯咖啡。

第三代沈培詩在父親鼓勵下，也到台灣讀書。沈培詩的興趣是服裝設計，並以此為第一志願，身為長女的她經過反覆思考，也希望將來運用所學為家鄉努力，進而選讀企業管理。也因為泰北家鄉種植咖啡，沈培詩主動到台北大學附近的老柴咖啡館打工，從實做中認識咖啡，畢業後，在家鄉規劃開設咖啡店。

創業緣起　農民喝不起咖啡

多數遠赴國外留學者，畢業後往往會留在當地找工作，沈培詩一心一意想要回到家鄉，運用在台灣所學的專業來就業，她認為從既有的資源（咖啡豆）去做，盡力就會有好成果。

Northern Thailand has long been known as part of the Golden Triangle, once used to cultivate poppies for opium production. However, the opium trade harmed Thailand's image and caused environmental degradation in the area. In 1969 Thailand's late king, Bhumibol Adulyadej, visited northern Thailand and initiated the Royal Project Foundation.

The Royal Project founded by King Bhumibol, the ROC's Vocational Assistance Commission for Retired Servicemen (now the Veterans Affairs Council), and agricultural assistance teams from the International Cooperation and Development Fund have since been working together to improve farming methods in northern Thailand and to replace opium poppies with other high-value cash crops.

After completing studies in Taiwan, Liz Shen's father, Shen Qingfu, returned to northern Thailand and began to cultivate cash crops. In 2009 he established the 93Army Coffee Plantation, beginning what would become a lasting involvement in the coffee business.

At the time Shen Qingfu was familiar only with coffee cultivation techniques. He had never had a cup of coffee, which was a completely foreign thing to him. It was not an uncommon phenomenon for the planters to be unable to afford a cup of coffee.

Her father's encouragement convinced Liz Shen to study in Taiwan. She wanted to put her academic studies to good use when she returned home and chose to focus on business management. She eagerly took up part-time work at Lao Chai Café House near the National Taipei University branch campus in Sanxia, and learned about coffee firsthand. She planned to open a coffee shop of her own in her hometown after graduation.

An entrepreneur's precious brew

While many students studying abroad end up staying in the host country and seeking jobs after graduation, Shen was intent on returning home to Thailand and starting a career that would put her studies to practical use. She worked hard to develop a business around the local coffee crop.

Pha Tang's coffee is cultivated in highlands between 1200 and 1600 meters above sea level. Production is limited by the paucity of arable land, and competition with large-scale producers is not possible.

Moreover, the retail price of roasted coffee beans is many times the wholesale cost of the raw beans. The coffee sold in the shop, which costs 100 baht and up per serving, is far too pricey for the farmers who grow it.

93 師咖啡店內布置充滿軍事風，連餐飲都有代表軍人的綠色元素。（沈培詩提供）

A martial atmosphere permeates 93Army Coffee, and army green is also featured in the food and beverages. (courtesy of Liz Shen)

家鄉帕黨的咖啡豆都種植在海拔 1,200 ～ 1,600 公尺的高山上，由於種植面積不大，產量有限而無法與量產的商業豆競爭。

加上收購價和烘焙過後成品的售價差距數倍以上。例如，收購價是 20 元，經過中盤商轉手，烘焙後的市場價是 100 元，咖啡店內販售的百元咖啡對咖啡農而言，卻是喝不起的奢侈飲品。

在泰國皇家計畫下生產的泰北農產品具有一定的品質，也深受泰國人支持，甚至外國遊客也常搶購成為伴手禮，遠近馳名的皇家牛乳片、皇家蜂蜜等是台灣訪泰遊客的必買清單。

沈培詩深感泰北咖啡知名度僅限於泰國境內，而在東南亞的咖啡產地，又以印尼和越南最為聞名，她在受訪時，流露些許落寞，但也更加深她推廣泰北咖啡的使命，讓世界循著「好咖啡」走進泰北的咖啡莊園。

「農民對於種植具有專業技術，不過，收入扣除生產成本後所剩無幾，利潤全由中盤商及國際食品企業掌控。」有心提升家鄉農民生活品質的沈培詩，願景是讓更多人認識泰北地區及泰北的精品咖啡。

「Good coffee can be bad coffee, but bad coffee is still bad coffee.」（譯：好咖啡有可能成為劣咖啡，然而劣咖啡仍是劣咖啡。）她說。

從種植到成為一杯香醇的咖啡，每個過程都是專業，咖啡農擁有種植技術，從採收到販售的過程，藉由技術可增加咖啡價值，而這些技術就是她在台灣所學的企業管理、行銷學、咖啡豆處理及辨識等專業，要成為好咖啡則每一階段都需重視。

這是創業最初的想法。

萬事起頭難，獲得家人支持的沈培詩決定在高度國際化的曼谷市創業。二十多歲的她在沒有任何規畫下就開店了，她回憶起當時的這股衝動還是覺得「太冒險」，沒有任何經驗的她不諱言曾經想要放棄，當店門一開面對的是能否服務周全，遞給客人咖啡時不知味道符合嗎？當每到晚上打烊時，集結一日的壓力與疲勞都顯現在倦容上。

「會喝咖啡不代表能開咖啡店，學習企管不代表就能經營。」吃足苦頭的她仍堅持做下去，邊做邊學並調整步伐，從 2014 年 10 月創業至今，93 師咖啡店不僅能喝到泰北有機栽種的純阿拉比卡豆咖啡，也能吃到有台灣味道的刈包漢堡。

勤學不倦的沈培詩不斷地自我精進，專注於咖啡領域的她也獲得美國咖啡師執照、烘焙師執照，現今常獲邀擔任咖啡比賽評審或是顧問。她是創業家也是教育家，常有慕名前來 93 師咖啡店的海內外遊客，向她學習咖啡技術及如何成為一名咖啡師。

永續經營　合理交易

沈培詩一直不忘創業初衷就是打響家鄉咖啡品牌，提升農民收入，以便專注於提高咖啡豆的品質。

收成時是農忙季，採摘的工人經常供不應求，結實累累的咖啡豆需要分批細心摘下已成熟的紅色果實，其他半熟或未熟的應該等成熟後再採摘。對比微薄的日薪，分批採收是耗費時間且沒有效率的事。

採收的咖啡豆成熟程度若不一致，會影響烘培時咖啡的品質，因此講究的沈培詩不僅教育農民如何採收，也藉由社群媒體號召國際志工一同上山，從實作帶領咖啡愛好者體會，一杯好咖啡的誕生是需要歷經一段辛苦過程才能實至名歸，同時也注入「永續經營、合理交易」的理念。

沈培詩是「泰國精品咖啡協會」（Specialty Coffee Association of Thailand, SCATH）的一員，定期與精品咖啡協會成員及志工一同到泰北山區協助當地咖啡農。

他們在野外搭著簡易帳篷，白天到咖啡莊園內分送並協助種植咖啡苗，不過，每個山區的氣候、緯度條件不一，適合的咖啡品種也不一，有時需要種植後才能評估是否合適此處，然而這些都需要長時間等待。

與當地農民形成的互動並非建立在買賣雙方的利益價值上，沈培詩穿著雨鞋，蹲下

沈培詩與泰國精品咖啡協會
定期前往泰北，協助種植咖啡苗。

（沈培詩提供）

////////////////////

Liz Shen and representatives of the Specialty
Coffee Association of Thailand regularly visit
northern Thailand to help with cultivation
techniques and planting. (courtesy of Liz Shen)

It is one of the high-quality products that have resulted from support by the Royal Project. They are popular among Thai customers and foreign tourists who often buy them as gifts.

Shen is well aware that the coffee grown in northern Thailand is widely known only in Thailand and that among the coffee-growing regions of Southeast Asia, coffee produced in Indonesia and Vietnam is more famous. During our interview this seems to pain her, yet it only increases her determination to promote northern Thai coffee and ensure that the world learns that good coffee is also to be found in the plantations of northern Thailand.

"Good coffee can be bad coffee, but bad coffee is still bad coffee," she says.

Each step in the process of making a rich cup of coffee, from planting to pouring, takes specialized professional skills. Cultivating coffee requires specialist knowledge through each step from harvesting to selling. The skillful application of professional knowledge can increase the value of the coffee. These were the skills she had learned in Taiwan—business management, marketing, how to process coffee beans and how to assess their quality. Each step must be given its proper attention to produce good coffee.

Such was her thinking when she started her business.

But looking back at how she opened her shop in her twenties without much of a plan, she thinks that her impulsiveness was really risky. She admits that the inexperienced entrepreneur that she was back then had thoughts about giving up on the business.

"Being a coffee drinker doesn't mean you'll be successful at opening a coffee shop, and studying management doesn't mean you'll know how to run it," she says.

She has persevered through all her hardships, learning through experience. Since the shop opened in October 2014, 93Army Coffee's customers have

一杯好咖啡的誕生
需要歷經一段辛苦過程才能完成。

A lot of hard work goes into
making a good cup of coffee.

身,一手拿著咖啡苗,一手拿鏟挖土,將每株代表未來希望的咖啡苗親手種下,她形容自己是個「農夫」。

每到晚上,蛙鳴蟲叫聲與夥伴們的笑聲攪和著,來自世界或全國各地有志一同的咖啡愛好者,一同喝咖啡、聊咖啡直到半夜。沈培詩還說,在山上煮的咖啡特別香醇美味。

沈培詩讓泰北的咖啡莊園走向精品咖啡,掛著93咖啡莊園招牌的咖啡豆都是兼顧品質及環境永續的理念,每一杯咖啡的生產履歷都是誠實揭露,包括來自那一山區、處理流程及時間。對於農民也提供合理交易價格,當農民生活改善,便會用心照顧咖啡豆,消費者也能喝到好品質的咖啡,這是正向的回饋,也是對農民的鼓勵。

93師咖啡在沈培詩一步一腳印的經營下,落實「永續經營、合理交易」用家鄉的咖啡豆創業,掌握原料品質及通路,讓喝下的每一杯都是被認可的好味道。

沈培詩定期往來台灣與泰國,除了參加咖啡展覽外,日前還曾在台北舉辦「咖啡分享會」,並宣布93師咖啡正式引進台灣販售。未來也希望能在台灣開設分店,93師咖啡帶來的不僅是泰北孤軍生命故事的延續,更多的是台灣與泰國深化的農業技術合作,以及永續經營、合理交易的農業消費模式。

———— 2017 年 8 月刊出

been able to drink a brew made from pure Arabica coffee beans and nibble on Taiwanese-style *guabao* sandwiches.

Interested in all things coffee, she also earned her barista certification in the United States and is often invited to serve as a judge or consultant for coffee competitions. She is both an entrepreneur and an educator and is frequently sought out by visitors from Thailand and abroad who want to study her specialized knowledge or learn how to become baristas.

Embracing sustainability and fair trade

Shen has never forgotten that her motivation for starting her business was to help raise the incomes of farmers by improving the quality of their coffee beans.

At harvest time, pickers are often in short supply. The ripe red beans must be painstakingly plucked one by one from the clusters, leaving semi-ripe and unripe beans for harvesting at a later date. It is very tempting for farmers to try to reduce their wage costs by harvesting all the beans at the same time.

But if the maturity of the harvested beans is not consistent, roasting and quality will be affected. Shen therefore uses her considerable understanding of coffee to advise farmers on harvesting. She also leads people involved in the coffee trade to experience coffee farming themselves, helping them to understand that a good cup of coffee earns its name only through an arduous process.

To this end Shen, a member of the Specialty Coffee Association of Thailand, regularly accompanies other association members and volunteers on visits to assist the coffee farmers in the highlands of northern Thailand.

They pitch simple tents in the countryside and spend their days at the coffee plantations distributing and planting seedlings.

Wearing rubber boots, Shen squats down and with a trowel in one hand digs a hole for the seedling that she holds in the other. Each seedling that she plants with her own hands represents hope for the future, and no matter what else she does in life, she likes to describe herself as a simple farmer.

Each night, the enthusiastic coffee lovers sip coffee together and talk about coffee late into the night. Shen says that mountain-brewed coffee is especially delicious.

Shen has turned the coffee from the northern Thai plantations into a boutique product. Coffee beans sold under the 93Army brand reflect her embrace of superior quality and sustainable growing methods, and each step of production is transparent. She also pays fair prices to the farmers, believing that as their quality of life improves they will also more meticulously care for the coffee plants, so that superior-quality coffee is produced for the enjoyment of consumers. This results in positive feedback and further encourages the farmers.

Shen has developed 93Army Coffee one step at a time, from implementing sustainable development and fair trade practices to building a business based on local coffee beans and on understanding and accessing the highest-quality resources, in the hope that each cup of coffee will win the approval of coffee drinkers.

Shen also travels regularly between Thailand and Taiwan, where she attends coffee exhibitions and recently held a coffee tasting event at which she launched the sale of 93Army Coffee in Taiwan. She also hopes to open a branch of her coffee shop in Taiwan. While the company helps keep alive the story of the stranded Nationalist soldiers, it also represents the increased sharing between Taiwan and Thailand of agricultural techniques, including environmentally sustainable methods and fair trade practices.

— Published in August 2017

Part *5*

心守護・為新住民發聲
POLITICS

制度化建置的推手：司法通譯硬漢──陳允萍
Making the Case for Judicial Interpretation—Peter Chen

為新住民姊妹發聲：首位新住民國策顧問──胡清嫻
National Policy Advisor Ho Thanh Nhan—Speaking Up for New Immigrants

倡議姊妹權益的守護者：邱雅青
Her Sisters' Guardian—Yadrung Chiou

台灣第一位新住民立委：柬埔寨「灰姑娘」林麗蟬勇闖國會
Taiwan's First New Immigrant Legislator: Lin Li-chan

 特別篇 台灣 NGO 扎根越南：教育改變孩子未來
Taiwanese NGOs in Vietnam: Changing Children's Futures Through Education

Making the Case for Judicial Interpretation—Peter Chen

制度化建置的推手

司法通譯硬漢——陳允萍

文‧李珊瑋　圖‧林旻萱
Lee Shan Wei / photos by Lin Min-hsuan / tr. by Phil Newell

每一種工作都是神聖的，尤其是當這種工作，有權力左右他人的利益得失時，更要用一種誠惶誠恐的心情，去面對和處理。

承辦外籍人士司法案件長達 25 年的陳允萍，對「司法通譯」現身說法。將自己從外事警察到移民署業務的親身經歷，撰寫成書，四方奔走宣揚，期待落實「司法前人人平等」的執法精神，讓當事人享有「知」的權利，並且透過良善的制度，保障通譯者的人身安全。

/////////////////////////////

All work is sacred, but work that affects other people's rights and interests should be approached with particular reverence and awe.

Peter Chen, who has been serving as a judicial interpreter for 25 years, is an ambassador for his profession. He has written two books based on his personal experience working for the foreign affairs police and later the National Immigration Agency, and is constantly on the go. His aims are to uphold the principle that all persons are equal before the law, to enable parties to legal cases to enjoy their "right to know," and, through sound institutional arrangements, to assure the personal safety of interpreters.

先行者，往往是孤寂的，但是隨著披荊斬棘，灌溉深耕的傻勁，綠洲已初現端倪。12年來，通過化蛹成蝶的煎熬，隨著司法改革的腳步，志同道合者的襄助，司法通譯的春天，已經不遠。

法律講求邏輯，經驗更是核心。執法人員對案件的精準判斷，需要學養，更需要歷練。

然而，由執法者來擔任司法通譯這種便宜行事的方式，是否能夠毫無偏頗地傳遞出真實的案情？

「中立」是通譯底線

司法講求的是公正合理的審判程序，如果當事人有語言障礙，何來正義可言？所以司法通譯是給予當事人公平待遇的起點，否則將會對人民的權利，造成嚴重的侵害。

所謂「通譯」，是要用當事人聽得懂的語言，加以轉述，讓他（她）理解。陳允萍指出，「通譯本身就不是一件容易的事，而作為司法通譯，更是一個需要嚴謹訓練的工作。」不僅要精通雙方語言，更要能精確掌握法律文件的語彙。

「就像『得』，在法律屬性中，具有可做，也可不做的意義。代表你有這種權利，但是也可以選擇放棄。」陳允萍舉一個最粗淺的例子說。當把這些法律文字，翻譯成當事人聽得懂的語言時，必然要字斟句酌，精準表達，絲毫不能偏離，才能保障當事人的基本人權。

法律的天秤，容不得絲毫偏頗。基於中立公正原則，擔任通譯者，理論上要和案件無關。但是警政單位，尚未設置全面性的通譯資料庫，可隨時提供調度運用。而且案件發生時，往往十分緊迫，為了講求效率，迫使執法者在第一時間，只能便宜行事，尋找最熟悉的人來擔任通譯，根本無暇顧及該名通譯者是否能秉持中立，或是否具有司法素養。更多時候，就由執法者自己來擔任通譯。球員兼裁判的狀況，屢見不鮮。

陳允萍用最常見的案例來說明：「如果今天有一名外勞脫逃，警方可能會請仲介來擔任司法通譯。」但是仲介往往歸於利害關係人，理應迴避。一個不適格的通譯，如何期待公允？「所以司法通譯倫理，是程序正義中，最重要的一環。」

雙向保障，才能圓滿

通譯，其實是一個具有潛在危險的工作，必須要有管理和相關的配套措施。陳允萍提到一個發生在2012年，通譯者遭他殺死亡，

陳允萍轉送善心人士捐贈的冬衣，給台東富岡漁港的外籍船工。（陳允萍提供）
Peter Chen passes along donated winter clothing to foreign fishing boat crew in Taitung County's Fugang Fishing Harbor. (courtesy of Peter Chen)

由警界到移民署，陳允萍的業務，始終和外籍移民相關。

From the foreign affairs police to the National Immigration Agency, Peter Chen's professional work has always been related to foreign immigrants.

Judicial systems strive for just and reasonable trial procedures. If there are linguistic obstacles for a party in a case, what justice can there be? Therefore, judicial interpretation is the starting point for providing fair treatment in cases involving different languages.

"Interpretation" means re-expressing spoken information in a language that a party to a case knows, so that he or she can understand it. Peter Chen says, "Interpreting in itself is not an easy thing to do, but to be a judicial interpreter is a job that requires even more rigorous training." Not only do you need to be fluent in two languages, you have to have an accurate grasp of legal terminology, for only then can you protect the basic human rights of the party.

Based on the principles of neutrality and fairness, in theory a person serving as an interpreter should be unconnected with the case concerned. But police agencies have yet to establish a comprehensive database of interpreters which they can use to call on qualified people at all times. Moreover, when an incident occurs, often there is great urgency, and in order to take effective action, law enforcers have no choice but to seek out a person they are familiar with to serve as interpreter, regardless of whether that person has legal training or not. Very often it is law enforcement personnel themselves who serve as interpreters. It is by no means rare to have a situation in which the player and the referee are one and the same.

Personal safety

In fact, interpreting is a job fraught with potential danger, so there must be proper management and procedures. Chen mentions an unsolved case from 2012 in which an interpreter was murdered, which should be a warning to the judicial community.

In early 2012, Peter Chen, the Judicial Reform Foundation and other non-governmental groups presented a petition at the Control Yuan to promote a formal management system for judicial interpreting. After investigation, the Control Yuan issued a

The law emphasizes logic, but experience is even more critical. For law enforcement personnel to make accurate judgments in a case, they need not only theoretical training, but also learning through experience.

Neutrality is the baseline

Can an approach of having law enforcement personnel serve as judicial interpreters, convenient as it may be for the agencies themselves, really enable the true facts of a case to be conveyed without bias?

懸而未破的案例，值得司法界警惕。「也許冥冥中，上天就是選定我，為大家發聲。」陳允萍回溯整個過程，又感到一股無可推卸的使命感。

2012 年初，陳允萍和司改會及民間團體，為了推動通譯制度化，到監察院陳情。監察院調查後，發出糾正報告書，但是獨獨漏了「保障通譯人員人身安全」一項。

兩個月後，監察院調查官主動聯繫陳允萍，談及宜蘭一名通譯人員遭殺害的新聞。

雖然警方調閱監視錄影帶，過濾出一名菲籍移工出現在案發現場，但隔日迅即離境，至今未破案。

據悉該名死者開設商店，並且擔任通譯人員多年。她死前，曾到地檢署為一名菲籍移工擔任通譯。但是該名移工，認為死者沒有站在同鄉立場，為他說話，心生不滿。事後，並多次向死者顯露出不友善的態度。

「不主動爭取，面對不合宜的對象，更要拒絕去做通譯。」陳允萍憑藉著職業敏感度，多

到全國各地演講和
上課的陳允萍，
致力提升司法通譯人員素質。

Peter Chen, who has lectured
and taught across the country,
is endeavoring to upgrade the quality of
judicial interpreters.

corrective report, but left out one thing: measures to protect the personal safety of interpreters.

Two months later, an investigator from the Control Yuan contacted Chen to talk about a news story that a Filipina interpreter in Yilan had been murdered. Although from surveillance camera footage the police had identified a Filipino worker who appeared at the scene of the crime, he hurriedly left Taiwan the following day and has never been interviewed.

It was reported that the deceased had a shop, and had served as an interpreter for many years. Before she died, she had interpreted at the district prosecutor's office for a Filipino migrant worker. But the worker felt that she had failed to speak up for him as her fellow countryman, and so he bore a grudge against her.

In view of the sensitive nature of the work, Peter Chen earnestly exhorts his students that to avoid conflicts of interest, "you shouldn't push to get any specific judicial interpreting assignment, and if faced with an inappropriate counterpart, you should refuse the assignment." There are even rules for where the interpreter should stand in court, to ensure their personal safety, he explains.

Lost in translation

In recent years, Taiwan's foreign-born population has been increasing steadily. No matter whether it is a case of a foreign national being harmed and in need of the protection of the law, or of a foreign national behaving improperly and infringing the law, in both circumstances there is a need for interpreters to protect the judicial rights and interests of immigrants. This is why systematic training of skilled interpreters is such an urgent task.

While courts do have lists of interpreting personnel, frankly the main purpose is to resolve problems for the judicial bodies themselves, not to assist disadvantaged foreign nationals. Peter Chen believes, "To ensure that interpreters can act fairly, the interpreting system should be independent, and not be under the jurisdiction and control of judicial bodies."

Unity is strength

Twelve years ago, this ideal pushed Chen to found the Taitung County Foreign-Language Interpreters Association, which received recognition

次向學員們耳提面命。「連在法庭上站立的位置，都有規範，確保通譯者的人身安全。」

通而不譯，譯而不通

近年來，外來人口日漸成長，無論是外籍人士受到迫害，須要法律的保護；或是行為失當，觸及法律，都需要通譯人員來保障新移民的司法權益。基於此，有系統的培育通譯人才，是刻不容緩的事宜。

陳允萍指出，目前通譯人員欠缺的關鍵，在於「通而不譯」或「譯而不通」，也就是說，具有通譯能力的，身分卻不符合；身分符合者，又往往沒有司法素養，能力不足。

雖然法院也有通譯人員名冊，但是憑心而論，主要目的是為司法單位解決問題，而不是協助弱勢的外籍人士。陳允萍認為，「為求立場公正，通譯制度，應該要獨立運行，而不是受司法單位指揮管轄。」

眾志成城，迎來春天

這個理念，促使陳允萍在 12 年前，成立了「臺東縣外語通譯協會」，並且獲得志同道合者的認同和贊助，2013 年進而擴大為「台灣司法通譯協會」。目前全國各地區都設有分會，受訓的會員逾千人，並且持續增加中。

期待透過協會的平台，進行篩選和媒合，及時提供警政和司法單位，適任的通譯人員。

「一路走來，要感謝的人太多，如果沒有他們的幫忙，我還是只能一個人在偏鄉，狂犬吠日，毫無建樹。」陳允萍誠摯感恩公益平台文化基金會董事長嚴長壽及江賢二藝術文化文教基金會的鼎力支持，以及就諦講堂執行長李三財的襄佐運行。

「要善用上天賜予的力量，維護語言不通者的基本人權。」做為改革者，陳允萍期許自己能扮演創世紀的角色。12 年來，繞著台灣跑了 3 圈，舉辦了上百場教育訓練和演講，期待建置語言公平的司法環境。

「我可以每天上課 7 個小時，連續上 3 天。」展現過人毅力的陳允萍，不僅把所有休假都奉獻給公益，更把原本堅決反對的太太，也感動到擔任無給職的志工，夫唱婦隨。

陳允萍第二本著作《司法通譯——譯者的養成與訓練》，除了宣揚理念，更加入實務技巧和能力考核，吸引更多有志之士，投入司法通譯，落實友善司法的目標。「把善念付諸實現，讓世界看到努力。」這是陳允萍對司法通譯，最終的願景。

2018 年 4 月刊出

陳允萍著書為推動司法通譯制度化而努力。

Chen has written books in an effort to promote systematic management of judicial interpretation.

法律的天秤，容不得絲毫偏頗。

The scales of justice must weigh each case with complete impartiality.

and support from like-minded people, and in 2013 expanded to become the Taiwan Judicial Interpreters Association. There are now branches all over Taiwan, and to date more than 1000 people have undergone training. The association hopes to provide a platform for the screening and recruitment of personnel, to provide competent interpreters for police agencies and judicial bodies in a timely fashion.

"Having come this far, there are so many people to thank, and without their help I would still be just one person in a rural backwater, unable to achieve anything much, like a dog barking at the moon." Chen is sincerely grateful to Stanley Yen, chairman of the Alliance Cultural Foundation, and to the Paul Chiang Arts and Culture Foundation, for their support, as well as to JiouDi Association CEO Li Sam Choi for his operational assistance.

Over the past 12 years, Chen has circled Taiwan three times, holding more than 100 educational training sessions and lectures, in hopes of building a judicial environment that is linguistically fair.

Chen's second book, *Judicial Interpretation—The Development and Training of Interpreters*, besides expounding his ideals, also incorporates practical techniques and information on competency assessments, to attract even more dedicated people into judicial interpretation and reach the goal of a linguistically friendly judiciary. "To put good ideas into practice, to let the world see our efforts"—this is Peter Chen's ultimate vision for judicial interpretation.

Published in April 2018

National Policy Advisor Ho Thanh Nhan
—Speaking Up for New Immigrants

為新住民姊妹發聲
首位新住民國策顧問胡清嫻

文・鄧慧純　圖・莊坤儒
Cathy Teng / photos by Chuang Kung-ju / tr. by Robert Green

皮膚黝黑，剪著短短整齊的妹妹頭，個子不高，胡清嫻在人群中不易被找到，但是她的聲音宏亮，講起話來又急又快，很容易依聲尋人。在人群中發聲，是胡清嫻現在的工作，擔任屏東縣好好婦女權益發展協會（簡稱「好好協會」）的多元文化課程宣導講師，多年來為新住民權益的付出與努力，使她在小英總統上台後，被聘任為總統府國策顧問。

///////////////////////////

Ho Thanh Nhan, a petite woman who wears her hair neatly in a bob, is not easy to spot in a crowd. But what does stand out is her powerful voice, speaking rapidly and with a sense of urgency. Ho currently acts as a spokesperson for her community. As a cultural diversity lecturer for the Juridical Association for the Development of Women's Rights in Pingtung, she has been working to promote the interests of "new immigrants." After Tsai Ing-wen became president, Ho was appointed a national policy advisor to the Office of the President.

胡清嫻描述當初接到府方來電徵詢,是否願意擔任國策顧問一職,她反問:「那是做什麼的?我可以做什麼?」府方說明:可以不定期跟總統開會,把新住民的心聲跟總統表達。「那時候我想,可以幫助我的同胞、幫助新住民,那我可以做。這是個機會,把大家的心聲和收集的意見帶到總統面前。」胡清嫻說。

家人是後盾

台灣首位新住民國策顧問胡清嫻來自越南,來台灣已十一年多了。當初離家到胡志明市在台商工廠工作了6年,不知道未來還能如何的迷惘,讓她選擇到台灣試試看。

胡清嫻與先生許志成是由仲介介紹認識,兩人相見不到一天,就辦了結婚登記,隨後到台灣開始新生活。胡清嫻的婆家開明,許志成說:「我媽媽的觀念是說,從那麼遠的地方嫁過來,就要疼人家,像自己的女兒一樣。」婆婆手把手地教胡清嫻做飯煮菜,帶她去市場買菜,把媳婦要學的事一點一滴傳授。

胡清嫻也好學,學中文、學電腦、參加司法通譯課程培訓、考取中餐證照,從小學讀到高中,現在的她正準備開始大學的課程,這一切,家人都給予她最大的支持。

在「好好」成長

好好協會可說是胡清嫻投身公領域的起點,協會長年關注新住民的人權議題,2011年更率先招募新住民加入工作團隊,胡清嫻就是其中之一。其後更有賴民間如浩然基金會、台灣證券交易所等單位經費支助,多年來讓新住民朋友能與好好協會一起工作、學習、成長。好好協會主任蔡順柔說:「當初我經常讓她們聽打會議的逐字稿,或是做訪視

讓孩子從小接觸不同的文化刺激,唯有了解才能消除偏見。(胡清嫻提供)
Only by exposing children to the stimulation of different cultures can prejudice be dispelled.
(courtesy of Ho Thanh Nhan)

胡清嫻的主持風格平易風趣，
她常把麥克風遞給攤位的姊妹，
讓她們「自己」介紹家鄉美食。

Ho Thanh Nhan has an easygoing humorous style when hosting events, often giving the microphone to other immigrant women and letting them introduce their traditional delicacies.

Ho recalls that when she was first asked to serve as a national policy advisor, she asked in return: "What would I be doing? What do I have to offer?"

They explained that she would have the opportunity to meet with the president from time to time and speak up for the immigrant community. "Then I realized that I would be able to assist my fellow countrymen and the immigrant community, so I decided to do it," she says. "This was an opportunity to express people's opinions and aspirations directly to the president."

Welcomed with open arms

Taiwan's first national policy advisor representing the immigrant community hails from Vietnam. She has lived in Taiwan for over 11 years. Originally she left home in Vietnam to take up work at a Taiwanese-owned factory in Saigon, where she stayed for six years. At a loss as to what to do next, she decided to give Taiwan a try.

Ho and her husband, Xu Zhicheng, were introduced by a marriage broker, and on the first day they decided to apply for a marriage license. Soon after, they started a new life in Taiwan. Her husband's family was supportive. "My mother feels that if someone has come so far to be with her husband, we should treat her like our own daughter," Xu says.

Ho's mother-in-law took her under her wing, taking her shopping and teaching her how to cook local dishes.

Ho is studious by nature, and she studied Chinese and computers, took a course on police and court translation and obtained certification for Chinese cooking. She completed the elementary and high school curricula in Taiwan and is now

紀錄，那很辛苦，卻可以訓練聽力、用字。當然一定鬧過笑話，像把『萬丹』聽成『完蛋』；但紮實的訓練，姊妹們多撐過來了，成長很快。」

蔡順柔也讓胡清嫻學習撰寫計畫書，向各單位申請經費。學習拿起麥克風，在人群面前表達自己的主張與訴求。我們初見胡清嫻時，她正主持好好協會舉辦的「哇！新住民市集——社區參與式多元文化活動」，來自各國家的新住民搬出烤架、鍋鏟，以自己最拿手的料理絕活，展現母國特色。當天只見她與另一名來自印尼的夥伴謝莉莉繞著市集會場，一攤攤介紹、光顧。兩人一搭一唱，穩健的台風，氣氛十分歡愉，胡清嫻還不時把麥克風遞給攤位的姊妹，讓她們「自己」介紹家鄉美食。

如此駕輕就熟，但胡清嫻坦言她第一次上台的時候，對著滿場的教師聽眾，手腳發抖、聲音也抖，腦筋一片空白，好不容易才照著簡報講完，完成她的處女秀。而如今的駕輕就熟，是靠著蔡順柔外出演講時，都帶著胡清嫻等人同行，讓她們上台發表，如此一次一次訓練膽識、修正口條，蔡順柔笑說：「現在叫她上台講3個小時，她都還不肯下來，她的潛力就這樣培力出來的。」胡清嫻則自述：「我的上課風格比較幽默一點，我盡量讓大家醒醒的聽我講。」乍聽之下，有點奇怪的句法與用字，但這也成為胡清嫻的特色，和她可愛的個性相應，果然會讓大家「醒醒的」開懷大笑。

多元文化講師

早些年，台灣社會對於多元文化的認識尚淺，為了修正社會大眾對新住民及移工的刻板印象，身為多元文化講師的胡清嫻及新住民姊妹們到學校、社區進行一場又一場多元文化的講座與課程，對象從小學、中學、大學、教師、社區長者都有。針對不同的對

許志成假日有空時也會陪同胡清嫻一起參與活動，解說越南文化。（胡清嫻提供）
On his days off Xu Zhicheng often joins Ho Thanh Nhan at events introducing Vietnamese culture.
(courtesy of Ho Thanh Nhan)

preparing to start college. Through all of it, her family has been extremely supportive.

Finding her voice

The Juridical Association for the Development of Women's Rights in Pingtung (JADWRP) launched Ho's career in public service. For many years the association has been concerned with issues of immigrants' human rights. In 2011 they began recruiting immigrants to join their team, and Ho was one of those recruits. With funding from the non-governmental Hao Ran Foundation, the Taiwan Stock Exchange, and other sources, the JADWRP has given immigrants the opportunity to work, study and grow together. "At the outset I used to have them listen to recordings of various meetings and type them out verbatim," says JADWRP director Tsai Shun-jou. "It wasn't easy for them, but it gave them the opportunity to practice their Chinese comprehension and word usage."

Naturally the participants sometimes made comical errors with the words they were learning, like mistaking the local "Wàndān" Township for *wándàn* ("done for"), which sounds the same except for the different tones. But the training allowed the immigrant women to make rapid progress.

Tsai also had Ho write program proposals and practice taking up a microphone and expressing her opinions in front of an audience. The day we first met Ho, she was hosting the JADWRP-organized "Wa! New Immigrant Fair"—a community-based multicultural event that gave immigrants the opportunity to showcase delicacies from their home countries. On that day she could be seen with Hsieh Lye Lye, an immigrant from Indonesia, weaving through the fair, introducing different stalls and visiting participants. The two kept up a lively banter and held their own as hosts in the happy atmosphere. Ho often turned the microphone over to the

姊妹們在市集上大秀才藝，展現自信。

Immigrant women confidently show off their talents at a multicultural fair.

象，胡清嫻也因人制宜的改變溝通方式，如面對社區的長者，她會比較台越兩地文化相似、相異之處，如端午節包粽子的習俗，越南也有，但粽子形狀不一樣，南越還有吃煎餅的習俗，讓社區的老人家知道家中媳婦的母國文化。

胡清嫻說剛接觸這領域時，心情很沉重，因為常常在學校遇到對自己媽媽母國文化自卑的孩子，讓她聯想到自己的孩子是否也是如此。因此在多元文化的課程中，她會留意觀察班上的學生，如果有特別安靜的，她便私下去接觸，了解孩子的背景是否為新二代。在課堂上，她鼓勵新二代的孩子分享自己的東南亞經驗，建立孩子的自信心，也讓其他同學了解多一種文化的優勢。

工作場合許可的情況下，她會盡量把自己的兒子、女兒帶在身邊，讓他們接觸不同的族群，看見大家的不同，「可能因為工作接觸過，所以他們不會隱藏媽媽的身分，反而會大聲說我媽媽是越南人。」胡清嫻說。

每年幾百場的多元文化教育課程，胡清嫻除了自己上台講課，她也努力提攜後進的新住民姊妹，更在各個社區尋找願意站出來服務的姊妹，希望培育更多的種子教師。台灣社會的多元融合其實有賴這群人幫忙溝通，促進雙方的瞭解認識，「如果台灣人和新住民融合起來，不就會爆發一些不一樣的知識和人才嗎？」她的話甚有道理。

胡清嫻說自己很愛講話，又很愛管人，因此她總成為新住民姊妹的帶頭大姊。自己個性直來直往，有話直說，不畏勢力。她曾質問屏東縣長潘孟安，新住民母語人才資源培力後，下一階段呢？培力出來的種子教師需要有發揮的舞台，還有姊妹的工作權也應予以保障。

她從沒想過自己會投身公領域，成為國策顧問。當年那個從越南到台灣，憧憬著人生有更多可能性的女孩，如今她勇敢地站到人前，為新住民發聲。

涉入複雜的政治圈，胡清嫻坦言也有些累

家人是胡清嫻最大的後盾。
Family is Ho Thanh Nhan's greatest source of strength.

了，也想如同一般姊妹過平凡的日子；可是想到如果不出來幫姊妹說話，姊妹的權益怎麼辦？

但她也不曾後悔到台灣來，她覺得這就是緣分，而且自己選的路，只有往前走。

2018 年 2 月刊出

immigrant women so that they could introduce the cuisine of their homelands.

Ho is now an experienced public speaker, but she admits that the first time she took to the podium and addressed an audience of teachers, she was trembling, her voice quavered, and her mind went blank. Her debut was a nightmare, and even with the help of her notes, she barely made it through the lecture. But she progressed with each performance and improved her delivery. "Nowadays even after she's been speaking for three hours, we can't get her off the stage," Tsai says with a chuckle.

"My lecture style is a little on the humorous side," Ho says. "I try to hold the audience's attention."

On first impression, listeners find her syntax and word usage a little quirky, but this has become Ho's hallmark. It suits her endearing personality and keeps her audiences laughing.

Teaching cultural diversity

In order to change public stereotypes about immigrants and foreign workers, Ho and other cultural diversity lecturers give talks and courses in schools and various communities. Hu tailors her teaching style to suit different audiences. When she visits elderly audiences, for example, she will highlight cultural similarities and differences between Taiwan and Vietnam. Vietnam shares many of the same traditions, such as the Dragon Boat Festival and the making of wrapped rice dumplings, though they are made slightly differently. Fried pancakes are also popular in southern Vietnam just as they are in Taiwan. This helps seniors better understand the native culture of their daughters-in-law.

When Ho first began this work she was saddened to see that the children of immigrant mothers often felt embarrassed and looked down on their mothers' cultures. She wondered if her own child would feel the same. So in her multicultural training programs, she invites the children of immigrant mothers to share their experiences of Southeast Asia with the class to help them build confidence and help other classmates understand the benefits of cultural diversity.

Whenever possible Ho brings her own son and daughter to work with her to let them meet people of various ethnic backgrounds and see that people are all different. "Perhaps after meeting different people through my work, they will not try to hide their mother's background, but instead say proudly that their mother is Vietnamese," Ho says.

Aside from lecturing in the hundreds of cultural diversity courses offered each year, Ho also guides students who need her help, hoping to cultivate new teachers from among the immigrant women. Taiwan's efforts at creating a multicultural society rely on the immigrant community to promote mutual understanding. "If the people of Taiwan and the new immigrants mix together, won't that lead to new understanding and cultivate new talent?" she asks with sound logic.

Ho says that she has always loved to talk and to get involved in other people's lives, so she naturally fell into the role of looking after other immigrant women. Straightforward by nature, she is unafraid to speak up when something needs to be said.

She never imagined a public service career or becoming a national policy advisor. When she first came to Taiwan, she was a young woman longing to see what life held in store. Today she stands fearlessly as a representative for the immigrant community.

Ho admits that she has found life in the complicated world of politics somewhat exhausting, and she sometimes misses the simplicity of her old life. But who would speak up for the interests of her fellow countrywomen if she didn't do it?

Ho has no regrets about choosing to live in Taiwan. She feels that it was both destiny and a self-chosen path. And she's not looking back.

Published in February 2018

Her Sisters' Guardian—Yadrung Chiou

倡議姊妹權益的守護者

邱雅青

文・鄧慧純　圖・林格立
Cathy Teng / photos by Jimmy Lin / tr. by Geof Aberhart

南洋台灣姊妹會 12 周年了，在陽光暖暖灑落的午後，姊妹會舉辦感恩茶會。舞台上一群新住民姊妹合唱著「是什麼樣的勇氣，揮別至親奔向未知……」，她們不是專業的歌手，卻用最誠摯的心唱出她們的心聲。邱雅青是台上的一員，她已經來台 17 年了。17 年，她從一個異國婚姻的新娘化身為一名投身公共議題的行動者。

The 12th anniversary of the Trans-Asia Sisterhood Association Taiwan is a warm, sunny day, perfect for the association's celebratory reception. On stage, a choir of Southeast-Asian immigrant women performs in Mandarin, singing about the courage to say goodbye to loved ones and journey into the unknown. While they aren't professional singers, they nonetheless sing with sincerity and passion. Among them is Yadrung Chiou, who came to Taiwan 17 years ago. In that time, she has gone from simply a "foreign spouse" to an engaged public activist.

1977 年出生，金牛座，AB 型，身形高挑纖瘦，說話的口氣和緩但堅定，咧嘴笑起來帶點美國影星茱莉亞羅勃茲的神韻，她是原籍泰國的邱雅青，有個美麗的泰國名字 หยาดรุ้ง ลาสา，意思是「日出的彩虹」。

雅青來自單親家庭，母親為了生活外出工作，雅青和兩個哥哥寄宿在不同的親戚家，成長過程一家子聚少離多。如此的背景培養了雅青的獨立自主，她打工、自己打理生活，不給家裡增添經濟負擔。大學讀的是商學院，主修會計，但她的社會學成績最好，也許在冥冥中就預告了雅青踏上社會運動的路子。

大學畢業後，她在百貨公司擔任銷售員，20 出頭的適婚年齡，家人曾介紹婚配的對象，但雅青覺得緣分未到，逃跑了。她的真命天子是個台灣男子，在跨國快遞公司工作，對於這段異國婚姻，她沒想太多，只是心想累積的工作經驗應該可以在台灣有一番發展，就決定來台灣。

婆婆幫忙找事做

初來台灣，語言不通的挫折比她想像的還大，雅青說：「自己明明是很獨立的個人，只是不會中文，在夫家卻被當成一個啥都不會的孩子，心態上難免沮喪難過。」無法藉由語言表達，這樣的情境讓她有苦難言，也跟夫家產生不少衝突。她整天把自己關在房內，不與人交往，還曾一度跑回泰國，不回台灣了。為此，夫家承受了來自鄰居「騙婚」的閒言耳語，是媽媽的一句話：「已經下的決定就要實踐到底，真不行了才放棄。」讓雅青再次回到台灣重新開始。

前後的適應期約有 3 年之久，婆婆很擔心，怕她整日悶在家中胡思亂想，鼓勵雅青多出門走走，為了讓媳婦早點適應台灣生活，婆婆還央求熟識的美容院讓雅青去工作，在美容洗頭打工，跟人群互動；為了讓媳婦學習台語，家裡買了一台卡拉 OK，每天午後是婆媳兩個人的 K 歌時間。

咧嘴笑起來帶點美國影星茱莉亞羅勃茲的神韻，言談間的邱雅青自信而從容，獨立自主是她的本色。

With a broad, winning smile, Yadrung Chiou is confident and calm when telling her story.

南洋台灣姊妹會以戲劇的方式表達她們的處境與訴求，圖為姊妹會 12 周年茶會上表演的劇目《看見我們》。

The Trans-Asia Sisterhood Association also uses drama to communicate their members' circumstances and aspirations. This photo shows members performing *Be Seen* at the association's 12th-anniversary reception.

Born in 1977, the tall and slender Chiou speaks with a firm but warm air, and sports a smile reminiscent of Julia Roberts'. Hailing from Thailand, her given name "Yadrung" is Thai for "rainbow."

Born to a single mother who had to leave them to seek work, Chiou and her two older brothers were sent to live with different relatives, and it is to this background that she credits her independent spirit. In college she majored in accounting, but her best grades were in sociology, possibly a hint to where her future would take her.

After graduating, she met a man who worked for a multinational courier company, and eventually married him and settled in Taiwan. She had given little thought to the nature of such cross-cultural marriages, simply hoping that Taiwan would be a great place to build on her past work experience and start building a future.

A little help from the mother-in-law

When she first arrived in Taiwan, the language barrier was bigger than she'd anticipated. "I'm very much an independent person," says Chiou, "but since I couldn't speak Chinese, my husband's family treated me like a helpless child, and inevitably this made me very upset." Her inability to voice her feelings led to no small number of clashes with her in-laws. At one point, she even ran off back to Thailand, planning to never return to Taiwan. While her in-laws were the victims of rumors of their son's "sham marriage," it was something her own mother said that inspired Chiou to return to Taiwan and start again: "Once you've made a decision, you need to see it through. If you really can't make it work, only then is it OK to give up."

During Chiou's adjustment period, about three years, her mother-in-law was concerned she was spending too much time cooped up indoors and encouraged her to get outside more. In addition, to help Chiou adjust to Taiwan life, her mother-in-law also asked a friend's beauty salon to hire Chiou, getting her work washing hair, but also giving her the chance to interact with more people.

雅青日後的社運之路，緣起於在美容院巧遇的越南姊妹引介她去永和社大上中文識字班，從而開啟了她的終身學習生涯。

在社大開啟新視野

識字班的課程不只是學習語言，更以議題討論的方式，把姊妹生活會碰到的問題帶到課堂上，它是啟蒙的、實境的，運用小組討論、議題探討等方式，培力姊妹的能力。加入永和社大後，她是班上最愛提問的學生，也被推選為班上的幹部，參與討論會議，參訪各地的社區大學，認識了各式各樣不同的人。老師覺得雅青有組織的潛力，提拔她為志工，而一步步走入南洋姊妹會。

雅青說：「姊妹會希望能成為姊妹的後盾，它的宗旨是給妳釣竿，要妳自己捕魚吃。」她們不計較學歷，只要有心向學，姊妹會提供各種學習的機會，同仁們也都會耐心地陪伴姊妹成長。

從姊妹會的理監事到執行祕書，在不同的角色裡，雅青取得許多學習的機會，一路跌跌撞撞的經歷成為她日後成長的養分。

自己的權益自己救

雅青的街頭運動初體驗是 2003 年姊妹們抗議政府草率成立移民署的議題。當時政府急就章地成立移民署，且其中 7 成 5 的人力調派自警政單位，相關的配套措施也都還沒準備好。姊妹會為此籌劃上街頭抗議，表明訴求。

身為姊妹會的理事，雅青必須走到人前代表發言，但中文不算好、發音鼻音很重，她擔心無法充分表達姊妹的心聲；其他姊妹則擔心還沒拿到身分證，走上街頭會被遣返。但她們覺悟：如果不主動爭取，權利是不會白白從天而降的。這是一次成功的運動，移民署最終延至 2007 年才成立。

邱雅青的街頭運動經驗多到數不清，進出立法院數千次，她認為，只要是對的事，就該站出來爭取。

因為切身才會關心，這群婚姻移民面臨了無

邱雅青的街頭運動經驗多到數不清，她認為只要是對的事，就該站出來爭取。（邱雅青提供）

Yadrung Chiou has countless experiences of taking to the streets. She believes that one's rights have to be fought for. (courtesy of Yadrung Chiou)

法加入勞保、健保、工作證，以及工傷無法申請補助等問題，這些案例讓姊妹們開始思考，開始研讀移民法、國籍法等自身權利相關的法條。且參與公共議題的討論不僅是一堂實用的公民課，還能引發許多姊妹參與，共創更好的明天。

為了鼓勵更多姊妹參與公共事務，姊妹會於 2005 年與世新大學社會發展研究所夏曉鵑教授合著出版《不要叫我外籍新娘》，2010 年，姊妹會再推出紀錄片《姊妹，賣冬瓜》，取泰文「ไม่ต้องกลัว」（不要怕）的諧音，這部片記錄了姊妹會上街頭倡議、培力成長的過

Chiou's journey into the world of social activism began with a chance encounter with a Vietnamese woman at the salon. The woman recommended that Chiou take Chinese classes at Yonghe Community University, igniting a new passion for learning.

New horizons through community university

Those classes not only taught basic Chinese, but also encouraged the women to discuss any problems they'd encountered in their everyday lives, using them to help further develop the women's skills. Chiou quickly proved to be the student with the most questions, and her engagement saw her elected as a class officer. Recognizing her organizational skills, Chiou's teacher recommended she start volunteering, and thus began her work with the Trans-Asia Sisterhood Association.

"The association aims to provide support to other women from Southeast Asia," says Chiou. "Their mission is to give us the tools we need, to give us the fishing rods we need to catch our own fish." They don't care about education level—as long as the women want to learn, the association is there to give them the opportunity to do so, as well as to provide patient assistance.

You've got to fight for your rights

Chiou's first experience of taking to the streets with the association came in 2003, when they protested the government's "reckless" establishment of the National Immigration Agency. The government had rushed through the establishment of the agency, having decided to get 75% of the staff through transfers from the police but not having made any preparations to cover the rest. As a director of the association, Chiou became its public spokesperson; however, her Chinese was still rough and her accent thick, making her worry she wouldn't be able to properly communicate the feelings of her sisters. Other women were more afraid that taking to the streets without having received their national ID yet would result in their being deported. Regardless, they all understood that one's rights don't just pop out of thin air—they have to be fought for. In this case, the protests were successful, and the NIA's establishment was postponed until 2007.

By standing up and doing the right thing, the women were able to secure their rights. These "marriage immigrants" were also unable to enroll in the National Health Insurance and Labor Insurance programs, get

姊妹會的工作分為三大類：組織培力、社會教育與法令政策倡議。圖為雅青（左 1）與姊妹會的工作人員合影。

The work of the Trans-Asia Sisterhood Association comes in three categories: organizational empowerment, community education, and political activism. This photo is a group shot of Yadrung Chiou (first from left) and other association staff.

雅青一路在組織中培力成長，從參與的成員到能獨當一面的講師，也曾任姊妹會的理事，雅青現為姊妹會的執行祕書。（邱雅青提供）

Chiou has always striven to become more capable as part of the association, whether just as a participant or as a speaker. She has even been a director of the association, and currently she works as their executive secretary. (courtesy of Yadrung Chiou)

程，雅青在裡頭掌鏡拍攝，還自學軟體剪輯影片；是一部南洋姊妹會成員的集體創作，透過姊妹之眼向台灣社會的傾訴。

以溝通經營家庭關係

從社大與姊妹會中學來的溝通方式，雅青學以致用地運用在經營家庭關係。夫家並非一開始即贊成雅青參與公共議題，婆婆雖然開明，但想到要走上街頭抗議，心中總有些許抗拒，但雅青舉例跟婆婆說：「大家都說新住民之子是遲緩兒，就是在說你的金孫，你願意被這樣貼上標籤嗎？」婆婆聽了當然不服，反而鼓勵雅青上街頭去矯正大家的刻板印象，「自己的權益自己救」是雅青從街頭的社會大學學來的一堂課。

對於小孩的教養問題亦然，雅青是一個嚴格的媽媽，且態度堅定，要求兒子作家事、自己洗便當，她認為讓孩子知道自己的責任，知道自己所為何事是家庭教育最重要的事。她容許兒子哭，等情緒宣洩完後，大家再來討論事情的癥結點。雅青的溝通方式也影響了兒子，當奶奶過度看重孫子的課業成績時，兒子也會堅定的跟奶奶反映：「請您不要看到我一次不理想的成績，就否定了我過去的努力。」

許多人以為雅青是個幸運兒，有先生與婆婆的支持，但她說：「每段婚姻、每個家庭都有其複雜且難以與他人言說之處。」她也是跟家人不斷地溝通，才擁有這樣的自由度去做自己的事情。即便家庭經濟不需她擔心，雅青也不認為她能因此依靠先生而不獨立。

接受了識字班的啟蒙、姊妹會的培養和街頭社會大學的洗禮，雅青於 2008 年獲得國家青年公共參與獎卓越貢獻獎的殊榮；2014 年獲超越基金會之邀，參與「超越達人」公益教育計畫，分享她突破困境、解決問題、超越自己的經歷。她把自己的時間、精力貢獻出來，為求新移民能獲得平等的權益，也為了這個已是她安身立命之地的台灣，能成為更公平、更友善新移民的社會。

───── 2016 年 5 月刊出

邱雅青於 2008 年獲得國家青年公共參與獎卓越貢獻獎。（邱雅青提供）

In 2008, Chiou was honored with an Outstanding Contribution Award at the National Youth Public Participation Awards. (courtesy of Yadrung Chiou)

婆婆是雅青生命中的貴人，她鼓勵雅青接觸人群，走入社會。（邱雅青提供）

Chiou's mother-in-law has been one of her greatest supporters, encouraging her to meet more people and get involved in the community.
(courtesy of Yadrung Chiou)

work visas, or apply for benefits after workplace injuries. Confronted by these and other problems, the women began thinking, studying the Immigration Act, the Nationality Act, and other laws related to their rights.

To encourage others like them to get involved in public affairs, in 2005 the Trans-Asia Sisterhood Association worked with Professor Hsia Hsiao-chuan of Shih Hsin University's Graduate Institute of Social Transformation Studies to publish *Don't Call Me Foreign Bride!* Five years later, the association released the documentary *Let's Not Be Afraid!*, which follows the association's growth and advocacy work. Chiou was part of the film as well, doing some of the shooting and even learning to use editing software. *Let's Not Be Afraid!* was the collective work of the association's members, and through it they strove to tell Taiwan their stories from their own perspectives.

Handling family relations through communication

Chiou also began using the communication skills she'd learned at community college and with the associ-

ation to work on her own family relationships. At first, her in-laws didn't agree with her activism. While her mother-in-law was an open-minded person, she was opposed to the idea of Chiou protesting on the streets. To help win her over, Chiou offered an example of what she was fighting: "Everyone says the children of Southeast-Asian immigrants are developmentally challenged; if it were your grandson they were talking about, would you be willing to have him labeled like that?" Obviously Chiou's mother-in-law was opposed, and after giving it some thought, she began supporting Chiou's efforts to fight back against such popular stereotypes.

When it comes to raising her child, Chiou is a strict mother, firmly requiring her son to do chores and wash his own lunch box. She is a strong believer in the idea that one of the most important things in childrearing is making sure your children know their responsibilities and the reasons for them.

Some people think Chiou is lucky to have such a supportive husband and mother-in-law; for her part, she says "every marriage, every family has its complexities and things they find hard to tell others." But through constant communication, she has been able to get the freedom to do her own thing. While her family's financial situation leaves her with no need to worry about money, Chiou doesn't want to simply rely on her husband.

From her start with Chinese classes through her work with the association and on the streets, by 2008 Chiou's activism earned her an Outstanding Contribution Award at the National Youth Public Participation Awards, and in 2014 the Eball Foundation invited her to participate in a public education project and share her experience of overcoming problems and pushing her own limits. Yadrung Chiou has given her time and her energy to fight for equality for immigrants to Taiwan and to make her new homeland fairer and friendlier to new arrivals.

Published in May 2016

Taiwan's First New Immigrant Legislator: Lin Li-chan

台灣第一位新住民立委

柬埔寨「灰姑娘」林麗蟬勇闖國會

文‧嚴思祺　圖‧林麗蟬提供
Peter Yen / photos courtesy of Lin Li-chan / tr. by Scott Williams

來自柬埔寨的林麗蟬是台灣第一位新住民立法委員，她操著流利中文和台語，為新住民和移工發聲。林麗蟬1997年嫁來台灣，從平凡主婦、志工、十大傑出青年、碩士到出任國會議員，一步一腳印，寫下動人的新住民奮鬥故事。

//////////////////////////

Lin Li-chan is Taiwan's first "new immigrant" legislator. Born in Cambodia, she now uses her fluent Mandarin and Taiwanese to give immigrants and migrant workers a voice. Lin arrived here in 1997, after marrying a Taiwanese man. In the years since, she has been a homemaker and a volunteer, been named one of Taiwan's Ten Outstanding Young People, earned a master's degree, and become a member of our legislature. With each step of her journey, she has added to her moving legacy of immigrant struggle and achievement.

憑藉崇高的社會服務精神以及本身新住民的多元背景，林麗蟬2015年底獲得當時國民黨主席朱立倫的邀請，出任該黨不分區立法委員候選人，名列國民黨不分區立委名單第4順位，並順利成為立法院第9屆立委，一躍成為舉國知名的政治人物。

2013年，林麗蟬因熱心社會服務工作而贏得十大傑出青年獎，首次成為媒體的焦點，當時她仍顯靦腆青澀。如今，林麗蟬站在國會殿堂上為民喉舌，犀利問政，再度吸引全國的目光，更多了一分幹練與自信。

心繫新住民與移工

從林麗蟬立委辦公室的擺設，就可看出她心繫新住民與移工。屏風上掛著斗笠和圍巾，門牆上展示著一對泰國掛軸，茶几上擺著東南亞各國紙幣，還有窗台上的大象布偶、衣帽架上的越南手提袋，再再散發著濃濃的東南亞風。

擔任立委以來，林麗蟬秉持一貫的志工服務精神，為新住民發聲。林麗蟬也發現，同樣是新住民的大陸配偶，卻和東南亞配偶待遇不同，她決定為她們爭取權益。林麗蟬主張一視同仁，把大陸配偶取得身分證的時間從6年改為4年，和其他新住民一樣，不要有差別待遇。

對於台灣境內的眾多外籍移工，也是林麗蟬關懷的對象。目前，2016年移工人數已逼近60萬大關，卻有高達51,000人行蹤不明。林麗蟬認為，基於治安以及人權保障的考量，勞動部應該更加重視移工的問題，運用「就業安定基金」從源頭加強他們的生活輔導和權益保障，才能緩解移工逃逸問題。

林麗蟬和超馬選手陳彥博、畫家李柏毅一同獲頒第51屆十大青年獎項。（彰化縣政府提供）

In 2013, Lin Li-chan was among the laureates of the 51st Ten Outstanding Young Persons award, along with ultramarathoner Tommy Chen and artist Leland Lee. (courtesy of the Changhua County Government)

身兼台灣新移民發展與交流協會理事長、彰化花壇長春社區發展協會總幹事的林麗蟬，投入社區服務為弱勢老人義剪，帶動地方潛力。

Lin Li-chan is both president of the Association for Development and Communication for New Immigrants, and director of the Changchun Community Development Association in Huatan Township, Changhua County. She has set up a service to provide free haircuts for the elderly, promoting local potential to the full.

Lin Li-chan's immigrant background and commitment to community service prompted Eric Chu, then the Kuomintang party chair, to invite her to run as a KMT candidate for a seat as a legislator-at-large in 2015. Entered into the KMT rolls as the party's fourth legislator-at-large candidate, Lin gained a seat in the Legislative Yuan for its ninth legislative term and was immediately catapulted into national prominence.

Lin's first experience with media attention came in 2013, when her passion for social work earned her a Ten Outstanding Young Persons award. In those days, she was still young and new to the public eye. Since being reintroduced into the spotlight as a legislator, she has been a confident and capable spokesperson for Taiwan's people who asks probing questions of the administration.

A feeling of connection

The decor of Lin's legislative office clearly demonstrates her connection to Taiwan's migrant workers and immigrants. A bamboo hat and shawl hang from a screen. A pair of hanging scrolls from Thailand decorate the wall by the door. Currencies from Southeast-Asian nations are displayed on the coffee table. An elephant doll sits on the windowsill, and a Vietnamese handbag dangles from the coat rack.

These connections manifest themselves the floor of the legislature as well, where she speaks for Taiwan's immigrants. She began fighting for equal rights for spouses from mainland China when she learned that they were treated differently than their counterparts from Southeast Asia. Advocating for equal rights for all, she succeeded in reducing the amount of time for a mainland spouse to obtain an identity card from six years to four, the same length of time as other immigrants.

She has also looked out for the interests of Taiwan's many onshore foreign laborers. When she learned that as of 2016, the whereabouts of some 51,000 of Taiwan's nearly 600,000 such workers were unknown, she pushed the Ministry of Labor to pay greater attention to foreign-worker issues in the interests of both public safety and human rights, encouraging the ministry to use the Employment Stability Fund to help alleviate the problem of worker flight by improving its guidance to these workers and strengthening its protection of their rights.

Training the second generation

Lin is also working to promote exchanges between Taiwan and the nations of Southeast Asia. As of 2016, citizens of seven of ASEAN's ten nations have to use ordinary visas or apply online for a visa

與丈夫謝水金結婚後，林麗蟬取得大學學歷，近年則致力於新住民交流，舉辦各種親子活動。

//////////////////////

After marrying her husband Xie Shuijin, Lin Li-chan gained a university degree. In recent years, she has become dedicated to improving communication between new immigrants by promoting a range of family activities.

推動新住民二代培育

林麗蟬同樣致力推動台灣與東南亞國家的交流。目前，台灣對東協 10 國，除新加坡、馬來西亞來台免簽，汶萊適用電子簽及落地簽，其他 7 國要用一般簽證或線上簽核。如今，行政院已決定簡化柬埔寨等 7 國以及南亞印度來台旅客簽證，背後可見林麗蟬努力爭取的身影。未來，她將致力推動台灣與東南亞國家進一步深化交流，尤其是台灣與柬埔寨的關係。

針對蔡英文政府力推的「新南向政策」，林麗蟬指出，新政府前進東南亞最大的問題是缺乏人才。她表示，台灣目前新住民已突破 51 萬人，新住民第二代已逾 36 萬人，其中許多人和東南亞國家關係密切，在血緣、文化與語言上佔有優勢，無疑是台灣布局東協國家的重要人力資本，新政府應該重視新住民的培育工作，讓他們成為台灣拓展東南亞經貿和外交工作上的尖兵。

在林麗蟬的構想中，培育新住民第二代，不但可以培養外交尖兵，也有助於提升新住民在台灣社會中的地位。先前，她和移民署共同推動的「新住民二代培力計畫」，讓新住民子女利用暑假回到外祖父母家，展開家庭生活、語言學習與文化交流，藉此培育多元化的人才，廣獲好評。

在此同時，林麗蟬同樣關切台灣對於新住民文化的認同與學習，以及東南亞語言人才的培育。她認為，這有助於相互了解，彼此尊重。其中，「十二年國民基本教育課程綱要總綱」預計 2018 年實施，新增新住民語文學習（以東南亞國家語文為主）。林麗蟬指出，柬埔寨、菲律賓和馬來西亞語教師仍然有待補強，以利教學工作的推動。

to visit Taiwan. Only citizens of Singapore and Malaysia are able to visit Taiwan without a visa, and those of Brunei are able to use electronic visas and visas-on-arrival. Lin's background efforts to change this situation are apparent in the Executive Yuan's decision to simplify visas for visitors from these other seven nations and India. Lin hopes to encourage still deeper exchanges between Taiwan and ASEAN in the future, and with Cambodia in particular.

Responding to the Tsai administration's promotion of the New Southbound Policy, Lin stated that the biggest issue facing the administration's push into Southeast Asia was a lack of personnel. She noted that Taiwan currently has more than 510,000 "new immigrants," and more than 360,000 second-generation immigrants, many of whom have close ties to Southeast-Asian nations. She argued that these

individuals possess ancestral, linguistic and cultural advantages in dealing with the region, and that they therefore represent an important human resource that belongs in the vanguard of our efforts to develop trade and diplomatic relationships with these countries.

But Lin believes that cultivating second-generation immigrants is more than a matter of training diplomats. To her, it also involves elevating immigrants' social standing. To that end, she has worked with the National Immigration Agency to promote the Second Generation New Immigrant Empowerment Program. The widely acclaimed program seeks to cultivate a diverse talent pool by enabling the children of immigrants to return to their immigrant parent's country of origin during the summer vacation to study the language and culture, and experience home life in that environment.

一步一腳印

首次成為政治人物，林麗蟬的表現絕無生澀，積極、主動而且勇於任事。這一切看似再自然也不過的事，對於林麗蟬來說，卻是突破重重障礙、辛勤耕耘得來的成果。

林麗蟬是典型的台灣新住民，透過婚姻仲介2小時就定親，從柬埔寨金邊飛來台灣，嫁入彰化花壇鄉尋常百姓家，先生謝水金從事五金加工，上有公公和婆婆。

她說，初來台灣之際，人生地不熟，語言又不通，充滿了未知和挑戰，這和來台前的生活明顯不同，頓時成為困擾與壓力的來源。

在金邊，身為華僑第三代的她，在經商父親的呵護下成長，生活尚稱優渥。但是，高中時，父親因車禍意外喪生，有如青天霹靂，家中也失去了經濟支柱，連學費都繳不出來。林麗蟬久久無法接受父親驟然離去，更失去了重要的心靈依靠。

每當林麗蟬遇上困難與挫折時，她都會向天上的父親哭訴，和父親對話，尋求支持與力量。

她說：「白天像是作夢，晚上才是生活。」來台最初的十年就是這樣度過的。

隨著女兒與兒子陸續出世，孩子成為林麗蟬新的動力來源。這位不服輸的媽媽學習中文，擔任志工，投入社區工作，努力融入台灣社會，背後都有保護子女的用心，也希望撕掉身上的負面標籤。

為了充實自己以及擴大助人的能量，林麗蟬先後就讀建國科技大學美容系、靜宜大學社會工作師學分班、暨南大學非營利組織經營管理碩士班，今年秋天更將進入暨南大學東南亞學系博士班就讀，希望能對新住民和台灣更盡一分力量。

看到和自己一樣的新住民，同理心油然而生，林麗蟬陪著她們學習成長，並創立「台灣新移民發展與交流協會」協助新住民姊妹們在台灣安居樂業，第二代能夠順利成長。

為此，林麗蟬產生了使命感，積極推動新住民的多元文化及親子教育。因為她深信，新住民和第二代是台灣未來的力量。

來台20年，從剛來時不懂台語、也不認得中文字，如今不但成為國會議員參與國家重大決策，未來更充滿無限的可能，林麗蟬的傳奇故事鼓舞了新住民，也帶給台灣這塊土地上的人民無限啟發。

2016年8月刊出

辛苦度過異鄉生活後，林麗蟬以行動抹去外界的刻板印象，如今更成為婆婆、丈夫與孩子眼裡最美麗的愛與驕傲。

After experiencing the difficulties of life in a foreign land, Lin Li-chan has worked to eradicate stereotypical attitudes towards new immigrants. She is now the pride of her family—especially of her mother-in-law, husband and children.

Lin has also focused on furthering Taiwan's recognition and study of immigrant cultures, and its training of teachers of Southeast-Asian languages, in the belief that such endeavors foster mutual understanding and respect. As a result of her efforts, the national guidelines for the 12-year basic education curriculum slated to be released in 2018 will include the teaching of immigrant languages (primarily those of Southeast Asia). Lin says that Taiwan needs to fill out the ranks of teachers of Cambodian, Filipino, and Malaysian languages if it is to facilitate this language education work.

One step at a time

Lin is a model immigrant whose bold and proactive performance has been anything but that of a political neophyte. For all that it seems to have come naturally, Lin says that it required diligent effort and surmounting numerous obstacles.

She agreed to marry her husband, Xie Shuijin, after just two hours with a matchmaker. She then flew from Phnom Penh to Taiwan to join his family in Huatan Township, Changhua County, where he operated a factory and lived with his parents. She recalls finding life in Taiwan strange, and having difficulties communicating when she first arrived. The differences between her life here and in Cambodia were a source of stress and perplexity—there were so many challenges and things she didn't know.

Lin grew up in Phnom Penh as a third-generation ethnic Chinese immigrant. Her doting father, a businessman, provided her with a comfortable childhood. But when he died unexpectedly in a road accident while she was in high school, it was like a bolt from the blue. His passing cost the family their provider, leaving them with no money for even her school tuition. She had a difficult time coming to terms with his death in other ways as well, as it took away an important source of emotional support.

Following his passing, she would tell her father's spirit about the frustrations and difficulties she encountered, talking to him in search of strength and support. "Daytime felt like a dream, and nighttime like life," she says, recalling her first decade in Taiwan.

With the birth of her daughter, and then her son, her focus switched to her children. She strove to integrate into Taiwanese society by applying herself to learning Mandarin, becoming a volunteer, and throwing herself into community work. Underlying it all was her desire to protect her children and to remove any negative stereotypes that attached to her as an immigrant.

Seeking personal fulfillment and a greater capacity to help others, Lin studied beauty science at Chienkuo Technology University and social work at Providence University College of Continuing Education before pursuing a master's degree in non-profit-organization management at National Chi Nan University. In the fall of 2016, she will begin work on a PhD in Southeast-Asian Studies at NCNU in hopes of doing still more for Taiwan and its immigrants.

Feeling empathy for the other immigrants with whom she studied and grew, she formed the Association of Development and Communication for New Immigrants as a means of helping her sister immigrants develop good lives in Taiwan, and enabling their children to grow up well.

Finding a sense of purpose in the association, she began actively promoting the diversity of immigrant cultures and the education of immigrant children in the firm belief that immigrants and their children will help shape Taiwan's future.

Lin arrived in Taiwan unable to read Chinese and unable to understand Taiwanese. Some 20 years later, she has become a legislator involved in national decision-making with an even brighter future ahead of her. Her story is more than encouraging to other immigrants: it offers inspiration to all of Taiwan's people.

— Published in August 2016

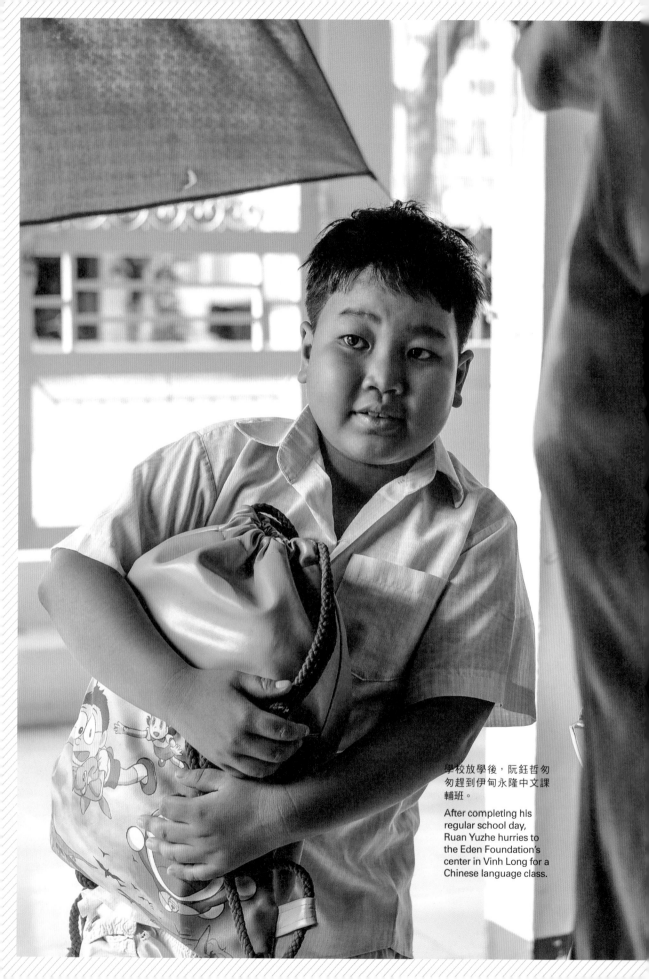

學校放學後，阮鈺哲匆匆趕到伊甸永隆中文課輔班。

After completing his regular school day, Ruan Yuzhe hurries to the Eden Foundation's center in Vinh Long for a Chinese language class.

Taiwanese NGOs in Vietnam:
Changing Children's Futures Through Education

台灣 NGO 扎根越南

教育改變孩子未來

文‧張瓊方　圖‧莊坤儒

Chang Chiung-fang / photos by Chuang Kung-ju / tr. by Scott Williams

台灣非政府組織（NGO）的援助版圖，向海外延伸已行之有年，慈濟、伊甸、家扶、路竹會……等基金會，都已是國際上知名的台灣 NGO。對於一向為台商重要投資地、又具有深厚「姻親」關係的越南，台灣 NGO 更是不該忽略。

然而，越南是共產國家，即便是 NGO，要在當地進行服務或援助仍困難重重、處處受限。無論是已扎根 10 年的伊甸基金會或 2015 年甫進駐胡志明市的家扶基金會，都必須因地制宜，發展一套不同於其他地區的服務方式。

在 63% 人口生活在國際貧窮線下的越南，教育是改變孩子未來最根本、直接的工程。伊甸與家扶在越南胡志明市以不同方式投入教育領域，無論是對台越關係的深化，或台越聯姻第二代的扶持，都有潛移默化的助益。

Taiwan's non-governmental organizations have been operating overseas for a number of years, doing valuable and important work in a variety of nations, including Vietnam, which is home to much Taiwanese business investment and many in-laws of Taiwanese families.

But Vietnam's communist government places many limitations on the aid services that NGOs can provide. In fact, the local regulatory environment has compelled Eden Social Welfare Foundation, which began working in Vietnam a decade ago, and the Taiwan Fund for Children and Families (TFCF), which established a Ho Chi Minh City branch just last year, to develop new ways of delivering services to those in need.

With some 63% of Vietnam's population living below the international poverty line, education services are perhaps the most effective means of offering children a better future. Though Eden and TFCF have leapt into the Vietnamese educational arena in different fashions, both are helping the children of Taiwanese–Vietnamese marriages and deepening Taiwan's relationship with Vietnam.

就讀小學 4 年級的阮鈺哲，學校放學後，外公和外婆兩人不辭辛勞、以三貼方式騎摩托車，載送他至半小時車程外，去上伊甸提供的中文課輔班。

伊甸在南越永隆省設立中文課輔班業已 10 年，輔導的對象是台越聯姻第二代，也就是俗稱的「新台灣之子」。

「選擇永隆是因為這裡很多女孩子嫁到台灣去。」伊甸基金會胡志明市辦公室組長高瑞蘋指出，永隆和芹苴兩省是越南婦女遠嫁他國人數最多的地方。伊甸一開始選擇在永隆設立兩個課室，一個在永隆市，另一個在更鄉下、距離永隆市車程 1.5 小時的永隆省茶溫縣，後來因為鄉下找老師困難，只好作罷。

親情不斷線

打從 2005 年 9 月教室開班就任教至今的老師文氏春梅表示，目前永隆課輔教室名單上有 13 名學童，小自 3 歲、大至 13 歲。但 3 歲的謝佩玲上個月已跟媽媽回去台灣，13 歲的孩子則因課業日益繁重，學習有一搭沒一搭，漸漸地就放棄課業之外的中文學習了。

「之前孩子還小，我們可以上半天的中文課，現在孩子大了，學校要上整天課，只能改成放學後來上一個半小時中文。」文氏春梅遺憾地說，除了時間受限之外，距離也是個障礙。因為孩子住在不同的地方，或遠或近都得靠外公、外婆、媽媽、舅舅或阿姨騎車接送，才得以往來教室學習中文。因此，中文學習除了孩子自己的意願，還得家人協助成全。

伊甸中文課輔班裡，目前有一到五年級各年齡層的孩子，他們有人會寫字，有人只會唸、不懂意思，即便年齡不一，程度也參差不齊，文氏春梅依舊不改初衷，教得賣力。她語重心長地說：「能進入這個班學中文的台越小朋友，將來回台灣才能跟爺爺、奶奶、爸爸溝通。」

對越南的新台灣之子而言，
中文是與家鄉台灣連結的臍帶。
（伊甸基金會提供）

Mandarin provides the children of Taiwanese–Vietnamese marriages living in Vietnam with a connection to their father's homeland.
(courtesy of the Eden Foundation)

課輔班文氏春梅老師教孩子注音符號和正體中文字。

Van Thi Xuan Mai teaches children *bopofomo* and traditional characters.

After school, fourth grader Ruan Yuzhe's grandparents pick him up on their motorcycle and drive him to his Eden Foundation Chinese class a half hour away.

For the last decade, Eden has been offering after-school Chinese classes to children of Taiwanese–Vietnamese marriages, known colloquially as "new Taiwanese children," in Vietnam's Vinh Long Province.

"We chose to set up in Vinh Long because many of its young women have married Taiwanese men." Gao Ruiping, head of Eden's Ho Chi Minh City office, explains that more women from Vinh Long Province and Can Tho City marry abroad than from any other area of Vietnam.

Staying connected

Van Thi Xuan Mai, who has been teaching at Eden's Vinh Long center since it opened in September 2005, says that it currently has 13 students on its rolls, ranging in age from three to 13 years old. But she adds that the three-year-old, Xie Peilin, went to Taiwan with her mother last month, and that a growing school workload has been causing the 13-year-old to gradually give up her extracurricular Chinese studies.

"When the kids were younger, we could provide them with a half day of Chinese classes. Now that they're older, they spend all day at school and have time for only an hour and a half of after-school Chinese." Van adds that distance is also an obstacle. Many of the children live in other areas, and have to rely on their mothers, aunts, uncles, or grandparents to get them to their Chinese classes. That means that not only do the kids themselves have to be interested in learning Chinese, but their family members have to be willing and able to provide logistical support.

Eden has students from first grade to fifth. Some can pronounce Chinese characters using the *bopomofo* phonetic system but don't know what the characters mean, while others can read and write characters. But Van remains committed to teaching all of them in spite of their different ages and abilities. "This class is the only thing around enabling these Vietnamese–Taiwanese kids to speak to their fathers and grandparents when they go to Taiwan," says Van.

Take Ruan, for example. His father is in Taiwan, his mother is working in Australia, and he lives in Vietnam with his maternal grandparents. Ruan has relied on the vocabulary he has learned through the center to communicate his feelings to his faraway father. In fact, he recently used his Mandarin to ask pointedly, "Dad, do you know what day my birthday is?"

Mandarin provides these "New Taiwanese kids" living in Vietnam with an important connection to their

來去台越兩地的孩子，語言學習經常是斷斷續續，難以連貫。以阮鈺哲為例，一家三口分居三地，爸爸留在台灣，媽媽在澳洲賺錢，他則和外公、外婆在越南生活。幾乎多在越南成長的鈺哲，缺乏中文學習環境，近來靠著在課輔班學的詞彙漸漸能與父親越洋聯絡感情。最近他講得最純熟的一句中文是：「爸爸，你知道我生日是幾月幾號嗎？」

大家都知道的「伊甸」

對返回越南生活的「新台灣之子」而言，具備中文能力，其實是日後與父親或出生地連結的重要臍帶，伊甸有心提供孩子中文教學服務，但卻困難重重。

「很難找到合作單位。」在伊甸服務7年的越南華僑高瑞蘋無奈地說，伊甸原本在胡志明市也打算開辦中文班，但因找不到合作單位而作罷。

伊甸在永隆除了開兒童中文班、農村婦女職訓班之外，其餘工作以發放物資為主，如：贈送殘障人士代步輪椅；中秋節發放花燈、月餅；新年發放米、油、醬油、餅乾、越南粽子等物資，對口的合作單位都是永隆省NGO友誼會。

NGO友誼會辦公室主任陳氏華指出，在永隆來來去去的NGO有四十幾個，長期服務的有29個，伊甸是其中之一。「在我們偏僻的永隆，大家都知道伊甸。」陳氏華感恩地說。

家扶胡志明市掛牌服務

在胡志明市同樣以兒童為扶助對象的，還有2015年9月掛牌運作的家扶基金會。

1950年成立，迄今已有65年歷史的家扶基金會，近年積極拓展海外據點，越南是繼蒙古、吉爾吉斯、史瓦濟蘭之後，第4個海外分事務所。

家扶越南代表鍾澤胤指出，基金會近年慢慢將資源放在東南亞區域，因為這裡是離台灣最近、最需要資源的地方。

家扶在越南服務的對象與在台灣一致，都是貧困兒童。但因為國家的環境不同，服務的方式有很大的差異。

家扶基金會媒合台灣認養人，以每月700元台幣的小額捐助方式，扶助越南貧童就學。扣除匯差，每月、每童約可獲得16.8美元的助學金。鍾澤胤指出，在胡志明市這筆錢雖不足以應付家庭開銷，但足夠繳學費。「我們告訴合作伙伴，助學金來源並非企業大筆捐贈，而是台灣認養人的小額捐助。因此，每一筆錢都很珍貴，要好好運用。」

截至2015年12月底，家扶已扶助623位越南學童，但後續仍有七十多位兒童在等候認養。值得關注的是，接受扶助的兒童當中，不乏拿台灣護照的新台灣之子。

家扶研究發展室專員鄧若瑜表示，目前扶助的學童中，新台灣之子人數不到十位，都是基金會與當地協同伙伴合作過程中無意發現的。換言之，因種種不同因素回越南居住的台越聯姻第二代，不可或免地仍有落入貧窮的危機。

窮不能窮孩子

「貧窮的樣貌各有不同，」鍾澤胤指出，越南鄉下因工作機會少，產業不發達，屬於普遍性的貧窮；但胡志明市以外來人口居多，以單親、隔代教養所產生的貧窮為首。「外來人口沒有戶籍，孩子沒有學籍，反而無法進入公立學校就讀。」

審閱近千份貧童資料的鄧若瑜也表示，有6成以上落入貧窮的原因是單親或撫養多名子女，再加上教育程度不高，無法從事技術性的工作，薪資相對較低。

「最近手邊的案例都是十幾歲的小爸爸、小媽媽，他們受教育程度不高，又不會照顧孩子，很容易就走上離婚一途，成為單親。」鄧若瑜感嘆。

受越南政府對NGO活動形式的限制，家扶在越南也必須透過與當地NPO或地方政府合作的方式，來提供服務。換言之，伙伴提出需求，家扶只能挹注資源，不能直接服

扶助兒童就學，是家扶的重點業務，在越南也不例外。（家扶基金會提供）
The Taiwan Fund for Children and Families' core mission is helping children get an education. (courtesy of TFCF)

fathers and their birthplace. Eden is happy to provide the classes, but faces many obstacles in doing so.

"It's hard finding organizations to work with," says a frustrated Gao, who has worked for Eden in Vietnam for seven years. She says that Eden had originally planned to offer Chinese classes in Ho Chi Minh City, but gave up the idea after failing to find a local partner.

Eden's partner in Vinh Long is the Vinh Long Union of Friendship Organizations. Tran Thi Hoa, the head of the association's office, says that while 40-some NGOs have been in and out of Vinh Long, Eden is one of 29 that have provided services on a long-term basis. "Vinh Long is pretty out of the way, so everyone here knows Eden."

Serving Ho Chi Minh City

Like Eden, the Taiwan Fund for Children and Families provides services to children. However, TFCF didn't set up shop in Ho Chi Minh City until September 2015.

Established in 1950, TFCF has in recent years been extending its operations overseas. In fact, its move into Vietnam was its fourth foreign venture, following forays into Mongolia, Kyrgyzstan, and Swaziland.

Frank Chung, TFCF's Vietnam representative, says that TFCF serves the same people in Vietnam that it does in Taiwan: poor children. However, the different environment results in a very different approach to those services.

TFCF finds Taiwanese sponsors to donate NT$700 per month to support the education of poor Vietnamese children. After accounting for currency exchange fees, sponsored children receive about US$16.80 per month to support their educations. Chung says that while this amount won't cover a family's expenses in Ho Chi Minh City, it will pay a child's tuition.

As of the end of 2015, TFCF was helping 623 Vietnamese students and had another 70-some kids on a list of those waiting for sponsors.

"Poverty has many faces." Chung notes that poverty is widespread in rural Vietnam because there is little

家扶駐越南代表鍾澤胤（右4）、專員鄧若瑜（右1）與當地培訓的社工人員共同打拚。

Frank Chung (fourth from right), the Taiwan Fund for Children and Families' representative in Vietnam, TFCF researcher Dee Deng (far right), and local social workers are working together to educate Vietnamese children.

務，也不能親自做家庭訪視。以扶助貧童就學為例，是由合作伙伴提供貧童資料給家扶，再由家扶依書面資料篩選出符合扶助條件的孩子。

「在台灣，家扶社工可以針對每位學童不同情況，提供不同服務。在越南沒辦法做到這麼細節，只能間接服務。與其說是社會工作，更像是做慈善工作。」鍾澤胤有感而發。

即便處處受限，只能間接服務，家扶仍努力在越南扎根，積極輔導、培訓當地7位社工人員，透過他們做服務與推展。

家扶2014年拿到的營運證只限於在胡志明市服務。今（2016）年家扶計畫要申請擴大營運範圍，往南拓展，距離胡志明市一、二小時車程的前江、永隆、同塔、芹苴等地區，都是考慮進入服務的範圍。

愛在越南

2015年9月，家扶基金會在越南的助學大業方才開始，伊甸基金會的台越第二代中文教育已十年有成。

2015年8月中旬，伊甸基金會在胡志明市辦公室舉辦「十週年感恩暨成果會」，伊甸董事長葉瀛賓親赴越南參與盛會。中文課輔班的孩子們又唱又跳地表演〈猜拳歌〉：「好朋友我們行個禮，握握手呀來猜拳，石頭布呀看誰贏，輸了就要跟我走。」

在孩子們天真無邪的歡樂歌聲中，伊甸的工作人員清楚地知道，馬步要蹲得更穩、根要扎得更深，因為教育是改變孩子未來的機會，不像孩子們玩的猜拳遊戲，只能贏，不能輸。

2016年3月刊出

阮鈺哲在課餘學中文，除了自己要有學習動機，還有賴外公、外婆不辭辛勞接送。

Studying Chinese after school not only requires that Ruan Yuzhe be motivated to learn, but also that his grandparents take him to class.

development and few jobs. But children in Ho Chi Minh City, which has a large population of migrants from the countryside, are more likely to be poor because they are being raised in a single-parent family or by their grandparents. "Rural migrants don't have household registrations, so their children don't appear on school rolls. In fact, they are unable to enroll in public schools."

Dee Deng, a child poverty researcher with TFCF in Vietnam, observes that nearly 60% of childhood poverty is the result of growing up in a single-parent household or in a household with several children. "All the clients we've been dealing with lately are teen fathers and teen mothers who don't have much education and are incapable of taking care of children. Such couples are prone to divorcing and becoming single parents," says Deng.

The restrictions the Vietnamese government places on the activities of NGOs make it necessary for them to seek a local partner (usually a local non-profit or the local government) to deliver services. In TFCF's case, its local partner provides documentation on kids, which TFCF then screens to find candidates meeting its criteria.

"In Taiwan, TFCF can tailor its services to students in all kinds of situations. In Vietnam, we have to go about providing services indirectly. It's more like charity work than social work," explains Chung.

Though severely constrained, TFCF has been actively training and guiding seven local social workers, working with them to deliver and even expand its services. This year, TFCF plans to apply to extend the scope of its operations southwards, and is considering providing services everywhere within an hour or two's drive south of Ho Chi Minh City.

Laying foundations

By the time TFCF began offering educational support in Vietnam in September 2015, Eden had already been there for a decade.

In fact, Eden held a ten-year-thanksgiving retrospective at its Ho Chi Minh City office in August 2015. There, many of its Chinese language students sang and performed the "Rock, Paper, Scissors" song: "My friend, let's bow to one another / Shake hands, and play rock, paper, scissors / We'll play the game and see who wins / And if you lose you'll come with me."

As the happy, innocent voices of the kids rang out, Eden's workers remained focused on the importance of establishing firm foundations. After all, education provides children with greater opportunities to succeed in life, and, unlike a game of rock, paper, scissors, with education everyone wins.

Published in March 2016

語言是溝通的橋梁，更是新台灣之子與家鄉連的文化牽繫，伊甸在永隆開設課輔班，目的在搭橋。（伊甸基金會提供）

Language is a bridge between cultures. Mandarin provides the children of Taiwanese–Vietnamese marriages with a connection to their father's homeland. The Eden Foundation's Chinese language classes in Vinh Long Province are bridge builders. (courtesy of the Eden Foundation)

〔光華畫報雜誌叢書 33〕

心南向 · 一家人

Bonds of Friendship, Bonds of Love—Taiwan and Southeast Asia

發 行 人	吳釗燮	**Publisher:** Jaushieh Joseph WU
社 長	陳銘政	**Director:** Henry M.J. CHEN
總 編 輯	陳亮君（代理）	**Editor-in-Chief (acting):** Ivan CHEN
副總編輯	陳亮君	**Deputy Editor-in-Chief:** Ivan CHEN
文稿主編	曾蘭淑	**Editor:** Esther TSENG
文稿副主編	郭玉平	**Deputy Editor:** Camille KUO
文字編輯	鄧慧純、陳群芳、蘇俐穎	**Writers:** Cathy TENG, CHEN Chun-fang, Lynn SU
攝影組召集人	莊坤儒	**Photographic Coordinator:** CHUANG Kung-ju
攝影組長	林格立	**Photographic Director:** Jimmy LIN
攝影編輯	林旻萱	**Photojournalist:** LIN Min-hsuan
英文編輯	陳瑩潔、唐樂榕	**English Editors:** Audrey CHEN, Robert TAYLOR
版面主編	胡如瑜	**Director of Layout:** HU Ju-yu
美術編輯	蕭郢岑、王敬勛	**Art Editors:** HSIAO Ying-tsen, Henry WANG
資深行政編輯	段蜀華	**Senior Administrative Editor:** DUAN Shu-hwa
出 版 者	光華畫報雜誌社	**Published by Taiwan Panorama Magazine**
地 址	中華民國台灣台北市 10051 中正區天津街 2 號	**Address:** No. 2, Tianjin Street, Taipei 10051, Taiwan, ROC
網 址	www.taiwan-panorama.com	**E-mail:** service@taiwan-panorama.com
讀者服務專線	**Tel:** +886-2-2397-0633	**傳真機 Fax:** +886-2-2397-0655

美術設計	四點設計有限公司	**Graphic Design:** 4Point Design
印 刷	上海印刷廠股份有限公司	**Printer:** Shanghai Printing Works Co., Ltd.
經 銷 處	光華畫報雜誌社	**Sales:** Taiwan Panorama Magazine

GPN	1010800021	
ISBN	978-957-9188-54-8（平裝）	
版次	中華民國 108 年 1 月 初版一刷	
定價	新台幣 360 元，美金 15 元（含郵資及處理費）	**Price:** NT$360 / US$15 (including postage and packing)

國家圖書館出版品預行編目（CIP）資料

心南向·一家人 / 陳亮君總編輯 . -- 初
版 . -- 臺北市 : 光華雜誌, 2019.01
面 ； 公分 . -（光華畫報雜誌叢書 ; 33）
ISBN 978-957-9188-54-8(平裝)
1. 移民 2. 社會生活 3. 臺灣
577.6 107021191